CASE STUDIES
in Forensic Accounting and Fraud Auditing
2nd Edition

D. LARRY CRUMBLEY, Ph.D., CPA, CFF, Cr.FA, MAFF
Louisiana State University

WILSON A. LaGRAIZE, CPA, Cr.FA
Kushner & LaGraize

CHRISTOPHER E. PETERS, MBA, CFE, CIDA, MAFF
GPS Consultants

Wolters Kluwer

EDITORIAL STAFF

Editor: Sandra Lim
Production: Jennifer Schencker, Vijayalakshmi Suresh, Prabhu Meenakshisundaram
Cover Design: Laila Gaidulis

This publication is designed to provide accurate and authoritative information in regard to the subject matter covered. It is sold with the understanding that the publisher is not engaged in rendering legal, accounting, or other professional service, and that the authors are not offering such advice in this publication. If legal advice or other expert assistance is required, the services of a competent professional person should be sought.

ISBN: 978-0-8080-4193-1

No claim is made to original government works; however, within this Product or Publication, the following are subject to CCH Incorporated's copyright: (1) the gathering, compilation, and arrangement of such government materials; (2) the magnetic translation and digital conversion of data, if applicable; (3) the historical, statutory and other notes and references; and (4) the commentary and other materials.

Printed in the United States of America

Preface

Willis Emmons, Senior Lecturer at the Harvard Business School, states that there are three levels of learning from using the case method to teach:

- **Level One:** Transmittal of information, concepts, frameworks, tools, and techniques.

- **Level Two:** Development of capabilities with respect to analysis, critical thinking/judgment, decision-making, and execution.

- **Level Three:** Development of values, self-awareness, leadership, temperament, and capacity for on-going learning.

Case Studies in Forensic Accounting and Fraud Auditing, 2nd edition, will reach these three levels of learning by bringing together in a single volume a number of short, medium, and longer case studies covering the broad approach to forensic and investigative accounting. These cases have been prepared by a variety of academic and practitioner authors. This book can be used as a supplement to any of the forensic accounting or fraud examination textbooks on the market. Or it could be used as a stand-alone text by an instructor who has extensive power point slides or prefers not to use a textbook. Auditing professors should find these cases to be helpful in an auditing or ethics class.

The use of case studies is a form of the scenario principle. A "scenario" presents information using characters performing activities in a specialized setting. Previous research indicates that applications of the scenario principle enhances students' communication and interpersonal skills, stimulates students' creativity, and enables instructors to improve their teaching performance. These benefits are due to the fact that students are either reading about or portraying characters interacting, formulating solutions to dilemmas, putting textbook information into practice and, hopefully, enjoying the process.

The cases in this second edition have been improved and include the following new cases:

- Is the Current Use of Impression Management by Professors in the Classroom Similar to Earnings Management by Corporate Executives?
- Is the Widespread Use of Test Banks by Students Fraud?
- Fighting International Fraud with the FCPA
- Consideration of Fraud in a Financial Statement Audit
- The Valuation of Economic Damages
- Adding Mathematical Statistics to the Auditor's Tool Box
- Green Tech Manufacturing: Fraud and the Independent Auditor
- The Fraud at High Flying Corporation: Developing Audit Interview Skills

- Uncovering Majority Shareholder Fraud in a Closely Held Corporation: A Case Study to Develop Forensic/Tax Investigation Skills
- Diamond Foods' Payments to Nut Growers
- The Dixon City Embezzlement: A Rita Crundwell Story
- Mani/Pedi? Credit Cards Not Accepted
- Exclusive Restaurant or a Front for Illegal Gambling

Dr. D. Larry Crumbley, CPA, CFF
Wilson A. LaGraize, CPA, Cr.FA
Christopher E. Peters, MBA, CFE, CIDA, MAFF

About the Editors

Dr. Larry Crumbley, Ph.D., CPA, CFF, Cr.FA, MAFF, FCPA is Emeritus Professor of Accounting at Louisiana State University. He is editor of the Journal of Forensic & Investigative Accounting and the Oil, Gas & Energy Quarterly. He created the Forensic & Investigative Accounting Section in the American Accounting Association, being its first president.

A frequent contributor to the forensic accounting literature, Professor Crumbley is an author of more than 60 books and 370 articles. His latest book entitled *Forensic and Investigative Accounting*, 7th edition, is published by Wolters Kluwer (900-224-7477). Some of his 13 educational novels, e.g., *Trap Doors and Trojan Horses* and *The Big R: A Forensic Accounting Action Adventure*, have as the main character a forensic accountant. His goal is to create a television series based upon the exciting life of a forensic accountant and litigation consultant. dcrumbl@lsu.edu

Wilson LaGraize, CPA, CFF, Cr.FA is a partner in Kushner LaGraize, LLC in Metairie, Louisiana. A 1965 graduate from Louisiana State University, his background includes experience locally in tax preparation work for corporations, partnerships, individuals, and real estate investments, as well as audit experience in both private and governmental sectors. He is experienced in litigation support, forensics, reasonable compensation, personnel searches, business valuations, and other management consulting engagements. He is a member of the Society of Louisiana Certified Public Accountants, the American Institute of Certified Public Accountants, and American College of Forensic Examiners (ACFEI). He has been an expert witness on numerous occasions. Wilson@kl-cpa.com

Christopher E. Peters, MBA, CFE, CIDA, MAFF is the founder of GPS Consultants, LLC, which is a management consulting and forensic accounting firm focused on assisting clients with improving operations and solving organizational problems through forensic accounting, litigation support, and data analysis. Prior to starting GPS in May 2011, Peters was the Chief Financial Officer for one of the largest home remodeling companies in the United States. As a CFO, Peters focused on improving the company's existing operations; he also spearheaded the company's expansion into two new markets: Dallas/Ft. Worth, TX (acquisition) and Philadelphia, PA (start-up). Prior to his CFO position, Peters worked for a regional CPA firm where he focused on advising clients with improving business operations and solving problems through forensic accounting, internal auditing, litigation support, and data analysis. Peters graduated from Louisiana State University (LSU) with a bachelor's of science degree in Management & Entrepreneurship. As a graduate assistant while obtaining his Masters of Business Administration in Finance & Entrepreneurship from the LSU Flores MBA Program, Peters advised and assisted Louisiana small businesses and entrepreneurs with preparing business plans and financial projections used for raising capital to start and/or grow their businesses. cpeters@GPSconsultants.com

Contents

Please visit *CCHGroup.com/Resources* for any periodic updates or clarifications that may become available related to *Case Studies in Forensic Accounting and Fraud Auditing* as well as CCH's *Daily Tax Day* news, tax briefings and other items of interest.

CASE STUDY 1:

What Is A One Cent Error Worth?

Dr. Donald L. Ariail, CPA, CFF, CGMA, CVA
Kennesaw State University

LEARNING OBJECTIVES

After completing and discussing this case, you should be able to:

- Appreciate the value of bank reconciliations.
- Understand that materiality is not important in a fraud investigation.
- Understand the purpose of a proper cut-off date.

A bar/restaurant that an accounting firm serviced for a number of years (compiling quarterly financial statements and preparing the annual tax returns) was audited by the IRS with an audit that was not a regular field audit. This Taxpayer Compliance Measurement Program (TCMP) audit (United States General Accounting Office, 1994) is now called the National Research Program (NRP; Department of the Treasury, Internal Revenue Service, 2005) and is used by the IRS to develop the statistical basis for selecting audit targets. This type of examination checks everything—including every number and every other representation (such as proof of incorporation, stock ownership, and citizenship).

After working on the audit for about a week, the IRS agent gave the CPA partner a list of questions which included a request to explain a one cent error in the bank reconciliation for the prior year-end (the compiled financial statements for the first quarter of the current year had not yet been prepared). When the accountant looked at the reconciliation, he saw that a staff accountant had reconciled the account and that the "checker," a CPA with 30 plus years of experience, had "passed" the reconciliation even though it was out of balance by one cent. He had written "Passed—Immaterial" on the reconciliation.

So the partner stayed at the office late that night and re-reconciled the account. What he found was disturbing and cost him his first and only IRS penalty for which he was (in 34 years of practice) responsible. How can a one cent error cause an IRS penalty? Is it not immaterial?

CASE STUDY 2:

That Trusted Employee

D. Larry Crumbley, Ph.D., CPA, CFF, Cr.FA
Louisiana State University

LEARNING OBJECTIVES

After completing and discussing this case, you should be able to:

- Appreciate the importance of skepticism with respect to employees.
- Understand the importance of segregation of duties.
- Appreciate the importance of reconciliation of bank statements.

Jim Aaron owned a successful energy service company in Baton Rouge, Louisiana for 14 years. Stacy Oxner helps Mr. Aaron with his recordkeeping. Mr. Aaron considers Stacy to be a trusted employee, having worked for him for eleven years. She has worked long hours, often coming in early and working late. She is an excellent employee.

Stacy had to go to the hospital for a hip replacement. While Stacy was away from work the canceled checks came from the bank to Mr. Aaron's home. Feeling somewhat guilty for forcing Stacy to work such long hours, Mr. Aaron opens the bank envelope. He is surprised to find several large checks made out to Stacy: one for $14,000, another for $17,500, and a third one for $11,300.

Mr. Aaron never signs blank checks. He does not have a check writing machine, and the signatures on these questionable checks are his signature. The signatures have not been forged.

How did this fraud occur? Discuss segregation of duties. Discuss opportunity in the fraud triangle with respect to this situation.

CASE STUDY 3:

Employee Fraud at Miami Rehabilitation Center

Jeffrey E. Michelman, Ph.D., CPA, CMA
University of North Florida
Bobby E. Waldrup, Ph.D., CPA
Loyola University
Alex Bird, MBA, CPA, CIA
Wells Fargo

LEARNING OBJECTIVES

After completing and discussing this case, you should be able to

- Understand investigative accounting where forensic data is scarce.
- Learn how to find missing cash.
- Recognize the importance of bank statements.
- Understand the importance of internal controls in a small business.
- Learn about the fraud triangle.

INTRODUCTION

Juan Martinez sat motionless in his small office and reflected on the day's events. By this time, the police were long gone. The police officer remarked that, without a confession, they really had no valid reason to arrest anyone. There were so many signs, and Juan had been certain that the police would be able to resolve the issue of the missing $1,400. Juan continued to rehash the recent events in his mind. He could not understand how things had gone wrong. He was heartbroken. He had always approached his employees like they were family. How could any of them have stolen from him?

It was almost 10:00 pm on Friday, November 22, 2009, and Juan was nowhere closer to fully understanding or solving the theft. After all the decisions that Juan had made relative to his business, he still had no clue what to do next. Was this problem merely a discrepancy due to sloppy bookkeeping, or did he have a bigger problem of fraud in his organization? As he gathered his thoughts and began to reflect on the company's history and how he had gotten to this point, he wondered what to do next. How would he tell his wife that he didn't have any answers? The business represented their children's future.

He called his wife.

Juan: Isabella, I can't determine what happened to the missing $1,400. I'm really angry that I didn't do something to avoid this.

Isabella: Juan, when are you coming home? I know you must be extremely tired. I'm certain that we will get this resolved. Please come home.

Juan: I am going to stay a little longer. I'll be home in a little while.

THE COMPANY'S HISTORY

Juan remembered how he and four other physical therapists had started the original company in 1994. It was a very exciting time, and everyone was thinking about the company's potential. The five physical therapists decided to name the company Miami Rehabilitation Services (MRS). The company was located in Miami, Florida and began in one office with five owners. During the next eight years, MRS grew steadily as the demand for physical therapy had grown. Juan reflected on all the conversations he had with his business partners about other healthcare providers that had been covered by the local press when they encountered difficulty and even fraud.

Juan felt strongly that one reason why MRS had a good reputation was the way they treated their patients. MRS had also developed a good reputation among insurance companies, HMOs, and local attorneys who referred patients from motor vehicle accidents, personal injury cases, and workers' compensation cases. Juan thought for a moment about these third-party payers. During 2008, third-party payers represented about 90 percent of Miami's annual revenues of nearly $1 million. These were the good times Juan was remembering. From 1994 until 2002, Juan and his partners expanded the business to seven locations. Juan even remembered all the attorney meetings when they separated the business into three corporations. The business had gotten so large he and his partners wanted to limit their liability.

In 2002, Juan and his partners took advantage of an opportunity to sell their business to the U.S. subsidiary of a publicly owned Canadian health care company called Canada Health. The opportunity provided the partners with cash from the sale, and the sale also allowed the partners to continue their physical therapy activity. For his part, Juan agreed to manage the Miami operations as a regional vice president. To take advantage of their brand recognition, the name of the business was maintained as Miami Rehabilitation Services.

Canada Health owned and operated numerous nursing homes, assisted living centers, and other health care providers in the United States and Canada. In 2005, Canada Health began to experience losses in the United States. The company's difficulty had stemmed from operational problems, Medicare and Medicaid reimbursement declines, and liability issues. Juan could definitely relate. At that point, Juan and one of his partners were able to repurchase the business. Juan bought two locations, and Don Smith bought one location. They closed the remaining locations. This time, each individual purchased their locations separately. However, they again retained the trade name, Miami Rehabilitation Services.

Juan thought about how problems were always arising in the billing and collection side of the business. These problems were the reason he and Don decided to establish a separate company to handle these functions. As he thought back on it, he remembered the frustration that he had experienced each year as the third-party payers had reduced reimbursement for physical therapy services, while at the same time the claims filing process continued to become more complicated. Estimating revenues became increasingly difficult. Juan and Don decided that they would create a separate billing company to handle the reimbursement for their three clinics. They had named it MS Billing (MSB). The ownership was 50/50. Juan had felt that MSB would be able to focus more closely on collections and reimbursement with the third-party payers. Later in 2007, Juan closed one of his two locations. MSB's office was then located within walking distance to Juan's remaining MRS location.

THE NEW EMPLOYEE AND THE DISCOVERY

Juan considered how Canada Health had run into trouble and several of the recent bankruptcies of healthcare providers that he had heard about from his physician friends. Juan felt he was now in a similar position. For Juan, the big issue was survival in a business where the healthcare provider was being squeezed out by the third-party payers. By 2007, payments from the third-party payers represented nearly all of the company's revenue. Juan did not like the payment percentages they were receiving from these third parties, but he had to accept it. The percentages were very inconsistent. In September 2009, he hired a new employee to work part-time as a second accounts receivable coordinator. After a few weeks on the job, Angelita López approached Juan because something didn't seem right.

Angelita: Juan, I offered to pick up the mail and receipts from the two physical therapy clinics, but Helen said it was on her way home, and she liked doing it. She seemed adamant that she would do it herself.

Juan: That is interesting. Helen has always been a good employee, and I am sure she is just trying to be helpful. However, if I recall that job was assigned to María Vega, my office manager.

Juan was wondering why he didn't act sooner when approached with his new employee's concern. Although he and Angelita started to look closer at the books and records after business hours, he wasn't able to put his finger on the problem. Juan spoke with Angelita a week later.

Juan: What you are finding scares me. Business has been really tough these past few years, and increasingly, I seem to have been spending less time managing the operations of the clinic and more time seeing patients. The office appeared to be running smoothly, so I didn't get involved.

Angelita: I am not sure yet what I have found, but if you give me a little time, I am happy to continue to investigate.

Juan: Yes, I think that would be good, but at this point, let's keep the investigation between us.

They had looked at the bank statements together, and there were a lot of inconsistencies. Some of the deposit slips were incomplete, and some were missing signatures. Together, they totaled some of the slips, and compared the bank copies with the office copies. They quickly noticed that the totals did not match. (See Exhibit 1). By quickly analyzing the difference between the two deposit slips in just this one situation, he started to get nervous. A quick comparison showed him just how bad this might be. (See Exhibit 2). Juan began to realize that there was very little control over the deposit slip books. The deposit slips were not sequentially numbered, and that was making it difficult to verify the deposit activity. Based on their efforts, Juan concluded that at least $1,400 had been stolen. Juan was really angry with himself. He simply could not understand how the deposits could have been wrong, and why the office manager had not made the discovery. How was his newest employee able to develop this suspicion when he had practically been clueless? (See Exhibits 1 and 2).

Exhibit 1: Deposit Slips

Bank Copy

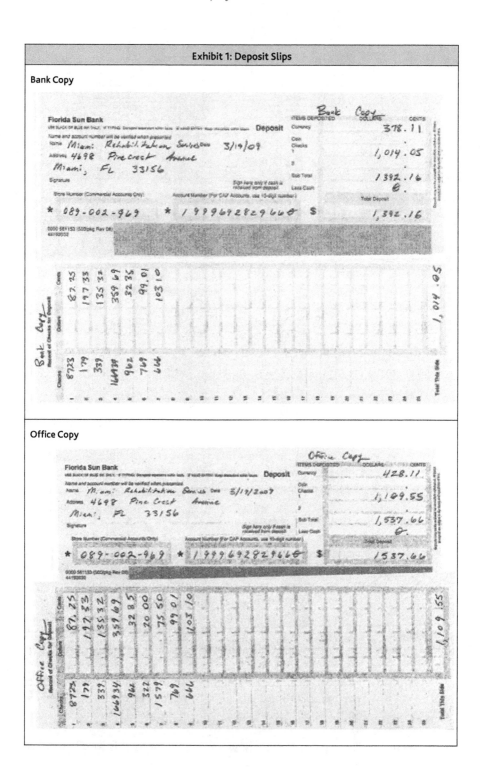

Office Copy

Exhibit 2: Deposit Reconcilement				
Office Copy			**Bank Copy**	
	Amount			Amount
Currency	$428.11		Currency	$378.11
Checks			Checks	
8723	$87.25		8723	$87.25
179	$197.33		179	$197.33
339	$135.32		339	$135.32
166934	$359.69		166934	$359.69
962	$32.35		962	$32.35
322	$20.00		769	$99.01
1579	$75.50		666	$103.10
769	$99.01			
666	$103.10			
Totals	**$1,537.66**		**Totals**	**$1,392.16**

HELEN, THE ACCOUNTS RECEIVABLE COORDINATOR

Helen Fagan was MRS's primary accounts receivable coordinator. Juan recalled that Helen was an employee that he and his partner had essentially inherited from one of their previous partners. She had worked for the organization since 1997. Except for one earlier period, around 2002, just after they split the practices, Juan remembered that Helen had complained to her coworkers about being underpaid, so he met with her and discussed the situation.

Juan: Helen, what is going on here? I have heard you complaining about your pay to others in the office. We discussed your compensation after the organization's split, and you decided to stay with me. I felt that your compensation level was appropriate. You have always been a satisfactory employee, but your pay is set and talking with others isn't going to raise it.

Helen: I know this was wrong, I really enjoy working here, but things have been really tight at home with medical expenses, you know.

Juan: I know that times are tough; they are for all of us, but if I hear you complaining again about your pay at work I will fire you on the spot. Are we clear?

Helen: Yes, Juan, I am really sorry. I really need this job; it will not happen again.

Helen got the message and stopped complaining. Around this time $600 was stolen from the business in 2003. Juan had no idea who had committed the theft. However, there was one woman who was suspected. She quit the company because the suspicions were widely known. Juan recalled how the woman said, "You all are crazy for thinking that I stole that $600." The scene created quite a commotion. Unfortunately, her resignation ended the inquiry.

Then there were the previous rumors about Helen's husband having a substance abuse problem. Her husband was a painter, and Juan also recalled that money was always an issue. Helen and her husband had three children. He thought about all her comments related to the oldest child's learning problems. She often spoke about his hyperactive behavior, and how they had tried several different schools. The second child had juvenile diabetes. He recalled the time that he had confronted her about her complaining. Juan always imagined how difficult that must have been. There were many occasions when Helen had to take time from work for the child's doctor visits. Juan thought about the fact that Helen, her husband, and their children lived with Helen's parents. She drove an old car, and she was always having money problems. She never seemed to be wearing any new clothes. This was despite the fact that he and his partner had paid periodic bonuses to their employees for obtaining certain business goals.

After he talked to her in 2002, Helen's attitude had improved and she received the bonuses when they were given out. If Helen had stolen the money, he could not figure out what she had done with it. He had never noticed any changes in Helen that would have tipped him to the fact that she was stealing money. It just did not make sense that she could have been the perpetrator.

Juan considered the tasks that Helen performed on a daily basis. She collected the mail from the post office box, opened the mail, and collected the patients' co-payments from the two physical therapy clinics. Helen also posted the payments into the patient account computer software system. He knew that these payments included both cash and checks. He also knew that she totaled the payments received from the clinics and through the mail, completed the bank deposit slips, and prepared the deposit. Helen made the bank deposits twice weekly on her way home.

But why did the office manager not check Helen's work. This was not the way he had designed Helen's job. She was doing practically everything. He was disappointed that he had never really followed her activities closer. This function was his business; why had he become so removed from the financial operations? Honestly, as the reimbursements became slower, he had to let a therapist go. After all, he had hired people that he thought he could trust. He knew that he had placed too much trust in his staff. He and his wife Isabella had strong values, and Juan expected that everyone operated with the same set of values.

Juan also recalled how the daily front desk logs listed patient and payment information. The front desk receptionist was supposed to tally the log amounts at the end of each day. The logs included whether the patient payments were cash, check, or credit card. Copies of patient receipts were attached to the logs.

In retrospect he recalled on several occasions Helen tallied the log amounts instead of the receptionist. He should have questioned that activity at the time, however, he failed to do so. Her involvement in the tallying activity was again contrary to the policy that he and his partner at MSB, Don, had established.

Helen also printed two computer reports daily that listed the payments received by mail and payments received at the clinics. These reports were supposed to be used to verify that all payments had been posted and deposited. He did not recall any discussion on the office manager's part about those reports being reviewed. Furthermore, when he and Angelita had tried to determine the amount of the theft, the reports were not found. In addition to these reports, Helen also made and received collection calls from patients. On a monthly basis, Helen would prepare a "write-off" list, and Juan would review the list. Occasionally, Juan would ask that an account be referred for collection. Beyond that, Juan didn't recall any further involvement on his or the office manager's part. Where was his office manager when all of this was happening? Was she just a bad supervisor or was she involved?

Juan never thought that something might have been wrong when Isabella, Juan's wife, complained bitterly about the waste of the time it had been for her to sit with Helen and learn her job. Isabella had volunteered to substitute for Helen during the upcoming birth of her baby. Juan reluctantly recalled his wife's displeasure with Helen and his unwillingness to act.

> **Isabella:** I am really getting tired of Helen's attitude. I really wanted to help when she had the baby. A mother needs to spend time with a newborn. Instead, she is bound and determined to immediately return to work. Doesn't she get any time off to have a baby?
>
> **Juan:** Yes, she has accrued sick leave, but she has always refused to take it.
>
> **Isabella:** I asked her numerous times to explain her job to me, but each time she had an excuse. She has never taught me anything about her job. Helen will not let anyone into her world.
>
> **Juan:** I don't understand what the big deal is. She is not planning on being gone more than a day or two.

Juan also remembered that Helen had not relinquished the post office box key despite the fact that she had been asked several times. He even thought about all the times he walked past Helen's desk and repeatedly noticed uncashed checks. He could not understand why he had accepted that as common practice. He was beginning to get angry with himself. He became more upset when he realized that he had noticed Helen making mistakes recently. She never asked for any vacation time, EVER.

Suddenly, he recalled a discussion with his friend, Will, who had bought a business in Tampa.

Will:	You remember when I bought the restaurant; I decided to keep all of the employees that were there. Some of them, including waitresses had been there over 15 years. I figured things were good and the business valuation had come in like I expected.
Juan:	Yeah, so what's your point?
Will:	Well I did not do any background screening on the employee that had been doing all of the bookkeeping and payroll. It turns out that she had a criminal record, had been stealing from the previous owner, and just continued the stealing when I took over the business. How was I supposed to know?
Juan:	Oh my, so what happened?
Will:	Well, the employee messed up her plan when she got pregnant and was planning on a single week of leave. Unfortunately for her that day happened to be payroll day, and a substitute employee discovered that "wonderful bookkeeper" had been embezzling money.

The similarities were startling. The pregnancy, Helen's unwillingness to let anyone into her world, and her refusal to relinquish the post office box key were all creating a sinking feeling in Juan's stomach. Over and over, he kept reflecting on how angry Isabella had been after trying to train with Helen.

MARIA, THE OFFICE MANAGER

María Vega had worked for Juan and Don for approximately seven years prior to her leaving in 2002. She was rehired as the office manager for MSB in 2005. María was responsible for managing the office staff and maintaining the control environment. She also was responsible for handling Medicare and workers' compensation accounts, reconciling bank statements, and entering information into the accounting system. Although María did check the copies of bank deposit slips against the bank statement amounts, she didn't compare the bank deposit slip copies to the office copies. Had she completed this step, she would have discovered the theft.

Thus, Helen was clearly involved with the missing $1,400. But was María involved? He simply couldn't understand why María had not discovered the theft. He and his partner had established certain policies long ago. But many of those polices hadn't been followed in years. There was no performance review system in place that might have contributed to why policies hadn't been followed. Also, Helen always seemed to volunteer for additional responsibility, particularly when money was involved. Was it possible that María and Helen had acted together to steal the money? At this point, it seemed like a distinct possibility.

BUSINESS DECISIONS

It was close to midnight, and Juan was tired and frustrated. He called Isabella again and explained,

> **Juan:** I want to stay at the office a little longer to work through this problem.

> **Isabella:** Juan, don't you remember how upset I was about the time when I tried to train with Helen....? Juan, everything is going to be okay. Do you want me to come to the office?

> **Juan:** No, I need to sort this out myself.

After the call, Juan recalled some of the decisions his partner, Don, and he had made in the early days of the billing company's establishment. One of the first decisions they made was to purchase software to perform the patient billing function. There were so many vendors and programs from which to select. Juan considered himself better suited to handling the clinical side of the business. He also was very comfortable making personnel decisions. His previous partners, including Don, were self-proclaimed business experts. He remembered how his previous partners would micro-manage expenses, particularly when an equipment purchase was being considered. The partners rationalized that they didn't want to spend money on anything they or their staff could do. So, Don persuaded Juan not to purchase the available report generation features offered by Health Payment Computer Services. These features included reports that separated patient payments from third-party payments. The features also separated the payments by cash, check, and credit card. Juan now realized that if he had purchased these software features, it would have been much easier to determine an estimate of the missing money. The current system only showed historic billings and payments.

When María reviewed and reconciled the monthly bank statements, she would pass them along to the CPA. Juan seldom even looked at the bank statements. Juan also recalled that he and Don had consulted with their CPA about the software. The CPA provided tax preparation and bookkeeping services as well as prepared monthly financial statements.

> **Juan:** Don and I are considering buying some new software that has a number of different features. I am not really sure what features we should be looking at.

CPA: I know. This stuff is even confusing to me. The only thing I really want you to pay attention to is how the G/L relates to the tax module. You know right now my staff and I have to do a lot of data entry, and we would rather not because your system is not compatible with ours.

Juan: The vendor has lots of options including one that will allow us to better track revenues by payer type. They have even offered to come by and make a presentation for us. Are you interested in attending?

CPA: Like I said, that stuff is all really great for complex businesses. Your business is pretty simple. My recommendation is just make sure that they include a download module so that I can complete the tax filing.

Reflecting back Juan wondered why the CPA had never offered to provide other services. Perhaps there might have been something she could have offered that would have prevented the theft. At least he might have been able to better understand what had been stolen. Was there a malpractice problem? Could he sue the CPA?

Juan thought about some comments from his neighbor, an accounting professor at a nearby university. The neighbor had mentioned from time to time how CPA firms had diversified their businesses and offered many types of consulting services, specifically for small businesses, but since his CPA seemed content to prepare the basic financial statement, quarterly tax filings and the annual tax return, he figured there was no need to spend any extra money.

Juan remembered when he suggested the purchase of a credit card processing machine to his partner. Don objected because of the $500 price. María also objected. Don claimed they would never be able to recover that investment; however, his presumption was wrong. They found that an increasing number of customers preferred to pay with credit cards, and the two found it necessary to buy a second machine. Juan realized that the credit card machine certainly must have reduced the amount of the theft. The arrangement with the credit card machine provider caused the credit card amounts to be deposited directly to the companies' bank accounts.

For a moment, Juan thought about why he and his partners never completed any background verification of their employees. He realized that Helen and María had both been employed prior to Canada Health's ownership; however, he and Don had never discussed doing a background check. He remembered some radio advertisements for local firms that completed those types of checks. He wondered if an employee check would have uncovered any unfavorable information. Perhaps they should have paid better attention to all current employees.

THE DAY'S EVENTS

The day had started with the packing of all the evidence in boxes and placing the boxes on Helen's desk. Juan and Isabella were in the office early waiting for the police, Helen, and María to arrive. They were prepared for the confrontation. Helen arrived and unsuccessfully tried her door key. Juan had changed the locks the previous evening. She had brought her new born baby to work that day, and she questioned why her key didn't work. After Juan let her in, Helen went in and out several times to ensure she had everything the baby needed. Helen noticed all the boxes on her desk and questioned Juan about them. He replied, "We are going to have to talk about that."

María arrived next, and she was suspicious immediately. Isabella was seldom at the office in the morning. María also noticed the boxes. Then two police officers arrived. One officer took Juan, Isabella, and Helen into one office. Juan was amazed how Helen maintained the straightest face during some very intense questioning by the officer. It was as if she had been in this position before. The other officer questioned María, and the officer determined that María was negligent in her oversight but not involved in the theft. After several hours of questioning, the police officers told Juan and Isabella that they didn't have anything concrete and were unable to make an arrest. María was feeling appropriately guilty, and she was blowing off steam. Helen went home.

THE NEXT STEP

By now, it was as if Juan had been in a terrifying daydream for several hours. He was exhausted. He left the office and arrived home fifteen minutes later. Isabella was waiting and once again offered her support. She wanted to know what they were going to do. Juan said they would talk about it in the morning. They could survive a loss of $1,400 if that was all it was, but what if it was more. How much more?

REQUIREMENTS

1. Like fuel, air, and heat come together to make fire, the likelihood of fraud increases when the three elements of the fraud triangle come together. Analyze how the three elements of the fraud triangle are important and how all three elements were present in Helen's case.

2. In 2006, The Committee of Sponsoring Organizations (COSO) published a small company version of their 1992 *Internal Control – Integrated Framework* model to help small public companies improve their internal control systems. The basis for this model is that internal control is composed of five interrelated components. Control activities represent one of the five components.

Define control activities and discuss at least two control activities and their application or lack of application in MRS and MSB's case.

3.   Two other components of COSO's model are the control environment and monitoring. Name and describe at least three recommendations that you would make regarding these two components.

4.   Brainstorm about the red flags that Juan and Maria missed during the commission of this financial fraud. Describe how you would go about conducting a forensic audit of Juan's records.

5.   With regard to segregation of duties, what recommendations would you make to Juan and his partner to improve this control activity?

6.   Analyze how the accounting system is both a preventive and detective control.

CASE STUDY 4:

Big Oil versus Big Ideals

Mary B. Curtis, Ph.D., CPA, CISA
University of North Texas
Eileen Z. Taylor, Ph.D., CPA, CFE
North Carolina State University

LEARNING OBJECTIVES

After completing and discussing this case, you should be able to

- Identify the laws and regulations governing whistleblowing and whistleblower retaliation in the U.S.
- Analyze the pros and cons of whistleblowing, especially from the individual whistleblower's point of view.
- Recognize the difficulty of changing an existing corporate culture.
- Apply the Ethical Dilemma Resolution Framework.

In writing this case, our goal is to provide a window into the life of a whistleblower, showing the long, often torturous path a whistleblower may follow. Although we do provide a time line for the events in his/her life, it is not our aim to document the detailed chronology of the court case. Indeed, we have obscured some facts and purposely omitted others, including the identity of the whistleblower and the company he worked for.

THE CASE

Part I:

After graduating from a large southwestern university in 1995 with a degree in accounting, George began his career at a Big-4 public accounting firm. He worked his way up to audit senior manager before taking a position in the spring of 2005 at a Fortune-500 company ("the Corporation") as Director of Technical Accounting Research and Training. George was directly responsible for supervising, evaluating, and improving technical research and training for the entire finance and accounting ("F&A") organization. During his job interview, the Corporation's Senior Vice President and Chief Accounting Officer (CAO)

emphasized that the Corporation had recently faced questions about its accounting practices and needed to 'clean up' its accounting. They were looking for
someone to keep abreast of SEC, FASB, and international rules and train their
in-house accountants at locations throughout the world. George was aware of
the negative publicity surrounding the Corporation's accounting practices, and
was wary of their offer. Despite his concerns, based on the CAO's statements,
George thought the job sounded like a great opportunity to 'fix a company in
need.' Besides, although George did not know them personally, several other
former auditors from his firm worked at the Corporation.

Similar to a consultation partner in the national office of a public accounting firm, George was the 'go-to' person for questions about proper application
of GAAP at the Corporation. His job took him around the globe. Some of his
presentations focused on accounting for joint ventures, while others taught
proper application of GAAP in revenue recognition. His technical presentations
were well-received by the Corporation's accountants, who were eager to learn
about appropriate treatment of unique, industry-specific transactions and FASB
developments. Individual accountants at the Corporation came to George with
their questions and he felt that they valued his opinion.

In summer 2005, George reviewed the Bill-and-Hold decision tree the
Corporation used to determine timing of revenue recognition (The decision
tree actually violated the Corporation's written policy on revenue recognition).
George concluded they were recording revenue prematurely, based on an improper
application of GAAP (the SEC's SAB104 and EITF-0021). In short, as part of
service contracts with their clients, the Corporation was required to manufacture
custom-designed equipment in order to actually perform the required services
for their customers. The equipment was manufactured in advance by the Corporation and stored in their warehouses until the service was performed. The
Corporation recorded the sale of the equipment when it was manufactured and
placed in the warehouse, before it was used in the service.

George considered this treatment to fit the characteristics of a classic Bill–and–
Hold scheme, which can result in improper acceleration of revenue recognition.
Prior year e-mails and documents from Internal Audit raised concerns that this
practice did not comply with company policy. The same documents made it
clear the Corporation responded by adding a clause to their sales orders in an
effort to evidence the passing title of such manufactured repair equipment to the
customer at the time the sales order was issued, although the company's policy
was never changed. Thus, accounting practice remained out of compliance with
GAAP. In fact, the passage of title or risk of loss is only one of the seven bill-
and-hold criteria, all of which must be met in order to recognize revenue. In
addition, the title passage clause did not change prior contracts, whose revenue
had already been recorded. George did some additional research and found an
article on Bill-and-Hold in the industry, written by a manager at the Corporation's external audit firm.

Based on his understanding of company practices and his research, George published an internal memo describing his findings; he also sent a copy to the audit firm's engagement team. The Corporation responded by conducting a survey to analyze the materiality level of the questionable transactions. According to George, they found the issue was widespread and material as it was 20-25% of total revenue. The third quarter was coming to a close and the external auditors were onsite. George discussed the issue with both the Chief Accounting Officer and the audit engagement manager. Both assured him the Corporation would restate revenue and correct the error. However, when the quarterly financial statements were issued, there was no correction or restatement. George was surprised, but he received no explanation. The controller, George's boss, left the Corporation soon afterward, and the CAO refused to meet with George to discuss the matter.

Faced with a dilemma, George considered his choices. He could go along with the Corporation's treatment and let the issue drop. In other words, he could 'take no action,' keep his job, and continue to train the Corporation's accounting staff. Or he could resign and find work at a different organization, leaving the Corporation to continue to file what George felt were inaccurate statements to the public. Alternatively, George could continue working within the Corporation, trying to gain support for his concerns internally. Last, George could pursue the issue and report his concerns externally, either to a regulatory body or to the media.

George carefully weighed his options. He had not faced a dilemma this serious in the past. His actions would affect his career, his family, the Corporation, and even the investing public. He took his wife and children on a short trip. He thought about the situation and asked himself, "What would my dad do?" In his heart, he just wanted the company to change its accounting practice, but he had been unsuccessful. In addition, the external audit manager knew of the situation, agreed with George, and still the audit firm gave the financial statements a clean opinion. George made a decision.

Required: Complete the following questions before proceeding with the case.

Prevention

1. Discuss how each of the following questions might have alerted George to the corporate culture of the organization when he was interviewing for the job. Could George have predicted ahead of time how the organization would react if he challenged their accounting practices?

    a. How is the company perceived in the media?
    b. How do employees describe the organization's culture? What could George have done to investigate the "mood in the middle" and the "buzz at the bottom"?

  c. Is it enough to know that others from your current firm work there?

  d. Do you have any information about how the firm has handled prior whistleblowing reports? For instance, have they required whistleblowers to sign arbitration agreements either before or after a whistleblower has made a report?

Choices

1. Professional guidance:

  a. Consult the AICPA Code of Professional Conduct. What components might guide a CPA working in a corporate environment?

  b. Consult the IMA Statement of Ethical Professional Practice. Describe how this case presents a conflict between Confidentiality and Integrity.

2. If you were in George's position, whom would you talk to at the company? Outside the company?

3. Complete the Ethical Dilemma Resolution Framework, contained in the Appendix.

PART II:

George's position:

George continued in his attempts to persuade the Corporation to modify their practices, but to no avail. Finally, in November 2005, after the Corporation had filed its third-quarter financial statements with no revised revenue recognition policies, George sent a confidential e-mail to the SEC and the PCAOB, outlining his concerns and implicating the CAO and external auditors. The SEC interviewed George about the Bill-and-Hold practice. After the Corporation filed their 2005 annual financial statements, the SEC opened an inquiry into their reporting practices. According to George, the SEC also encouraged him to contact the Corporation's audit committee. On February 4, 2006, George learned the Corporation had been contacted by the SEC and so he sent what he believed would be a confidential e-mail, outlining his concerns, to the audit committee via a link on the company's webpage. George was not prepared for what happened next.

  The Corporation hired a law firm to investigate the Bill-and-Hold practices; after approximately 5-6 months, they reported that any issues with improper revenue recognition were immaterial to the company's financial statements. The SEC also closed their case.

  Meanwhile, contrary to promises made on the website, the legal department, rather than the Board of Directors, was first to receive George's e-mail. The General Counsel forwarded the e-mail to the Chief Financial Officer, who shared it with others including the VP of Investor Relations, the Chief Accounting

Officer, and the external audit partner. The CAO then sent e-mails to others in the company identifying George and his complaints to the SEC and company hotline; he further instructed his staff to investigate whether George had violated the company's Code of Business Conduct by contacting the SEC. The audit committee eventually also received the e-mail. When the SEC notified the Corporation they were opening an investigation of accounting practices, the General Counsel sent out an e-mail notifying key individuals the SEC was investigating "George's complaint"; this e-mail was shared widely throughout the organization.

Disclosure of George's e-mail to these parties resulted in retaliation in many forms. George was shunned by Corporation employees. The Corporation's executives excluded him from all meetings with the external auditor, removed him from major projects and, worst, they took away his training responsibilities. With his job decimated, he asked to go on administrative leave.

Stunned by the Corporation's actions, George sent the SEC a 50 page report with over 100 exhibits detailing the accounting practices he felt were questionable. He supplied his estimates of the amount in question, which he later found out were much larger than those the Corporation had reported to the SEC. George did not meet with the SEC until March 28, 2006. About the same time, April 1, 2006, George agreed to a 6-month administrative leave of absence from Corporation.

In September, the Corporation notified George his leave would expire at the beginning of October, and they expected him to return to work. George believed the Corporation had not provided the SEC with enough evidence about the case, and that the SEC's decision to close the case was based on incomplete evidence. The Corporation refused to allow George to have access to their final report to the SEC. On October 17, 2006, George submitted his resignation and retained his own counsel. In his letter of resignation, George stated, "I have every reason to believe that the Corporation intends to persist in violating securities laws and filing inaccurate and misleading financial information. Professionally and ethically, I cannot return to active employment under these conditions."

The Corporation had informed him that when he returned to work in October, he would be reporting to someone at his own level. In addition, the conditions that existed before his leave would persist. He would not be placed back on projects, he would continue to be excluded from meetings, and he would not be able to train in-house accountants. He would not be able to meet with the external auditors, who George was told refused to include him in their meetings, which precluded him from carrying out his responsibilities as the company contact person in regard to accounting policy. George believed all of these changes were retaliation for his whistleblowing actions.

The Corporation's Position:

Although company personnel initially did not disagree with George's concerns, they did ask for further analysis of the issue in the fall of 2005. Because the person to whom he reported, the CAO, felt George had invested too much time and effort on this one accounting issue, they asked a senior accounting manager to perform the analysis (who did not consult George during this process), and this individual arrived at a conclusion opposite to George's position. George's superiors were also concerned about George's leadership, stating that he was not collaborative or acting in the best interest of the company.

The Corporation further investigated the accounting issue by asking their internal lawyer (from the U.K.) to consider the issue. That attorney concluded the accounting treatment met revenue recognition requirements.

The SEC investigated George's claim and formally notified the Corporation in September of 2006, that no enforcement action was being recommended. The Audit Committee's investigation likewise concluded that no changes in the company's accounting practices were needed.

EPILOGUE

Between May 2006 and September 2011, George pursued his cause through the U.S. Court system. The Sarbanes-Oxley Act (SOX) was the prevailing regulation protecting whistleblowers at the time. Under SOX, George claimed he whistleblew in good faith and the Corporation retaliated against him. The retaliation included the disclosure of his identity to other employees and constructive discharge from his job. George lost his initial case, and the Department of Labor (DOL) Administrative Law Judge dismissed his appeal.

After these losses, George's attorney gave up, but George did not. He put together a petition for review and submitted it to the DOL Administrative Review Board (ARB). In September 2011, the ARB ruled that George was protected under SOX, and the Corporation did retaliate against him. They remanded the case back to the lower court. After more back-and-forth between the courts, George was notified in early 2013 of the appeal court's finding in his favor. This landmark decision took George years to reach.

George has moved on professionally; he is employed as an accountant again and despite his long and arduous journey, feels he has been able to effect positive change for future whistleblowers.

While you may never come across as serious a situation as George has, you will likely encounter situations where accounting judgments and decisions appear unclear. You may have to make a choice to stay, go, or whistleblow. It is beneficial to consider what you might do in such a situation, before the situation presents itself. Below are some discussion questions and exercises that can help you develop a strategy and perhaps lessen the chance you will find yourself in a dilemma like George's.

Required: Complete the following questions.

PROTECTION AND THE REGULATORY ENVIRONMENT

1. What is the SEC authority for and policy on investigating financial statement misstatement?

2. Read the whistleblower provisions of the Sarbanes Oxley Act (SOX). Note that some provisions address required hotlines and others address retaliation against those who use the hotlines. Now, search the business press for articles and opinion pieces on these provisions. Based on your research, discuss whether SOX has sufficiently increased the likelihood an individual will report fraudulent financial reporting. Examples of questions you might address include: What real protection does SOX offer whistleblowers? How are whistleblower retaliation reports investigated under this law? Is the law producing its intended effect?

3. Read the section of the Dodd-Frank Act of 2010 related to whistleblowers. How does this newer act change protections and motivations for corporate whistleblowers? Search the business press for articles and opinion pieces on these provisions. Describe the provisions and contrast them to those of SOX. Based on your research, discuss whether the Dodd-Frank Act of 2010 is likely to be more effective than SOX.

4. Based on your research, is there evidence whistleblowers are not equally protected and taken seriously across industries, company types (public/private), or levels of authority (their own) in the organization? Consider the reactions of the SEC and the PCAOB to George. Did each organization react as you would have expected?

INDIVIDUAL EXERCISES

1. Research a recent (past 2 years) whistleblower case. Summarize the details of the case, including its resolution, if known. Identify and discuss key factors that influenced the whistleblower's actions. Consider the individual's personal characteristics, the corporate culture, and the subject of the whistleblower's report.

2. Visit the SEC and PCAOB websites. Locate each agency's confidential hotline and analyze and evaluate their policies regarding their hotline use.

Case Learning Objectives and Implementation Guidance

In Part I of this case, we describe an actual ethical dilemma faced by an accountant and, in Part II, we discuss his actions and the resulting ramifications. Our goal is not to discourage whistleblowing - quite the contrary. However, it is important for accounting professionals and students to understand the possible consequences of corporate misconduct and regulatory failure by humanizing the discussion.

We divided the case into two parts in order to encourage students to think through the full array of possible actions available to "George," before they narrow their perspective by reading about the course George actually took. Possible solutions to the questions are provided in the Teaching Notes, although you may be surprised to find your students suggesting answers that you, and we, had not considered. Ethical dilemmas are a uniquely personal conundrum, and individuals must forge a solution that is satisfactory to their individual combination of ethical, religious, cultural, and social influences. However, the resolution framework (see Appendix) encourages them to pay particular attention to laws, regulations, and codes of conduct to which they may be subject.

Our goal is to stimulate thought and discussion among accounting students, as an aid to ethical reasoning development. While this case is based on actual events, we write primarily from the whistleblower's perspective. We do not assert that "George" was correct in every evaluation he made regarding the actions of the Corporation and regulators. That is for the courts to decide.[1]

We provide questions compatible for either in-class discussion or outside completion. To develop research and critical thinking skills, we include questions requiring students to form opinions based on news stories and published articles. Our students have greatly enjoyed discussing the case both in groups and in an open class setting. We wrote the case to address primarily ethical decision-making, which is accounting issue-neutral. However, for those instructors who would like their students to delve more deeply into Bill-and-Hold, we suggested they refer students to the related article accessible at http://www.trinity.edu/rjensen/BillandHold.pdf.

REFERENCES AND ADDITIONAL RESOURCES:

1.   American Institute of Certified Public Accounting (AICPA). Code of Professional Conduct. http://www.aicpa.org/Research/Standards/CodeofConduct/DownloadableDocuments/2008CodeofProfessionalConduct.pdf.

2.   Christopher, John C. 2004. Bill-and-hold transactions in the oilfield services sector. http://www.trinity.edu/rjensen/BillandHold.pdf.

3.   EthicsWeb: http://www.ethicsweb.ca/resources/decision-making/index.html.

4.   Ethics Line: http://www.acfe.com/resources/ethicsline.asp.

---

[1] The press covered the actual lawsuit. Related news stories and legal filings are located online. It is possible that students may locate these items and bring them into class discussions.

5. IMA Statement of Ethical Professional Practice: http://www.imanet.org/ PDFs/Public/CMA/Statement%20of%20Ethics_web.pdf.

6. Markopolos, Harry. 2010. No One Would Listen: A True Financial Thriller. New York, NY: Wiley& Sons, 376.

7. Public Companies Accounting Oversight Board (PCAOB) – Auditing standards: http://pcaobus.org/Standards/Auditing/Pages/default.aspx.

8. Rittenberg, L. E., J. Johnstone and A. Grambling. 2012. *Auditing: A Business Risk Approach* 8th Edition. Florence, KY: Cengage Learning, Inc.

9. Securities and Exchange Commission (SEC). 2002. Sarbanes Oxley Act (SOX): http://www.sec.gov/about/laws/soa2002.pdf.

10. Securities and Exchange Commission (SEC). 2010. Dodd-Frank Wall Street Reform and Consumer Protection Act (DFA): http://www.sec.gov/about/ laws/wallstreetreform-cpa.pdf.

11. U.S. Department of Labor. 2010. Procedures for Handling Retaliation Complaints. http://webapps.dol.gov/federalregister/HtmlDisplay.aspx?D ocId=24196&AgencyId=17&DocumentType=2.

APPENDIX:

ETHICAL DILEMMA RESOLUTION FRAMEWORK*

1. Determine the facts and identify the ethical dilemma involved

    Facts: List the facts relevant to the ethical dilemma - describe the situation and how the person or firm got into the situation.

    Dilemma: Identify from whose perspective you are analyzing the case and explain the ethical dilemma the person or firm is facing.

2. Determine the affected parties and identify their rights[2]

---

[2] Rights are having a claim or title to an item or a particular behavior. Many individual rights arise from basic human rights, such as life, liberty and the pursuit of happiness. Beliefs about such rights may differ among individuals; for example, one person may believe that individuals have a right to gainful employment, while others may view this as a privilege. Additionally, laws and moral obligations confer rights upon a person, such that individuals have the right to meet their obligations or legal responsibilities. The critical point here is that individuals affected by this dilemma have 'rights' that could be impeded by our decision regarding resolution of the dilemma. Additionally, one person's rights can conflict with another's rights, and the individual with the ethical dilemma must first recognize all rights, and then prioritize them.

For each party currently affected by the problem or who could be affected by the solution, describe their interest and identify their rights in regard to this situation. (Note: Just because someone may want or prefer something, doesn't mean it is their *right* to have it.)

3.   Determine the party with the most important rights

Identify who you feel has the most important (prevailing) rights. Obviously, if you are resolving the situation, you will be the one determining the most important rights — recognize in your write-up that this is only one person's opinion.

You must pick only one party here. Two parties typically have at least some rights in conflict and you cannot give the two conflicting rights equal status. Thus, when selecting your solution strategy, you must know whose interests must prevail when those interests are mutually exclusive.

4.   Identify the applicable laws or codes of conduct

For each law or rule, completely identify its origin. Then describe what the rule or law is and why it is applicable to this particular case. It must be applicable to the person or firm having the ethical dilemma (identified in Step 1).

5.   Develop alternative courses of action

This is a brainstorming process. List *all* the options available to the individual or firm with the ethical dilemma. Do not evaluate the options at this point, but do completely explain each.

Then use the results of your brainstorming to create 3 or 4 possible courses of action. These should be mutually exclusive. Additionally, when you pick the best alternative in step 8, you can pick only one of the courses of action you list here; thus, each must be complete as to the process.

Example: it may be that a person is violating company policy. Two options are to speak to the person about it or to report them. Therefore, one course of action might be to first speak to the person, and if they don't correct their behavior, you will report them to their superior. An alternative course of action would be to report the violation, without taking the step of speaking to the person first.

Note: In resolving an ethical dilemma, you can only decide on your own actions; you cannot decide on the actions of others. Others may or may not act as you desire, therefore you must build contingencies into your plan. You also cannot change what has already occurred, you can only plan for what will happen in the future.

6. Determine the possible consequences of each proposed course of action.

Again, this is a brainstorming process. For each possible course of action, list ALL of the possible consequences to each affected person for each alternative. Some may not be very probable, but now is not the time to eliminate them. An incomplete solution to this step is a common cause of unsatisfactory resolution of a dilemma. Then, organize your brainstorming ideas. Consider each of the affected parties in finalizing your list of possible consequences.

7. Assess the likelihood of each possible consequence of each proposed action.

For each possible consequence you listed in step 6 above, assess the likelihood of the consequence occurring, if the individual or firm with the ethical dilemma takes that course of action.

8. Decide on the appropriate course of action

Based on your analyses in steps 1 through 7, select one of the alternatives as your solution strategy. This should be an action favoring the party with the most important rights, as identified in step 3. If there are multiple steps you would like to take, they must be completely contained within one alternative in step 5. For example, if you want to talk with management and then withdraw if they don't agree to your recommendations, then this must be completely explained in one alternative in step 5.

Note: Why can we not select two alternatives? The reason lies with the possible consequences of the alternatives. Consequences of possible courses of action should significantly impact your selection of the most appropriate course of action. Unfortunately, when you string two courses of action together, the first action may change the consequences of the second action, compared to taking only the second action alone.

Example: You win $25,000. Possible courses of action include: (1) buying a pool table, (2) buying a car, (3) investing for retirement, (4) paying off credit cards. Each is less than $25,000, so any one course of action alone is possible. But, if you buy a car and then invest for retirement, the investment you could make would be significantly less than if you chose this as your initial and only option. Thus, the first action has changed the scenario for the second.

Example: You get stopped by the police for running a yellow light. Your possible courses of action include: (1) scream at the officer for inconveniencing you, (2) explain to the policeman the sun was in your eyes and you couldn't see, (3) tell him the person behind you was going so fast that you thought they might rear-end you if you didn't go on through the light, (4) take the ticket and pay it. Alternative 3 may be very productive and result in a positive solution, depending on how convincing you are. However, if you take course of action 1 (screaming) before taking action 3, you probably won't care for the ultimate outcome. Taking action 1 changes the possible consequences and the likelihood of those consequences for action 3. Although this is an extreme example, there are many parallels in the business world.

---

* This framework is derived from that presented in Rittenberg, Johnstone and Grambling (2012). Alternative decision frameworks may be employed, including Rest (1986).

CASE STUDY 5:

American Food Suppliers Inc.: A Case Study in Fraud and Forensic Accounting

Maria H. Sanchez, CPA, Ph.D.
Rider University
Christopher P. Agoglia, Ph.D.
University of Massachusetts

LEARNING OBJECTIVES

After completing and discussing this case, you should be able to

- Understand the basics of accounting for vendor rebates.
- Understand the dangers of over relying on third party confirmations as an audit procedure.
- Understand the responsibilities of the external auditor for detecting fraud.
- Appreciate the importance of professional skepticism.
- Understand the difference between a financial statement audit and a forensic audit.
- Appreciate the importance of ethical behavior in the accounting profession.

INTRODUCTION

American Food Suppliers was acquired by the company Barnacle in 2000. American Food Suppliers was the largest distributor of food to restaurants, hotels, schools, hospitals, and Barnacle's extensive chains of U.S. grocery stores. A material portion of American Food Suppliers' balance sheet was promotional allowances receivable from vendors (vendor rebates). As part of their normal audit procedures for American Food Suppliers, Barnacle's independent auditors, Doodle Auditors LLP, sent confirmations for these receivables. Confirmations were mailed to vendors' salespeople and were returned without exceptions. For the first two years after the acquisition, the auditors issued unqualified opinions. During the 2002 audit, however, Barnacle's independent auditors discovered problems and promptly withdrew their audit opinions for 2000 and 2001, and suspended their 2002 audit. On February 28, 2003, Barnacle announced that it would restate earnings downward for the fiscal years 2000 and 2001, and for the first three quarters of 2002 by a combined total of at least $500 million and that a forensic accounting investigation would be launched, mostly because of irregularities at Barnacle's subsidiary American Food Suppliers.

The company's stock price lost nearly two-thirds of its value on the day of the announcement. Barnacle's chief executive and chief financial officers resigned when the announcement was made, and subsequently other high-level managers at both the parent company and American Food Suppliers also stepped down. On March 28, 2003, Barnacle's audit committee ordered investigations at the parent company and at 22 Barnacle subsidiaries to look for accounting errors, irregularities, and other issues as well as assess internal controls and management integrity. After a forensic audit, Barnacle eventually reported that the overstatement of American Food Suppliers' earnings was more than $900 million. A large component of the overstatement resulted from improper recognition of promotional allowances. Several American Food Suppliers' employees and vendors either admitted to or were convicted of playing a role in the fraud.

In this case, students will gain insights into the proper accounting for and disclosure of promotional allowances and also the risk of over-reliance on third party confirmation as an audit procedure. Students will also distinguish between a financial statement audit and a forensic audit.

SOME BACKGROUND

Accounting for cash consideration from vendor rebates, also known as "promotional allowances," was at the center of the American Food Suppliers's earnings restatement. Rebates of this type are common in the grocery and foodservice industries and are frequently material in amount, sometimes exceeding 5% of sales. Vendors can offer rebates to customers in exchange for favorable display space in stores, or they may give volume rebates to provide an incentive to a retailer to increase sales of the vendor's products, with the rebate percentage increasing as the retailer's sales volume increases. However, these rebates are problematic in several respects. At the time of American Food Suppliers's accounting irregularities, there was no standardized accounting treatment of these rebates. Companies have accounted for them differently, and there have been differing levels of disclosure regarding their amounts. The investigation at American Food Suppliers revealed that determination of rebates receivable can be problematic.

Even before the investigation into American Food Suppliers's accounting practices, supplier rebate issues have come under scrutiny and have even resulted in regulatory action against other retailers. The Securities and Exchange Commission (SEC), as an example, alleged that among the accounting irregularities that occurred at Rite Aid in the late 1990's was how the company accounted for its vendor rebates. In June 2002, the SEC's Accounting and Auditing Enforcement Release No. 1581 indicated that Rite Aid improperly recognized $75 million in vendor rebates, which represented 37% of the company's pre-tax income in 1999 (SEC, 2002). Kroger Co. of Cincinnati had to restate its earnings from 1998 to 2000 as a result of how one of its acquired companies had accounted for such rebates. Similar irregularities and allegations of impropriety regarding recognition of vendor rebates have led to earnings restatements and/or regulatory actions at other companies, including Just for Feet, Fleming Cos., and Great Atlantic & Pacific Tea Co. More recently, the SEC filed a suit with Penn Traffic grocery stores in which the SEC alleged that Penn Traffic intentionally inflated income by prematurely recognizing income from promotional allowances (SEC, 2008).

GENERALLY ACCEPTED ACCOUNTING PRINCIPLES FOR VENDOR REBATES

Prior to 2002, there was no standardization regarding the accounting for or disclosure of these vendor rebates. Companies often "buried" the rebates in their financial statements, even though they were frequently material in amount, particularly for retailers such as American Food Suppliers. In August 2002, the Financial Accounting Standards Board (FASB) released Emerging Issues Task Force (EITF) Issue No. 02-16, *Accounting by a Reseller for Cash Consideration Received from a Vendor*, which addressed the accounting for and disclosure of these rebates. In the EITF, the FASB outlined three possible views of these rebates. Depending upon the circumstances under which it is being offered, a vendor rebate may represent: 1) a reduction in the cost of sales to the reseller; 2) a reduction in some other expense, e.g., advertising; or 3) a type of revenue for the reseller. Generally, cash consideration from a vendor is presumed to be a reduction of the price of the vendor's products or services and should, therefore, be a reduction in the cost of sales when recognized in the reseller's income statement. That presumption can be overcome, however, under two different sets of circumstances: 1) if the cash consideration is intended to reimburse the reseller for costs incurred (e.g., advertising), then the consideration received by the reseller should be recorded as a reduction in that expense; or 2) if the cash consideration is primarily payment for the reseller's expertise and efforts in a particular endeavor (e.g., market research), then the consideration should be recognized as revenue by the reseller (FASB, 2002).

Additionally, the Task Force concurred that if the cash consideration is primarily an incentive for the reseller to achieve certain sales levels, or to remain a customer of the vendor for a specified period of time, then the consideration should reduce the reseller's cost of sales. This reduction in cost of sales should be systematic and rational, reflecting the underlying progress of earning the incentive, assuming that the reseller's progress is probable and reasonably estimable. If the progress is not probable, or it cannot be reasonably estimated, the consideration should reduce the reseller's cost of sales as the relevant milestone is achieved (FASB, 2002).[1]

As an example, assume that retailer ABC Company is entitled to a 10% rebate of the purchase price of merchandise purchased from vendor XYZ Company if ABC Company is able to sell $1,000 of XYZ Company's products during the

---

[1]   This EITF has been codified into FASB ASC 605-50.

coming year. If it is probable that ABC will meet the $1,000 target and the company can also reasonably estimate its progress towards achieving the milestone, ABC should recognize the 10% rebate in a systematic and rational manner. If, on the other hand, the probability of ABC achieving the $1,000 sales level is uncertain or if ABC cannot reasonably estimate its progress in reaching the milestone, ABC should recognize the entire 10% rebate as a reduction in cost of sales only upon reaching the $1,000 target. The Task Force's position was clear that *immediate* recognition of cash consideration as a reduction of cost of sales or as revenue was *not* acceptable. American Food Suppliers appears to have been recognizing the vendor rebates as it *purchased* the product not when it was sold. Additionally, federal authorities alleged that American Food Suppliers deliberately booked vendor rebates to which they were not entitled. Thus, not only is this an accounting issue with respect to the *timing* of recognition of the rebates, but it is also an issue of fraudulently recognizing rebates that did not exist.

WHAT HAPPENED AT AMERICAN FOOD SUPPLIERS

During their 2002 audit of Barnacle's financial statements, as part of their confirmation process at American Food Suppliers, Doodle Auditors LLP discovered that certain accrued vendor allowance receivable balances were overstated. Doodle uncovered a series of accounting irregularities at American Food Suppliers and other Barnacle subsidiaries. Doodle immediately withdrew their audit opinions for 2000 and 2001 and suspended work on the 2002 audit.

There appeared to be a confluence of economic conditions, managerial "inventiveness," and failures of internal controls that led to the accounting irregularities at American Food Suppliers. Company sales for the year 2002 had been decreasing. In last quarter of 2002, upper management held a conference call with its divisional managers advising them that their annual bonuses were at risk if sales were not boosted. According to testimony provided by those inside the company, in that conference call, the company's chief operating officer described an "initiative" that would increase the likelihood of managers receiving their bonuses and help the company achieve its sales target for the year. Quite simply, the strategy was to order large amounts of inventory and immediately recognize the vendor rebates that accompanied them. The rebates were in many cases substantial and, according to some sources, ranged from 8.5% to 46% of the purchase price. Divisional managers stated that they were told by upper management that if they did not place orders for additional inventory, then it would be done for them. These managers reported that it was made clear that if they did not go along with the "initiative," not only were their bonuses in jeopardy, but perhaps their jobs were as well.

Soon the warehouses at American Food Suppliers were overflowing with inventory of food-related items and paper products. The amount of inventory the company purchased was so large that it had to rent additional space and refrigerator trucks to store it. As purchases increased, the vendor rebates to which

American Food Suppliers were entitled also increased. Supplier rebates increased from approximately $150 million in 2000 to about $800 million in 2003. These rebates were recognized immediately as products were purchased in an attempt to boost earnings. The excess inventory was so immense; however, that even after the announcement of the earnings restatement, it was questionable whether the company would be able to sell it. In an effort to unload the massive amount of product in its warehouses, the company had to reduce its selling price below its original cost in some cases.

During the audit of American Food Suppliers, third party confirmations of rebates receivable had been provided by the vendors' salespeople, not their accounting departments. According to complaints filed by the SEC, employees at American Food Suppliers urged their vendors to complete and return to the auditors false confirmation letters with dollar amounts intentionally overstated, sometimes by as much as millions of dollars. Some vendors were pressured, some were provided with secret "side letters" assuring the vendors that they did not owe the amounts listed on the confirmations.

In a span of several months, the "initiative" proposed by the company's COO unraveled. Rather than helping the company out of its economic doldrums, the scheme instead resulted in earnings restatements, plunging stock price, several high-level managers losing their jobs, regulatory investigation of the company's accounting practices, and allegations that company officers had criminal intent to deceive and defraud the investing public. In September 2003, officials raided Barnacle's headquarters and began a criminal probe. One year later, U.S. officials announced that three former American Food Suppliers executives were being formally charged with conspiracy, securities fraud, and making false filings. Prosecutors also announced at the same time that four other American Food Suppliers managers had admitted to their roles in the same alleged scheme of overstating earnings.

THE FORENSIC AUDIT

After the irregularities were uncovered by the external auditors, a criminal investigation was launched by the U.S. Department of Justice. In addition, Barnacle appointed a team of forensic accountants to work alongside the SEC. The forensic accountants had to sort through tens of thousands of documents.

The forensic audit revealed fraud at American Food Suppliers totaling over $900 million, with over $150 relating to 2000, over $300 million relating to 2001 and the rest relating to 2002. The fraud related to fictitious and/or overstated vendor allowance receivables and improper or premature recognition of vendor allowances and an understatement of cost of goods sold. Numerous American Food Suppliers employees were involved in the fraud, and it was discovered that the fraud went back as far as 2000. American Food Suppliers employees were found to have been using inflated recognition rates for vendor allowances and intentionally misapplying GAAP. Doodle's audit testing using third party confirmations failed to detect management's misrepresentation of the reduction in cost of sales resulting from these manufacturer rebates.

The probe of American Food Suppliers expanded to investigate several of the company's suppliers to determine if they might have been complicit in American Food Suppliers intent to misrepresent certain financial statement assertions. The investigation revealed that American Food Suppliers employees asked salespeople at their vendors to sign false documentation for Doodle and that some vendors cooperated with this fraudulent scheme. Four salespeople at Vendor A admitted that they had signed off on, and forwarded to American Food Suppliers external auditors, erroneous documents that reflected inflated amounts owed to the company by Vendor A. Similarly, at Vendor B, three salespeople also admitted to signing off on inflated amounts for manufacturer rebates due to American Food Suppliers. Vendor B claimed, however, that the erroneous confirmation amounts were discovered and that American Food Suppliers external auditor was notified before news of the accounting scandal broke. The forensic examination at American Food Suppliers also revealed numerous weaknesses in internal controls, including failure to properly record and track vendor allowances, inadequate accounting and financial reporting systems for vendor allowances, and failure to follow GAAP.

The investigation revealed fraud at not only American Food Suppliers, but also at several other Barnacle subsidiaries and the parent company. It was discovered at one subsidiary that fictitious invoices were used to conceal payments, and in some cases, payments were improperly capitalized rather than expensed. It was also discovered that the consolidation of certain joint ventures into Barnacle's financial statements was in error and that secret side letters had been concealed from Barnacle's audit committee and external auditors. Further, accounting irregularities and earnings management were uncovered at other subsidiaries and at the parent company.

Overall, more than 800 separate items related to internal control weaknesses and accounting issues were identified at Barnacle and its subsidiaries. This extensive forensic examination led to a lengthy delay in the announcement of 2002 audited earnings numbers. Barnacle's 2002 annual report was released on December of 2003, which included restatements for the years 2000 and 2001.

The total fraud at Barnacle was revealed to be over $1.2 billion. Of this, approximately $925 million related to American Food Suppliers. Upon conclusion of the forensic investigation, Barnacle announced the creation of a task force reporting to the audit committee to address the internal control weaknesses and improper accounting practices uncovered during the investigation. Barnacle announced in their 2002 annual report that the internal audit department would now report directly to the CEO and the audit committee, rather than solely to the CEO, as was the case previously.

According to press releases from Barnacle, after the accounting scandal, American Food Suppliers made substantial improvements in the company's financial systems and controls, as well as its financial organization, to strengthen financial monitoring and reporting. They also established a new office of governance, ethics and compliance.

LESSONS LEARNED: AUDIT CONFIRMATIONS

In designing the tests to be performed during an audit, an auditor must obtain adequate assurance to address audit risk. The greater the risk of a particular financial statement assertion (e.g., the existence and amount of vendor rebates), the more evidence an auditor should gather to support the assertion. Statement on Auditing Standards (SAS) No. 67 states that, "confirmation is the process of obtaining and evaluating a direct communication from a third party in response to a request for information about a particular item affecting financial statement assertions" (AICPA, 1992, SAS 67.06, AU 330). According to SAS No. 67, confirmation from an independent source is generally viewed as having greater reliability than evidence obtained solely from client personnel. Confirmation with a third party helps the auditor assess the financial statement assertions with respect to all five of management's assertions: existence or occurrence, completeness, rights and obligations, valuation or allocation, and presentation and disclosure. The auditor may design a third party confirmation to address any one or more of these assertions (AICPA, 1992). However, existence is usually the primary assertion addressed by confirmation of receivables.

Even though evidence obtained by a third party confirmation is generally viewed as being more reliable than evidence provided by the entity being audited, SAS No. 67 cautions that an auditor should maintain a healthy level of professional skepticism. The auditor should consider information from prior years' audits and audits of similar entities. Further, an auditor has an obligation to understand the arrangements and transactions between the audit client and the third party so that the appropriate confirmation request can be designed. SAS No. 67 states that "[i]f information about the respondent's competence, knowledge, motivation, ability, or willingness to respond, or about the respondent's objectivity and free-dom from bias with respect to the audited entity comes to the auditor's attention, the auditor should consider the effects of such information on designing the confirmation request and evaluating the results, including determining whether other procedures are necessary" (AICPA, 2002, SAS 67.27). The statement al-lows for the possibility that the party responding to the confirmation may not be completely objective or free from bias and requires the auditor to use other evidence to confirm financial statement assertions in such cases (AICPA, 1992).

Confirming accounts receivable is a generally accepted auditing procedure and is required unless the amount involved is immaterial, a confirmation would be ineffective, or if the auditor can substantially reduce the level of audit risk of the financial statement assertion through the use of other substantive and analytical tests. Accounts receivable, for the purpose of SAS No. 67 (AU 330), represent claims against customers that have arisen in the normal course of business and loans held by financial institutions (AICPA, 1992). The Statement does *not* specifically address confirming a receivable that arises when a vendor owes a rebate to a reseller, a situation that differs substantially from the typical trade accounts receivable from a customer. Confirming vendor rebate receivables give rise to different risks that likely were not envisioned when the Statement was adopted in 1992.

In adopting SAS No. 67, two (of the seventeen) Board members, while assenting to the Statement, expressed a reservation that the language used in the Statement usurped the freedom of the auditor in exercising professional judgment in how best to confirm accounts receivable and that the language might also lead auditors to place undue reliance on third party confirmation when circumstances might suggest that the auditor choose a more effective test (AICPA, 1992). With the benefit of hindsight it is clear that the auditors of American Food Suppliers could have, and should have, designed a more "effective test," one that would have helped overcome the inherent weakness that existed in this situation where parties providing the confirmation may have either been uninformed about the existence and/or amount owed to the retailer or may have had a vested interest to overstate the amount that was owed to American Food Suppliers. While some practitioner literature has made reference to biases of confirmation respondents, scant attention has been given to this particular concern regarding responses to auditor confirmations by vendors' sales personnel.

THE AFTERMATH

- Three former purchasing executives for American Food Suppliers pleaded guilty to participating in the scheme and to conspiring with suppliers to mislead the company's auditors. They later agreed to pay approximately $400,000 in civil penalties.

- U.S. courts approved a $1.3 billion global class action settlement between Barnacle and shareholders.

- The former CFO of American Food Suppliers pleaded guilty and was sentenced to eleven months of home detention and five years' probation.

- Fifteen American Food Suppliers vendors pleaded guilty from 2003 to 2006 to criminal charges related to the fraud, admitting that they submitted false confirmations to the auditors.

- Former American Food Suppliers CEO reached an agreement with Barnacle in which he agreed to pay $10 million but did not acknowledge liability.

QUESTIONS

1) What lessons can be learned from the American Food Suppliers case with regard to over reliance on third party confirmations?

2) What alternative substantive tests may have been available to the auditors of American Food Suppliers? How do the alternate procedures differ from typical accounts receivable confirmations when confirming vendor receivables?

3) What mistakes were likely made by auditors of American Food Suppliers and what responsibility does the auditor have to uncover fraud?

4) The FASB has reduced the wide latitude that companies once had in accounting for vendor rebates by issuing EITF Issue No. 02-16. What recommendations would you suggest to the FASB for further improving the accounting and auditing guidance in the area of vendor rebates?

5) Define professional skepticism. Do you think that the auditors of American Food Suppliers exercised enough professional skepticism? Why or why not?

6) What is the difference between a financial statement audit and a forensic audit? When would each type of audit be performed?

7) Who acted unethically in this case? What were the consequences?

8) Apparently, many people within American Food Suppliers knew of the fraud and either helped perpetuate the fraud or at a minimum did not notify the auditors or regulatory agencies. What options were available to the employees who knew about the fraud and wanted to do something about it?

REFERENCES

American Institute of Certified Public Accountants (AICPA). 1992. *Statement on Auditing Standards No. 67.* New York: AICPA.

American Institute of Certified Public Accountants (AICPA). 2003. *Statement on Auditing Standards No. 99.* New York: AICPA.

Financial Accounting Standards Board (FASB). 2002. FASB Emerging Issues Task Force No. 02-16: Accounting by a reseller for cash consideration received from a vendor. Norwalk, CT: FASB.

U.S. Securities and Exchange Commission (SEC). 2002. *Accounting and Auditing Enforcement Release No. 1581.* Washington, DC: U.S. Securities and Exchange Commission.

U.S. Securities and Exchange Commission(SEC), 2008, September 30. "Litigation Release No. 20760 SEC Charges East Coast Supermarket Operator Penn Traffic with Accounting Fraud."

CASE STUDY 6:

Dr. Sterling's Disability Insurance Claim

Diane M. Matson, Ph.D., CFE
University of St. Thomas
Wen Yu, Ph.D.
University of St. Thomas

LEARNING OBJECTIVES

After completing and discussing this case, you should be able to

- Spot some red flags of fraud.
- Recognize that fraud investigations proceed in stages, with information coming in at various times.
- Develop analytical skills in a specific context.
- Focus on where funds are spent.
- Learn how to search for more information.

Dr. Albert Sterling, a fictitious surgeon, submitted a disability income claim to Guardian Professional Protection Insurance Corporation, a fictitious insurance company. Dr. Sterling is making a disability claim, stating that he cannot continue to work as a surgeon, due to debilitating depression. While the doctor and the insurance company are fictitious, several aspects of this case are real.

You assume the role of an insurance investigator who is assigned to assess the validity of the claim. The case is divided into two phases, Phase 1 and Phase 2. Phase 1 contains most of the information and questions, and requires most of the analysis. Phase 2 contains six additional sources of evidence, and allows for a more in-depth investigation about the validity of the claim. Phase 1 is effective by itself, but Phase 2 shows that a fraud investigation usually proceeds in stages, with information coming in at various times.

This case provides an opportunity to practice forensic accounting techniques in the specific context of disability insurance. You will find several "red flags of fraud" to investigate. Tracy Coenen, CPA, CFE, an insurance investigator, notes: "For insurance claims that deal with illness or injury, such as workers compensation, disability or personal injury the key to finding red flags of fraud is looking for financial information that doesn't add up or is inconsistent with the claims submitted" (Drax, 2006).

APPLICATIONS

This case is appropriate for a forensic accounting course at the undergraduate or graduate level. We have primarily implemented this case in the advanced auditing course in our Masters of Science in Accountancy (MSA) program, which includes significant coverage of forensic accounting and fraud investigations. This case was tested and found effective in three sections of this course. We have also provided this case in independent studies in forensic accounting to both undergraduate and graduate students many times, and received positive feedback from these students.[1]

FEATURES

Several features of this case may be of interest to instructors. These features include the development of analytical skills in a specific context, the focus on where funds are spent, and the search for additional information.

Use Analytical Skills in a Specific Context. This case is set in a specific context, the insurance industry, where accounts, amounts and relationships are of particular concern when viewed in the light of a disability claim. This case encourages students to develop their analytical skills, as they will identify accounts, amounts and relationships that do not make sense for a high-earning individual and his family. For example, students should notice that Dr. Sterling has taken a loan against his pension, which may seem surprising for a high-income person to do. In addition, students are provided two guidelines or "rules of thumb" commonly used in determining the validity of disability claims. When students investigate the relationship and patterns with a specific purpose in mind—determining the validity of a disability claim—they should find that Dr. Sterling has not built up his net worth as much as would be expected. Students can transfer such analytical skills to other types of fraud investigation cases, even at a corporate level.

Consider Accounts that are Not Included. Students are encouraged to consider the reasonableness of accounts that are listed. Furthermore, students are directed to consider what accounts could be missing and what the potential impact (of those missing accounts) is on the validity of the claim. For instance, the Sterlings do not report any investments in stocks, or a vacation home. High-earning families often own these types of assets. In addition, these families may have other sources of income, such as interest and dividends from investments. Under some policies, the existence of other sources of income could decrease disability insurance benefits.

Focus on Where Money is Spent. This case also requires students to take a different perspective about the funds, than do other cases based on an

---

[1]   The university at which the authors work does not currently offer an undergraduate forensic accounting course in the regular curriculum, due to the time constraints of the other required accounting courses.

investigative technique. In a typical net worth analysis problem, students are provided some limited base year information and more detailed information for two or three years, from which they can list assets and liabilities, compute net worth, and add various expenditures (such as living costs, alimony, vacations and school tuition) to arrive at a measure of total increase in net worth. This measure is then compared to known sources of funds (such as salaries and inheritances) to arrive at unexplained sources of funds (if any). The possible presence of unexplained funds may indicate that the person is getting funds from illegal activities. The focus of this type of problem is: Where is the money coming from?

In this case, however, students should discover that the person does not seem to have a lot of assets or an extravagant lifestyle, as might be expected for a high-earning professional. Understanding where the money is being spent will help the investigator determine the validity of the claim. This case provides a completed net worth analysis (a short version, with only assets, liabilities, and net worth) and other relevant information on the person's salary and the family's lifestyle. The focus in this case is: Where is the money going?

Search for Useful Sources of Information. This case gives students a chance to consider what information would be useful in making a decision about this claim. In our experience, students tend to be unfamiliar with the types of information that are available in an investigation. This is not a surprise, as they often have limited experience with company documents, and even personal documents. So, this case encourages students to think about what type of information would be useful, and what documents would be relevant. For instance, to learn more about the family's spending, they could request bank statements, and to learn more about the value of the home, they could ask for an appraisal report.

CASE

Phase 1

This case asks you to apply your forensic accounting skills to a specialized area of forensic accounting, insurance fraud. In particular, you should consider the possibility of a fraudulent claim for long-term disability insurance. The **Background Information** provides a brief description of disability insurance. The **Disability Insurance Claim Information** gives details about the policyholder's claim and financial condition. In the **Questions for Phase 1**, you will identify and discuss issues and concerns you might have as an insurance fraud investigator.

Background Information

Disability insurance, also known as disability income insurance, provides income if a person is unable to work. This form of insurance protects the earned income of the beneficiary (the insured policyholder). A disability policy protects income against the risk that disability will make working (and therefore earning) impossible. Such a policy is designed to pay for living expenses if the policyholder becomes unable to work due to accident or illness. There are several sources of disability insurance, including federal government social insurance programs, employer-supplied disability insurance, and state-run workers' compensation benefits. In addition, policies can be sold and issued to individuals through insurance companies, which is applicable in this case.

There are two types of disability policies: Short-Term Disability (STD) and Long-Term Disability (LTD). STD policies typically take effect after 14 days of disability and may extend for two years. LTD policies usually take effect after several weeks of disability and may provide benefits for a few years, to the time when the person can collect social security payments, or even the remaining years of the person's life.

Disability insurance policies differ in the definition of "disability." One definition views the disability as a condition that prevents the person from performing the major duties of his or her chosen occupation. So, if a person cannot perform the main duties of his or her chosen occupation, this person will receive benefits. This is the "own occupation" approach, applicable in this case. Another definition views disability as a condition that prevents the person from performing the main duties of any gainful occupation. So, if a person cannot perform the main duties of his or her chosen occupation, he or she will be expected to obtain employment in another area. Earnings from another occupation may offset the disability insurance benefits. This is the "any occupation" approach.

DISABILITY INSURANCE CLAIM INFORMATION

Guardian Professional Protection Insurance Corporation File
February 10, 2010

Assume that you are a claims investigator with Guardian Professional Protection Insurance Corporation (GPPIC), a large insurance company based in Chicago. You have received a claim on the long-term disability policy for Dr. Albert Sterling. His policy is of the "own occupation" type. You are responsible for determining the validity of the claim. Here is the information that you have at this time:

1.   Dr. Albert Sterling is 59 years old.
2.   He is a general surgeon.
3.   He is the sole owner of his medical practice. There are two offices, one in downtown Chicago and one in Lake Forest.
4.   He has ten employees between the two clinics. They are nurses, office managers, medical records specialists and receptionists.

5. He has hospital privileges and does his surgery at two well-known hospitals.
6. He works around 60 hours a week performing surgery, visiting patients in the hospital, and conducting office appointments.
7. Mrs. Melissa Sterling and Dr. Sterling have been married for 35 years.
8. Mrs. Melissa Sterling has been a full-time homemaker since her marriage.
9. They have two children, Lauren and Albert Jr. (A.J.).
10. Lauren works in her father's Lake Forest office. She attended college for 2 years. She is married with one child.
11. A.J. graduated from a local university with a degree in business administration and is employed with a local market research firm.
12. Dr. Sterling reports the following salary information:

Year	Amount
2012	$550,000
2013	575,000
2014	610,000
2015	620,000
2016	630,000

13. The combined federal and state individual income tax rate is approximately 40%.
14. Dr. Sterling states that he has been suffering from debilitating depression recently. He has filed a claim for long-term disability insurance, asserting that he cannot continue to work in his profession, as a surgeon.
15. Dr. and Mrs. Sterling's personal financial statement (Personal Statement of Net Worth/Balance Sheet) has not changed significantly since the policy was issued in December of 2012. Copies of the Personal Statements from December 31, 2012; December 31, 2013; December 31, 2014; and December 31, 2015 are in GPPIC files. The Personal Statement for December 31, 2016 is provided next.

Dr. and Mrs. Albert Sterling Personal Statement of Net Worth/Balance Sheet As of December 31, 2016	
Assets	
Cash	$10,000
Automobile	50,000
Personal Property	60,000
Boat	100,000
Collectables	350,000
House	600,000
Pension	210,000
Interest in Professional Corporation	1,200,000
Total Assets	$2,580,000
Liabilities	
Automobile Loan	$25,000
Home Mortgage	400,000
Pension Loan	15,000
Total Liabilities	$440,000
Net Worth =	
Total Assets – Total Liabilities	$2,140,000

Under federal penalties of perjury, I do swear and affirm that the information provided above is true and correct to the best of my knowledge and belief.

Signed: Albert Sterling, M. D.   Date: January 15, 2017

Note: All persons, organizations and companies in this case are fictitious. However, many aspects of the case are realistic.

QUESTIONS FOR PHASE 1

1.   What type of income is Dr. Sterling hoping to replace?

2.   In general, do you notice anything unusual about the Personal Statement? Consider that Dr. Sterling is 59 years old and his children are adults. He is a surgeon, and surgeons usually work a lot, and are usually high-income professionals.

3.   What accounts on the Personal Statement should you investigate? Why? Please be specific as to why these accounts are of concern.

4.   Consider accounts that you do not see on the Personal Statement. Please identify these accounts and discuss what concerns you would have because these accounts are not reported by the Sterlings. In other words, what accounts might you expect to see on such a Personal Statement for a high-income family?

5.   Here are two guidelines usually used by claims investigators in these types of cases:

   (1)   If a person is trying to accumulate wealth, his or her home should cost at least twice as much as his or her take-home pay.
   (2)   A commonly-used formula for expected net worth is:

   Expected Net Worth =
   $$\frac{(\text{Age} - 10 \text{ years}) \times \text{Current Yearly Pretax Household Income}}{10}$$

   Please apply these guidelines to the Sterlings. Show your calculations. How do the Sterlings "measure up" here?

6.   What concerns do you have about Dr. Sterling and his disability insurance claim?

7.   What additional sources of information (documents, interviews, etc.) should you request or search for?

CASE

Assume you have found, requested and received some additional information and documents after starting your investigation. These documents provide more information about Dr. Sterling. Please find these documents attached, as follows.

Exhibit 1: Disability Insurance Policy

Exhibit 2: Credit Card Statement

Exhibit 3: W-2 (Selected Information)

Exhibit 4: Memo of Interview with Dolores Jones, Office Manager of the Clinic

Exhibit 5: Appraisal Report for the Sterlings' Home

Exhibit 6: Statement of Activities for Dr. Sterling's Clinics

Exhibit 1: Disability Insurance Policy

Guardian Professional Protection Insurance Corporation
115 North LaSalle Street
Chicago, IL 60602

Disability Income Policy
Schedule Page

Insured – Albert Sterling

Owner – Albert Sterling

Loss Payee – Albert Sterling

Occupation Class – Medical/General Surgeon

Date of Birth – January 14, 1951

Policy Number – A123456

Date of Issue – December 31, 2012

Age at Issue – 54

Last Renewal Date – December 31, 2016

Term – 12 months

Annual Premium for:

Basic benefits $25,000

Table of Basic Benefits:

Monthly Indemnity Payments $30,000

Lifetime Extension for Total Disability:

If you become totally disabled between age 54 and age 65, the monthly indemnity amount will be paid.

Benefits and Premiums after Age 65:

If you renew this policy when you are age 65, we will issue a new contract at that time. Premiums for this policy may increase on renewal at or after age 65.

Licensed Resident Agent's Countersignature

_____ Edward J. Feldman

Edward J. Feldman, Senior Agent
Licensed, State of Illinois

Exhibit 2: Credit Card Statement

Finance One Bank

Credit Card Statement for January 3 to February 2, 2017

Account #
1714 9600 4444   **Albert Sterling, MD**   **VIP Platinum**   **Since 2002**

Beginning Balance	$45,100.00	
– Payments	–$27,800.00	
+ Purchases	$31,300.00	
+ Finance Charge	$1,200.00	
= Ending Balance	$49,800.00	
Minimum Balance	$3,500.00	
Due Date	**28-Feb-10**	

Detail for January 3 to February 2, 2017

Payments

Payment—Thank you	$27,800.00

Transactions

10-Jan-16	Java Joe Coffee Shop Chicago	$14.00
14-Jan-16	Boca Chica Restaurant Chicago	590.00
15-Jan-16	Brooks Brothers Evanston	3,699.00
18-Jan-16	Delta Airlines CHICA VEGAS FLTS 3489, 2378 FST CLS RT	2,100.00
20-Jan-16	Access Check #17 Cash	12,000.00
25-Jan-16	Mirage Hotel Las Vegas Deluxe Suite Jan 18-25	8,397.00
29-Jan-16	Continental Airlines RES—4 Flts 345, 458 First Class Rd Tr Atlantic City	4,500.00

Exhibit 3: W-2 (selected information)	
Wages and Salaries	$630,000
Federal Tax Withholding	$189,000
State Tax Withholding	$63,000

Exhibit 4: Memo of Interview with Dolores Jones, Office Manager of Clinic

Memo for File

Date: February 16, 2017

I interviewed Dolores Jones, Office Manager of Dr. Sterling's downtown Chicago clinic. We met on Monday, February 13, 2017, from 10:00 to 11:15 am in a coffee shop, Java Joe's, near the clinic. Here are some relevant excerpts of our conversation:

Ms. Jones has been the office manager for 10 years. Before that, she had been home with her three children. She works about 45 hours a week, 5 days a week. She lives in Evanston. She supervises the receptionists and medical records specialists. She also is in charge of billing the patients and their insurance providers. She reports that much of her time is spent filing the necessary paperwork with insurance companies (for patients covered by their employers or other private insurance plans) or with various government agencies (for patients covered by medical assistance plans or Medicare).

She reports that she likes her job and plans to stay indefinitely. She says she gets along fine with Dr. Sterling, and that he is a fair boss. When I asked her if she has any concerns about Dr. Sterling, she said that he has been somewhat moody lately, and seems a bit "down." When I asked her for more specifics, she said that he has snapped at the office staff and even a few patients recently. This is out of character, she explained, but she figures that he is just tired. She did not have any other comments relative to this.

Ms. Jones does not know Dr. Sterling's family personally very well. She has seen Mrs. Sterling and A. J. at the clinic a few times. Lauren, the Sterlings' daughter, is the office manager at Dr. Sterling's clinic in Lake Forest. As such, Ms. Jones and Lauren do talk on the phone and correspond by e-mail about various scheduling and patient matters, but apparently do not interact on a personal level. Ms. Jones could not say if there seemed to be issues in the family, as she does not know the family in that way.

Exhibit 5: Appraisal Report for the Sterlings' Home

February 20, 2017

To Whom it May Concern:

I conducted an appraisal of the property at:

1415 Birchwood Road
Lake Forest, IL 60045

To arrive at the appraisal value, I considered the age, size, condition and location of the house. Other factors in this case included the small lot size and lack of a swimming pool. I researched the sales prices of similar properties in the same and adjacent neighborhoods.

In my professional judgment, the value of this property is:

$625,000

Thank you for allowing me to be of service.

Very sincerely yours,

Barbara Belle

Barbara Belle, Appraiser
Barbara Belle Real Estate Services, Inc.

Specializing in Residential and Commercial Real Estate
Sales and Appraisals
233 LaSalle Street South
Chicago, IL   60606
312-444-0077

Exhibit 6: Statement of Activities for Dr. Sterling's Clinics					
Upon request, Dr. Sterling provided his clinics' Statement of Activities for the last five years. A local accounting firm, Phipps LLP, has performed annual audits and issued unqualified opinions. The following is a copy of the Statement of Activities.					

Statement of Activities

	2016	2015	2014	2013	2012
Revenue, gains and other support:					
Net medical service revenue	$2,100,000	$2,050,000	$2,500,000	$2,220,000	$2,150,000
Investment returns allocated to current activities	(50,000)	(120,000)	100,000	50,000	48,000
Contributions available for current activities	15,000	20,000	40,000	38,000	35,000
Other	81,000	80,000	110,000	105,000	95,000
Total revenue, gains and other support	$2,146,000	$2,030,000	$2,750,000	$2,413,000	$2,328,000
Expenses:					
Salaries and benefits	1,300,000	1,290,000	1,260,000	1,180,000	1,150,000
Supplies and facilities	470,000	450,000	510,000	480,000	450,000
Provision for uncollectible accounts	45,000	41,000	55,000	48,000	46,500
Finance and investment expenses	12,000	12,000	18,000	16,000	15,500
Total expenses	$1,827,000	$1,793,000	$1,843,000	$1,724,000	$1,662,000
Income from current activities	$319,000	$237,000	$907,000	$689,000	$666,000
Non-current and other items:					
Contributions not available for current activities, net	$10,000	$10,000	$25,000	$20,000	$18,000
Unallocated investment returns, net	(125,000)	(300,000)	250,000	125,000	120,000
Pension and postretirement expenses	(24,000)	(22,000)	(30,000)	(28,000)	(26,500)
Total noncurrent and other items	$(139,000)	$(312,000)	$245,000	$117,000	$111,500
Increase in net assets	$180,000	$(75,000)	$1,152,000	$806,000	$777,500

QUESTIONS FOR PHASE 2

1. How does this additional information affect your judgment about the validity of the claim? Why?

2. What should you do now?

CASE STUDY 7:

Detecting Shell Companies with Dynamic Text Comparison Using Levenshtein Distances

Mark W. Lehman, Ph.D., CPA, CFE, ACDA
Mississippi State University
Marcia Weidenmier Watson, Ph.D.
University of North Carolina at Charlotte

LEARNING OBJECTIVES

After completing and discussing this case, you should be able to

- Search for shell companies.
- Learn how to use fuzzy duplicates using Levenshtein distances.
- Analyze employee and vendor tables.
- Appreciate the disadvantage of using a simple join.

INTRODUCTION

This case uses ACL's fuzzy duplicates analysis to identify potential shell companies that employees have established within a purchasing system to commit fraud. To search for these shell companies, auditors traditionally compare the addresses of vendors with those of the company's employees using a simple join of the vendor and employee tables. A simple join, however, only identifies exact matches. If the fraudster has altered the shell vendor address by just one letter (e.g., Dear versus Deer, Street versus Str.), the join will not flag the vendor as a potential shell. A new method introduced in ACL 9.3, fuzzy duplicates, uses Levenshtein distances to identify exact as well as similar values. Levenshtein distances measure the number of characters that must be changed to make two values identical. This case requires you to identify potential shell companies by analyzing employee and vendor tables. Specifically, you must (1) prepare the data for analysis with SUBSTR and OMIT functions and (2) perform a fuzzy duplicates analysis to identify potential matches of employee and vendor addresses. A SPLIT function and Look for Duplicates analysis are then used to reduce the number of false positive matches.

I. FACTS

In 2007, you were hired as an internal auditor by Integrity Company. One of your first tasks was to investigate a potential fraud in the purchasing department. Specifically, a call on the fraud hotline claimed that some purchasing employees were living extravagant lifestyles bankrolled by the company. To see if these claims were true, you analyzed company data for shell companies. Shell companies are fictitious vendors created by an employee to commit fraud and embezzle money from an organization. If a company does not have independent vendor authorization, (purchasing) employees may be able to add these shell vendors. The employee, or fraudster, often uses his/her home address as the shell company's address.

To test for these shell companies, auditors traditionally compare the addresses of vendors with those of the organization's employees using a simple join of the vendor and employee tables. However, you weren't satisfied with the results from the simple join because, unfortunately, this method only identifies *exact* matches. Slight variations in how addresses are entered (e.g., Street versus Str. versus St.) prevents obviously identical addresses from matching. So, you developed a script in ACL, a leading data extraction and analysis software used by both internal and external auditors, which used SOUNDEX functions to improve the probability of matching addresses having slight variations. A script (similar to an Excel or Access macro) is a series of stored commands that can be easily executed over and over again using a single command. SOUNDEX is a hashing system for English words based on how the word sounds rather than its alphabetical spelling. ACL's SOUNDEX function generates a four digit code for words by ignoring duplicate letters, numbers, punctuation, and the letters a, e, i, o, u, h, w, and y. This script has been used by Integrity since that time as it was the "best" way to identify matching vendor and employee addresses.

Now after years of service, you were recently appointed as the training director for the Internal Audit department. Your first task was to update the training manual on detecting shell companies. Since you developed your shell script, new technologies have become available that are easier to use and more effective in detecting non-exact matches. Specifically, ACL has introduced fuzzy duplicates analysis. Your new training manual on shell companies will walk new internal auditors step-by-step through the detection process.

II. SHELL COMPANY TRAINING MANUAL

This training manual has been designed to help you understand how to best detect shell companies. The classic audit test for shell companies is to join the vendor and employee master files on the address fields. Unfortunately, this method only catches *exact* matches. If the fraudster has accidentally keyed or intentionally altered the shell vendor address by just one letter, the join will not flag the vendor as a potential shell. Thus, slight variations in how addresses are entered (e.g., Street versus Str. versus St.) prevents obviously identical addresses from matching. This training manual shows you how to overcome this problem using fuzzy duplicates analysis. The instructions that follow assume you are able to create expressions using functions and extract data.

Before you learn the procedures involved, it is important that you understand how the fuzzy duplicates analysis works. Your understanding of these concepts is necessary to enable you to make appropriate audit scope decisions.

Fuzzy Duplicates and the Levenshtein Distance

The fuzzy duplicates analysis uses the Levenshtein distance to compare pairs of characters values. The analysis starts with the value in the first row of the data and compares it with every other subsequent value in that column. Fuzzy duplicates then performs the same comparison for the second value, third value, etc. (in the column).

The Levenshtein distance is the number of characters that must be changed to make two values identical. Examine the shaded characters in Figure 1:

Figure 1: Values having one different character

value #1:	M	A	R	K		S	M	I	T	H
value #2:	M	A	R	C		S	M	I	T	H

The C in value #2 needs to be changed to K in order to make it identical to value #1. Thus, the Levenshtein distance is one. One of ten characters, 10%, would have to be changed to make the values identical. Now consider the values in Figure 2:

Figure 2: Values having three different characters

value #1:	M	A	R	K		S	M	I	T	H		
value #2:	P		M	A	R	C		S	M	I	T	H

The Levenshtein distance is three. Three characters in value #2 (change C to K and delete the P and space) or 30% of the number of characters in value #1 (the smaller length of the two values) would have to be changed. Fuzzy duplicates analysis includes all characters – letters, numbers, spaces, punctuation, and special characters.[1]

Your first decision is to select the maximum difference threshold, the maximum Levenshtein distance that will identify two values as possible matches. The larger the difference threshold, the greater probability that two values will be identified as possible matches. However, larger difference thresholds also yield a

---

[1]   Recall that the prior SOUNDEX method ignores duplicate letters, numbers, punctuation, and the letters a, e, i, o, u, h, w, and y.

greater number of false positives, two values that have no obvious similarity. You will need to exercise your professional judgment to assign a difference threshold that balances these opposing results.

Similar to the SOUNDEX approach, fuzzy duplicates analysis can yield a large number of false positives. ACL provides the following two methods to control the number of false positives.

Difference Percentage – A percentage between 1 and 99, the difference percentage is the Levenshtein distance divided by the number of characters in the shorter of the two values. The maximum difference percentage is entered in the fuzzy duplicates dialog box. If the difference percentage of two values exceeds the maximum percentage, the values are not identified as matches. For example, consider the values ABC and ADF. The values have a Levenshtein distance of two and a difference percentage of 67%. Given a difference threshold of three, the values would appear to qualify as a match. However, if the maximum difference percentage is 50%, the values would be disqualified.

Result Size – A percentage from 1 to 1000, the result size is the number of records in the output divided by the number of records in the source data table. If the result size exceeds the percentage entered in the fuzzy duplicates dialog box, the operation is terminated.

Enhancing Fuzzy Duplicates Analysis

The Levenshtein distance performs a character-by-character comparison of two values. Although you can visually identify the two addresses in Figure 3 as a match, several characteristics of these values create an excessively large Levenshtein distances, thus preventing fuzzy duplicates analysis from matching the values.

Figure 3: Impact of Street Directions and Designations

value #1:	1	2		N	o	r	t	h		E	a	g	l	e		R	o	a	d
value #2:	1	2		N	.		E	a	g	l	e		R	d	.			

The Levensthein distance is seven and the difference threshold is 39%. North and N. have four different characters. Road and Rd. have three different characters. Yet these differences do not prevent the human eye from recognizing these values as being the same address. For this reason, fuzzy duplicates analysis is enhanced through the removal of punctuation (including spaces) and generic values, such as street directions (e.g., North, South) and street designations (Street, St.).

Performing Fuzzy Duplicates Analysis

Use the following five sequential steps to find the matching addresses in the sample data provided.[2]

---

[2]   In order for students to work with this problem, an Excel data file with a worksheet for Employees and a worksheet for Vendors is included in the Instructor's Guide material.

STEP 1: Prepare the data

Fuzzy duplicates analysis requires that the data be contained in a single table. In this case, the data is employee and vendor addresses. Other information, such as employee and vendor names, can be included to enhance the usefulness of analysis results. To merge data from two tables into a single table, the column[3] lengths must be identical. One way to accomplish this task is using the SUBSTR function, setting the length larger than any of the columns. For this sample data, a length of 50 should be ample. Use the SUBSTR function to create new columns for the vendor name and vendor address (both in the vendor table) as well as employee name and address (both in the employee table). Two slight modifications will be useful to make the final report easier to interpret:

- Employee name. The SUBSTR function for employee name should concatenate the employee's first, middle, and last names. It may be necessary to use the ALLTRIM function to remove padded spaces from any of the name fields.
- Vendor name. To allow you to more easily distinguish between employee and vendor names, uppercase the results of the SUBSTR function.

Label the new columns Address50 and Name50 in each table.

STEP 2: Extract fields to create combined table

Fuzzy duplicates analysis requires that the data being analyzed is in the same column of a single table. Therefore, the Address50 and Name50 columns need to be extracted from the employee and vendor tables into a combined table. The new table (use the name Combined in this example), should have two columns, one for Address50 and one for Name50.

STEP 3: Eliminate punctuation and generic values

Slight variations in the address name may affect fuzzy duplicates analysis. Therefore, it is helpful to eliminate punctuation and generic elements, such as street directions (e.g., N., North, S., South, etc.) and street designations (e.g., Street, Str., St., Road, Rd., etc.) before comparing the values. Integrity's previous method used massive, clumsy, embedded REPLACE functions in a script to remove these generic elements. ACL 9.3 and later versions include an OMIT function which allows for the easy removal of all these items. Review the data to determine what generic elements should be deleted. In the Combined table, create a new column for Address50 that uses the OMIT function to remove generic elements. Make sure that the OMIT function is not case sensitive. Then use the EXCLUDE function to eliminate all punctuation from the results of the OMIT function. Label the new column Address_Clean.

---

[3]   We use the term columns because ACL uses this terminology. The columns are the equivalent of fields in database terminology. Fuzzy duplicates require all data to have the same length (STEP 1) and be in the same column (STEP 2).

STEP 4: Fuzzy duplicates analysis

The SOUNDEX approach looks for similar matches instead of just exact matches (e.g., Charlotte versus Charlote, Deer versus Dear). The SOUNDEX function available in early versions of ACL was a useful tool for detecting similar addresses. However, ACL version 9.3 introduced fuzzy duplicates analysis which replaces the need for both SOUNDEX and the classic join of the employee and vendor tables.

Conduct a fuzzy duplicates analysis on the Address_Clean column. Keep the default settings: a difference threshold of 1, a difference percentage of 50, and a result size of 10. Select the options to include exact duplicates. Include other available columns in the results. Save the results to a table named FuzzyDup. Your dialog box should appear as follows.

Figure 4: Fuzzy Duplicates Dialog Box

Does this analysis work? Repeat the test using the same parameters as before except set the result size to 100. Does this analysis work? A portion of these results are shown in Figure 5. Group numbers represent the record number of the first value in a group of values that have a Levenshtein distance of zero or one. The original record number is the record number of the value in the Combined table. How many items are identified as matching? Do all of the items appear to be real matches?

Figure 5: Results of Fuzzy Duplicates Analysis

STEP 5: Use the SPLIT function to reduce false positives

STEP 4 identified many false positives (i.e., items that pass the fuzzy duplicates test but a visual comparison reveals are not matches). Examination of these false matches is likely to reveal that the primary difference is the street number. False matches having only a street number difference can be removed by using a combination of the SPLIT function and the Look for Duplicates analysis. Basically, we want to compare just the numeric portions of the employee and vendor address street names to see if they are the same. Using the FuzzyDup table, create a new column called Split using the SPLIT function to isolate the numeric portion of the address. Then use the Look for Duplicates analysis to select only those records where the numeric portion of the address matches within each group. How many items are identified as matching now? Do all of the items appear to be real matches?

III. EPILOGUE

All of the matches identified in STEP 5 as potential shell companies need to be manually verified by the internal auditor. In addition to reviewing information about the companies to see whether they are shell companies, internal auditors may also want to check the list of vendors against banned vendors lists provided by the government or developed internally within the organization.

CASE STUDY 8:

Knottyville Country Club: Asset Misappropriation

Srinivasan Ragothaman, Ph.D., C.A.
University of South Dakota

LEARNING OBJECTIVES

After completing and discussing this case, you should be able to

- Evaluate misappropriation risk factors.
- Evaluate internal controls.
- Design new control.
- Understand governance in non-profit sector.
- Analyze materiality decisions.
- Apply SAS 99, PCAOB AS5, and SAB 99.
- Perform cost benefit analysis.

KNOTTYVILLE COUNTRY CLUB:
AN INSTRUCTIONAL CASE ON ASSET MISAPPROPRIATION

There was a stunned silence in the courtroom as the Circuit Judge was about to announce the sentence. "You are sentenced to 15 years in prison for grand theft. Your abominable conduct ran long and deep, and it is now time to pay for it," said the judge. The judge also suspended an additional 25 years in prison time for Fancy Rockbottom. One of the members of the country club told Fancy that she was trusted as a family member by the patrons of the club and that trust was betrayed by Fancy.

OVERVIEW OF THE CLUB:

Knottyville Country Club (the Club) caters to the desires of its 1,800 dues-paying full members, 800 associate members and their guests. It also rents out its halls and ballrooms for weddings, reunions, and other gatherings. Built on the banks of the Missouri river, Knottyville Country Club offers a variety of exciting, fun-filled activities for its members. The Club was established in 1944 with a nine-hole golf course and an outdoor swimming pool. Since its opening, the Club has steadily continued to expand. It now (in 2007) has one of the most impressive 27-hole golf courses in the upper Midwest, six tennis courts, a spectacular clubhouse with lovely views, two swimming pools, an indoor basketball court, beautiful dining rooms with chandeliers, a restaurant, a bar and other opulent amenities. The Club facilities were in great demand and there was a six-month waiting time to book the halls for company picnics, banquets, family reunions, wedding receptions, and the like. There was also a waiting period to gain full membership.

Knottyville Country Club is a member-owned, private country club. The seven member board of directors is elected every two years by the members. It includes four officers—the president, vice president, secretary and treasurer—and is responsible for the day-to-day management of the Club. The board has broad powers to borrow money and to enter into contracts necessary for the normal operation of the Club. The Club has five committees – membership committee, the finance committee, the nominating committee, the construction and maintenance committee and the special events committee. The finance committee has three members elected from the membership at large and the treasurer is an ex-officio member of the finance committee. The finance committee met just twice a year. The Club was taking in approximately $8 million each year in membership fees alone. In addition, the restaurant, the bar, banquets, rentals and a variety of other programs brought in an additional $18 million each year. The president of the club was a friendly, jovial fellow and treated everyone with great warmth. He had no accounting or finance background. He was very trusting of people, in general and considered all employees and members as belonging to one big happy family.

SHENANIGANS OF THE GENERAL MANAGER:

Fancy Rockbottom was employed by the Club in a variety of capacities for twenty-two years including the bookkeeping function. The last six years she served as the general manager and continued to serve as the bookkeeper for the Club. Fancy was also in charge of ordering all supplies. The Club policy required two signatures on each check. As the general manager, Fancy had check signing authority. The other signature had to come from another employee, Sarah or from Robert, who is on the board of directors and is the treasurer. Fancy often asked Sarah to sign blank checks in advance so that she can pay the bills on time and does not have to wait for the second signature. Unsuspecting Sarah would readily oblige and would sign several blank checks from time to time.

As the bookkeeper, Fancy was in charge of maintaining the accounting records. She did the monthly bank reconciliation as well. Every three months Fancy would meet with the finance committee of the board and report about the financial situation. She would prepare simple profit and loss statements and a balance sheet. Working with the treasurer, she also presented the annual budget to the finance committee for its approval. Because Fancy was in charge of ordering supplies, she would often insist that they buy alcoholic beverages from a particular supplier who was her college classmate.

Members of the Club were allowed to charge their meals and drinks and pay for them later when the monthly statements are mailed to them. Fancy would charge a few dollars extra to some members' monthly restaurant/bar bills. If the members did not notice the extra charge, she would keep the money. If the members complained that they did not order that item or were not at the club on that day, she would apologize, blame it on clerical error and give credit to the complaining members. She would then accuse the server of punching in the wrong member number and take small amounts of money ($50, $36, $84 etc.) out of the paychecks of servers. Fancy's argument was that the servers had to pay for the mistakes they made. The amounts taken from the servers were quite small when compared to the gigantic amount stolen.

Fancy has been spotted by her co-workers at various video lottery parlors over the years. There is a rumor that she had a mild gambling addiction. She had acquired a couple of expensive sports cars in recent years and has taken several expensive vacations to exotic places including the French Rivera, Bangkok, and the Bahamas. It was revealed in court that Fancy had paid off large personal credit card debts of her family using the stolen money. The grand theft occurred evenly over a six-year period from 2001 to 2006. Ironically, it was a bank official who got suspicious about some transactions and alerted the president of the club. The bank official did some investigation when he found out that the business account of the Club was overdrawn. His investigation revealed that Rockbottom was depositing high dollar amounts from her personal account to take care of the balance. Alarm bells rang. He blew the whistle by informing the Club president about his suspicions. The Club terminated Fancy's employment in February, 2007 and ordered an internal investigation. A month later, the Club also filed a police complaint about the grand theft.

When Fancy was sentenced to 15 years in prison, she had already paid back $400,000 of the $1.2 million she had embezzled. She has sold her home and other assets to pay back this money. The Club is unlikely to get any more money from Fancy and the remaining $800,000 is gone. This whole episode has made many club members rather uneasy and 400 of them have already quit the club. The debt is mounting for the Club and its future looks rather bleak.

Note: Only a few of the facts mentioned in this case actually occurred in a real life situation. Several more fictitious information pieces were added to enhance the learning objectives of this auditing case. All names are fictitious. You can consult a couple of documents readily available in the public domain: COSO framework for auditing internal control for small companies and a fraud checklist from the Association of Certified Fraud Examiners.

REQUIRED:

(Questions below are independent questions.)

1. List in detail the various internal control weaknesses and weaknesses in the monitoring system that existed at the Knottyville Country Club.

2. You are hired as an expert CPA to institute effective internal controls and monitoring systems at the Knottyville Country Club. What controls and monitoring systems would you recommend? List them in detail.

3. The Knottyville Country Club wants to construct an $8 million addition to the clubhouse. They have approached ABC Bank. The bank required the Club to get an external audit done by a CPA firm for years 2005 and 2006. You have been hired as the external auditor. Hint: Read SAS No. 99 first.

    A) List the risk factors (red flags) for asset misappropriation that are present in this case.

    B) What audit procedures would you perform to make sure that there was no embezzlement at the Club and that its financial position is fairly stated? List them in detail.

CASE STUDY 9:

Blackstone Valley Chiropractic Clinic: International Deferred Compensation

Kevin E. Dow, Ph.D.
University of Nottingham Ningbo China
B. Charlene Henderson, Ph.D.
University of Illinois at Urbana-Champaign
Marcia Weidenmier Watson, Ph.D.
University of North Carolina at Charlotte

LEARNING OBJECTIVES

After completing and discussing this case, you should be able to

- Make a recommendation for tax compliance.
- Evaluate a proposed and implemented tax plan.
- Consider an individual's liability for criminal fraud.
- Describe the geographic limitations of nonqualified deferred compensation plans.

INTRODUCTION

This case presents students with an active-learning setting in which to conduct tax research and tax planning via a developing four-part timeline. Students first evaluate an international deferred compensation plan that a potential client is considering. The focus is on determining whether the plan complies with U.S. tax law, and if not, on developing recommendations on modifications to make the plan compliant. Next, students learn the individual has acted, and they must evaluate the implemented plan. Third, students learn the individual has been indicted for tax evasion. Then, they must consider whether their firm should agree to work with the individual and whether relying on the advice of professionals can be used as a defense against tax evasion charges. Finally, students learn that the individual has been convicted of criminal tax evasion. Moreover, the trial evidence suggests that the tax evasion extended beyond the facts known from the prior timeline, i.e., the individual participated in the evasion. Students must re-evaluate whether their firm should agree to work with the individual in appealing his conviction. The case materials are based on an actual case.

ASSIGNMENT 1: INTRODUCTION AND INITIAL FACTS

Following graduation from West Point with a degree in Basic Science and an emphasis in Anatomy and Physiology, Glenn E. Rachis entered the United States Army. There, he served as a Second Lieutenant line infantry officer and earned a Bronze Star. While active in Army service, he discovered his true calling and entered the New York Chiropractic College's Doctor of Chiropractic Program. Upon graduation, he joined the Army Medical Services Corps. Eventually, Dr. Rachis was promoted to O-4 (Major) and served as Clinic Chief in Darmstadt, Germany until his retirement and honorable discharge from the service (at age 46). At retirement, Dr. Rachis was earning military compensation of $119,920. The breakdown of his final year's pay from the Army can be found in Table 1 below.

After retiring from the Army, Dr. Rachis relocated to Worcester, Massachusetts where he purchased a 10 year-old personal injury practice in the Blackstone Valley area from a retiring chiropractor. The building exceeded 2,000 square feet, including reception, four exam/treat rooms, two diagnostic rooms, a management office, massage room, radiology room, and dark room. The building was equipped with state of the art equipment.

Table 1: Dr. Rachis' Final Army Payments		
Monthly Base Pay	$6,252.30	
Monthly BAQ (Basic Allowance for Quarters)	$1,131.60	
Monthly BAS (Basic Allowance for Subsistence)	$192.74	
Monthly Variable Special Pay for Medical Officers	$666.66	
Monthly Board Certified Special Pay	$500.00	
Total Monthly Pay	$8,743.30	
Total Annual Pay		$104,919.60
Additional Annual Pay for Medical Officers		$15,000.00
Total 2000 (Annual) Military Pay		$119,919.60

Dr. Rachis was excited about opening his own practice and moving his family back to the U.S. The practice was well-established in the community, with a very strong network of referring attorneys and other legal entities. The focus of the practice was personal injury (80 percent of total services). Well care, acute care, rehab, and expert witness testimony together comprised the remaining 20 percent of total services. The patient population was diverse and lived within a 10 mile radius. The sources of patients were as follows: 75 percent attorney referral, 15 percent direct mail, 6 percent employer referral, 4 percent patient referral. The practice accepted only cash and direct billing from attorneys.

For the initial year 2001, Dr. Rachis operated his practice as a sole proprietorship. Given that, he reported the income on his personal tax return (Schedule C,

Form 1040). However, upon the advice of counsel, Dr. Rachis incorporated his practice under the name Glenn E. Rachis, DC, PC. The practice then operated as a C corporation and under the name "Blackstone Valley Chiropractic Clinic." During the first three years (2001-2003), the practice generated gross revenues of more than $700,000 per year and net income in excess of $600,000 per year. In 2003, the practice had more than 2,000 patient visits, including more than 600 new patients. Dr. Rachis' take home pay before income taxes in 2003 was $480,620. Federal income taxes totaled $138,308.

"THE CAPS PROGRAM"

Due to the rapid and significant change in his personal income, Dr. Rachis became interested in succession planning, asset protection, and retirement funding. In early 2004, Dr. Rachis' personal attorney (also a practicing CPA) shared with him a brochure (Appendix 1) he received from an entity by the name of Concept Asset Protection Systems (CAPS), LLC. The brochure described a seminar titled "Asset Protection-Tax Deferral-Investment Strategies" to be held in Las Vegas, NV in March 2004.

Following the recommendation of his personal attorney, Dr. Rachis traveled to Las Vegas, Nevada to attend the two-day seminar. The seminar leader's introduction indicated that he had extensive experience in asset protection, estate and succession planning, and establishing income deferral programs and planning through tax treaties and appropriate domestic and international structures. The seminar leader also stated that he had represented numerous clients throughout the world and represented the U.S. in the China International Trade Talks. The advice that Dr. Rachis received spanned several topics including the utilization of an international nonqualified deferred compensation plan. The seminar provided Dr. Rachis with a retirement plan analysis, complete with the backing of legal opinions supported by numerous cases and regulations (see Appendix 2 for seminar materials). After meeting with the seminar leader and prior to agreeing to adopt the CAPS program, Dr. Rachis sought the independent opinion of his attorney (also a CPA), who reviewed the legal opinions and seminar documents provided to Dr. Rachis.

TIMELINE: PRIOR TO DECISION

Task #1

Dr. Rachis also sought an accounting firm to evaluate the plan. Martin Zingales is currently employed by a regional accounting firm. Not only does he have his CPA, but he is also a CFE. Ray Bertman, a partner in the accounting firm, asks Martin to determine if using the CAPS program would cause Dr. Rachis, a potential client, to commit fraud or income tax evasion. Martin must prepare a research memo to address the items below using the tax rate schedule in Table 2.

1.   Determine the potential tax savings had Rachis used the CAPS program in 2003 to defer $400,000 of taxable income (taxable income of $80,620 rather than $480,620).

2.   Analyze the materials provided by Dr. Rachis (Appendix 1 and Appendix 2), and assess whether the proposed program is consistent with the objective of retirement planning. Specifically, using seminar materials as facts, evaluate whether the proposed program is in compliance with U.S. tax law. If it is not in compliance, develop recommendations on how to change it to comply with the U.S. tax law.

Table 2: Schedule Y-1 — Married Filing Jointly or Qualifying Widow(er)		
If taxable income		
Is over—	But not over—	
$0	$16,700	10% of the amount over $0
$16,701	$67,900	$1,670.00 plus 15% of the amount over $16,700
$67,901	$137,050	$9,350.00 plus 25% of the amount over $67,900
$137,051	$208,850	$26,637.50 plus 28% of the amount over $137,050
$208,851	$372,950	$46,741.50 plus 33% of the amount over $208,850
$372,951	no limit	$100,894.50 plus 35% of the amount over $372,950

ASSIGNMENT 2: DR. RACHIS IMPLEMENTS THE CAPS PROGRAM

Following the two day seminar, Dr. Rachis, with the assistance of his attorney (who is also a practicing CPA), made several changes to his business consistent with the CAPS program. Dr. Rachis had no formal training in accounting, law, or business, and as a chiropractor, little experience. He relied on the advice and expertise of others.

Dr. Rachis first created the corporation entitled "Glenn E. Rachis, PC". The corporation continued to do business (DBA) under the name Blackstone Valley Chiropractic Clinic (BVCC). Dr. Rachis reported on his tax returns that he devoted 100 percent of his time and services to the corporation. Then, Dr. Rachis resigned from Glenn E. Rachis, PC and signed a long-term personal services contract to become an employee of Executive Recruitment and Leasing Services (ERLS), an existing employee leasing and deferred compensation company operating in Ireland. The contract terms provided that Dr. Rachis was to be assigned duty at the location and discretion of ERLS, and that Dr. Rachis would make himself available whenever and wherever ERLS required. ERLS agreed to promote Dr. Rachis' services worldwide. The contract specified that ERLS would pay Dr. Rachis a salary of $72,000 per year, and that ERLS would place $360,000 per year in a deferred compensation account (offshore trust) for Dr. Rachis.

Soon after, a Nevada company, Domestic Executive Leasing Services (DELS), contracted with ERLS for the exclusive rights to the professional services of Dr. Rachis. Glenn E. Rachis, PC was understaffed and was fortunate enough to find a chiropractor (on contract with ERLS), Dr. Rachis, for an annual lease payment of $480,000 (summary in Table 3).

Table 3: Rachis' Program		
	Prior to CAPS Program	After CAPS Program
Salary / Payment by Glenn E. Rachis, PC	$480,000	$480,000
Total Administrative Fees		($48,000)
U.S. Income Tax	($138,362)	$0*
Net to Dr. Rachis	$341,638	$432,000
Deferred Income	$0	$360,000
Disposable Income	$341,638	$72,000

*Dr. Rachis claimed the foreign earned income tax exemption.

TIMELINE: IMPLEMENTED THE CAPS PROGRAM

Task #2

Ray Bertman provided Martin with the updated facts and asks him to prepare a research memo to address the items below, using the tax rate schedule in Table 2.

1. Compare the actual program implemented by Dr. Rachis to the model outlined in the CAPS seminar materials.
2. Examine the tax savings to see if it matches what was claimed in the seminar and the estimates in your original memo (Task #1).
3. Determine whether the implemented program complies with U.S. tax law. If it does not, outline the modifications needed to make it firmly in compliance with U.S. tax law.

Suggested extension: Dr. Rachis implemented the CAPS program as part of retirement planning. Evaluate the retirement savings accumulated using $360,000, $400,000, and $300,000 of annual deferrals. Use a five percent rate of return and a ten year horizon (to retirement date).

ASSIGNMENT 3: DR. RACHIS INDICTED FOR TAX EVASION

Glenn E. Rachis was indicted by a federal grand jury on charges of tax evasion in May 2009. According to the indictment, Dr. Rachis evaded federal income taxes for the years 2004, 2005, and 2006, with actions that fraudulently reduced his taxable income. Specifically, Dr. Rachis entered into an improper offshore executive leasing and deferred compensation scheme by contracting his professional services to Executive Recruitment and Leasing Services (ERLS), an Irish entity, which leased his services to Domestic Executive Leasing Services (DELS), a U.S. company, which then leased his services back to Glenn E. Rachis, PC. All charges were in violation of I.R.C. Section 7201. Pending trial, Dr. Rachis was released on a $150,000 bond, with travel restrictions requiring him to surrender his passport.

Dr. Rachis has asked your firm to represent him before the I.R.S. and to work with his defense attorney to develop a strategy for dealing with the legal charges. Dr. Rachis claims that he does not know the tax law, and because he relied on the advice of his attorney (also a CPA), the liability for incorrectly setting up the plan should be his attorney's problem.

TIMELINE: INDICTMENT FOR CRIMINAL TAX EVASION

Task #3

Ray Bertman provided Martin with the updated facts and asks him to update his prior research. Martin must prepare a research memo to address the following items.

1. Analyze the facts and law and recommend whether your firm should work with Dr. Rachis and his attorney to resolve the charges. Your firm's policy is to represent only clients that are in compliance with tax law.
2. Evaluate whether and how Dr. Rachis' liability for fraudulent tax evasion changes, given his reliance on his attorney (also a CPA).

ASSIGNMENT 4: RACHIS CONVICTED OF TAX EVASION

Glenn E. Rachis was convicted on four counts of tax evasion in March 2011. Dr. Rachis was sentenced to serve five years in prison (three years of supervised probation after his release), and paid a $10,000 criminal fine and $100,000 in prosecution costs. At trial, in addition to the grand jury evidence, the prosecution presented evidence that Rachis' deferred compensation funds were returned to the U.S. using nominees to conceal his involvement. Once the funds were directed back to Rachis, he invested the funds in real estate. Further trial evidence revealed that beginning in 2008, the I.R.S. attempted to audit tax returns filed by Dr. Rachis for 2004, 2005 and 2006. Throughout 2008, all I.R.S. communications mailed to the street address of Blackstone Valley Chiropractic Clinic were returned (though unsealed) marked as "addressee not known." On five different occasions in 2009, when an I.R.S. agent visited the clinic to personally contact Dr. Rachis, the clinic receptionist reported Dr. Rachis was traveling and unavailable. Dr. Rachis failed to keep three appointments set up by the examining agent.

Dr. Rachis plans to appeal the original court's conviction. He has asked your firm to represent him before the I.R.S. and to work with his new defense attorney to develop a strategy for the appeal. Dr. Rachis expressed regret for getting into such an aggressive arrangement and provided plausible assurances that he wants to pay the taxes owed and resolve the matter.

TIMELINE: GUILTY VERDICT AND APPEAL

Task #4

Ray Bertman emailed Martin the news that Dr. Rachis was convicted. He asks Martin to prepare a research memo to address the following items.

1. Re-analyze the facts and recommend whether your firm should work on the Dr. Rachis appeal. Firm policy is to represent only clients that are in compliance with tax law.
2. Evaluate Dr. Rachis' liability for tax evasion, taking into consideration his reliance on his attorney (also a CPA).

In responding to both 1 and 2, explicitly address the impact, if any, of the trial evidence of Rachis' efforts to avoid I.R.S. contact as well as his personal access to deferred compensation funds on your assessment.

REFERENCES

American Institute of Certified Public Accountants (AICPA). 1999. Core Competency Framework & Education Competency Assessment Website. Available on-line on March 18, 2016 at: http://www.aicpa.org/interestareas/accountingeducation/resources/pages/corecompetency.aspx

Chatzky, M. G. and H. K. Scholz. 2000. "Tripartite Planning: Using an International Employee-Leasing Program Combined with a Nonqualified Deferred Compensation Plan and a Transnational Rabbi Trust," *Journal of Asset Protection* May/June: 24-35.

Chu, L. and T. Libby. 2010. "Writing Mini-Cases: An Active Learning Assignment." *Issues in Accounting Education* 25(2): 245-265.

Gunnett, G. J. 2000. "Nonqualified deferred compensation plans," *Physician's News Digest* October. Available on-line on March 18, 2016 at: http://www.physiciansnews.com/2008/10/12/physician-deferred-compensation-arrangements/,

Hurt, B. 2007. "Teaching What Matters: A New Conception of Accounting Education," *Journal of Education for Business* May/June 82(5): 295-299.

McDermott, Will & Emery. 2004. Nonqualified Deferred Compensation Provisions Added to the International Tax Bill. Available on-line at: http://www.mwe.com/publications/uniEntity.aspx?xpST=PublicationDetail&pub=4795 on March 18, 2016.

Pomierski, W. R. and D. S. Lee. 2009. "New Nonqualified Deferred Compensation Rules Extend to US Employees of Certain Foreign Corporations" *International Tax Journal* May-June: 75-94.

APPENDIX 1: WPC TRIFOLD RECRUITMENT BROCHURE

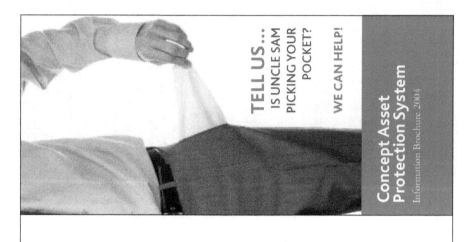

TELL US...
IS UNCLE SAM
PICKING YOUR
POCKET?

WE CAN HELP!

**Concept Asset
Protection System**

Information Brochure 2004

Wealth Protection Concepts, LLC
Lovell & Lovell Attorneys at Law
2801 S. Valley View Blvd.
Las Vegas, NV 89102
1-888-610-8990

allen@wealthprotectionconcepts.com

Our strategies are scrutinized for safety, profitability and legality by a leading wealth preservation attorney who has made it his mission to "clean up" the financial industry that makes advisors rich at the expense of their clients.

Remember, we do not sell insurance or investment products. This little known tax strategy will work to save you taxes this year, *but only if you act fast!* If this sounds too good to be true then you really need this program.

APPENDIX 1: WPC TRIFOLD RECRUITMENT BROCHURE (CONT.)

QUALITIES OF OUR CLIENTS:

Our clients share a few common traits. You may find a bit of yourself in the following.

- An increasing net worth with income which substantially exceeds that which they need to meet their living expenses
- A desire to take advantage of all legal means available to reduce their level of taxation, in present and future years
- An interest in eliminating estate taxes without losing control of their assets
- A history of listening to the advice of others, then making the final decision based on their own evaluation
- A desire to ensure that their estate will serve members of the family for generations to come and/or to endow a religious, scientific, educational or other philanthropic institution
- A personal desire to reverse the demoralizing effects and disincentives of taxation, coupled with a drive to be a highly contributive person
- A belief that if their concerns over the potential for financial loss from occupational litigation could be relieved, they would enjoy renewed focus on being even more productive
- Management expertise in and ownership in a successful enterprise with future years of growth potential
- An ambition to make significant social contributions and to leave the world a better place than they found it.

Whether or you are inclined to charitable giving, we can show you strategies to ...

1. Increase your discretionary income.
2. Reduce or in some cases even eliminate:
   - income taxes
   - capital gains taxes
   - estate taxes
3. Provide a tax-free inheritance for your heirs.
4. Leave a lasting family and social legacy.

Your current plan probably was designed for people making less income than you. Think about it; your current plan will only give you a lower standard of living when you retire.

TESTIMONIAL: *"I was skeptical when I first read the letter from Concept. I thought, 'what do I have to lose, so I'll at least call.' Well now I am happy I did. The $200,000 I saved in taxes this year is in my plan. I can finally see how to make an early retirement."*

– B.H. (Physician)

Our program is based on a treaty between the United States and Ireland. This treaty has existed for many years. The United States Senate in 1999 revised this treaty, and both countries have since ratified the changes.

Our experience is that 99% of you who are reading this do not have any discernible asset protection.

Your wealth represents your life's work and your family's current and future dreams. You need to find an advisor who will be with you for the long run, who has your best interest at heart, not someone who is only pushing financial products for a quick buck.

TAX SAVINGS **is an ongoing concern of most successful professionals like you. Are you being penalized for being successful?**

If you are paying too much income tax and not saving enough money to achieve the financial freedom you desire, there is a solution.

TESTIMONIAL: *"I was making about $500,000 a year but could live on $150,000. My tax bill was painful at $200,000. I ... saved about $150,000 in tax the first year. We set aside over $300,000 in the first year before tax and invested the funds where they would be safe from litigation and will grow tax-free. The best part is, we will reach our retirement goals without sacrificing the quality of life."*

– D.S. (Dentist)

APPENDIX 2: CAPS SEMINAR MATERIALS

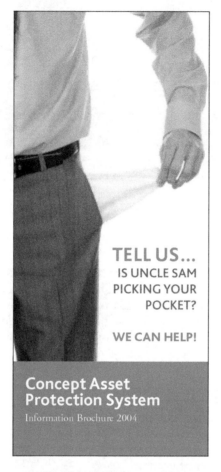

TELL US...
IS UNCLE SAM
PICKING YOUR
POCKET?

WE CAN HELP!

**Concept Asset
Protection System**
Information Brochure 2004

Wealth Protection Concepts, LLC
Lovell & Lovell Attorneys at Law
2801 S. Valley View Blvd.
Las Vegas, NV 89102
1-888-610-8990

allen@wealthprotectionconcepts.com

The report that you are about to read is based on a treaty between the United States and Ireland. The U.S. maintains similar treaties with five other countries. We currently use the U.S./Ireland treaty because we feel that it offers the greatest flexibility. The U.S./Ireland treaty has existed for many years. In 1999, the U.S. Senate made a few minor revisions to the treaty, and both countries have since ratified the changes.

APPENDIX 2: CAPS SEMINAR MATERIALS (CONT.)

CONTENTS   PAGE

PROGRAM BENEFITS

A little-known, tax advantage strategy is available that can dramatically improve your tax savings and financial picture. This strategy will allow you to put away all of the money that you do not need to maintain your lifestyle with before-tax dollars. There is no ceiling on the amount that you can defer annually, and all of the funds placed in The Program will grow and compound tax free.

The Program will benefit you in the following ways:

1.   Dramatic reduction of your taxes
2.   Your deferred funds are before-tax dollars, so you'll have more money to grow and growth will compound tax deferred
3.   No ceiling on the amount of income that you can defer annually
4.   Deferred funds are tax deductible to your business annually
5.   Impenetrable asset protection
6.   You will not be required to include other employees in this program
7.   You may take distribution of funds at any age, with no penalties
8.   This program is custom tailored to meet your financial goals and objectives

The Program is individually designed for you, the highly-compensated professional, business owner, or executive who has significant disposable income. This little-known strategy is carefully supervised by our attorneys and accountants as an alternative to traditional tax planning, and it has proven workable since 1954. It provides unparalleled opportunity to build and preserve your personal wealth.

APPENDIX 2: CAPS SEMINAR MATERIALS (CONT.)

OUR GOALS

- To expand the influence and affluence of successful members of society beyond their current level of activity
- To facilitate our clients' wealth accumulation by reducing their current taxable income without sacrificing their standard of living, and allowing for a compounding of tax deferred growth of before-tax dollars
- To educate and guide our clients on global financial matters and encourage a more independent approach to personal wealth accumulation
- To create a network of professionals and executives in various fields of expertise who recognize the advantages of using the global business environment to enhance their wealth accumulation

THE PROGRAM

The Program works on the basis that you become a leased employee to your business. Your current company pays the leasing company. You go to work at the same place, you perform the same services but your paycheck is issued to you from a leasing company. The Program provides you with global representation while creating a legal structure which maximizes asset protection and tax deferred accumulation of wealth. We educate and guide you in international financial and tax matters while allowing you to network your skills with other individuals who can either use or take advantage of them. Our meetings bring you together with top experts speaking on business issues relevant to today. Through these actions, we seek to improve the prosperity of the most productive members of society.

The Program begins with a comprehensive analysis of your current financial and tax situation as well as your future goals. Mandated expense contracts between you and your business entity are put in place as part of the leased arrangement. As a "key person" and a leased employee, you receive benefits as a result of your employment arrangement. The international employee leasing company, your employer, creates a non-qualified retirement plan that allows you to defer paying taxes on income above current needs. Your skills are promoted with the intent of finding additional business opportunities for you.

The unique combination of benefits offers not only peace of mind and security for the future but also a means to live better now.

THE BENEFITS

Reasons to take advantage of this incomparable asset protection and income tax reduction strategy include the following.

APPENDIX 2: CAPS SEMINAR MATERIALS (CONT.)

1. **Defer paying taxes on an unlimited amount of income above actual needs.** Retain more money to invest with the government's full knowledge and permission. If you can defer one hundred thousand dollars ($100,000) or more from annual pretax income, this program provides incomparable benefits.

2. **Grow retirement assets tax deferred and take advantage of compounding wealth accumulation.** You will accumulate wealth much faster than with traditional alternatives and are free to choose your investment vehicle.

3. **Begin distribution of your retirement assets at any time without penalty of mandated distribution schedules.** You have complete flexibility on the use of your money with no additional tax requirement because of unneeded distribution in any given year. You may begin withdrawal at any age and take only what you need to live on, preserving the principal for continued wealth creation.

4. **Selectively establish this plan for yourself and other key personnel.** A business or professional practice with highly compensated personnel can create an incentive to retain or reward important expertise without jeopardizing government regulated qualified plans already in place.

5. **Insulate yourself from frivolous lawsuits while protecting your assets from predators or creditors.** Apply the same methods used by entertainers and wealthy families to make your assets virtually litigation proof.

6. **Take advantage of periodic opportunities for new business ventures or consulting contracts.** Your skills are promoted to provide you with additional employment opportunities.

7. **Gain access to global financial expertise unavailable to most U.S. citizens.** Through our international connections, you can take advantage of global investment options which may offer superior alternatives to strictly domestic choices.

8. **Deduct a wider array of corporate business expenses.** Through the use of mandated expense contracts; your business can pay for various items which are commonly paid with after-tax dollars. This deduction represents an additional savings to an owner or corporation over and above the non-qualified retirement plan established for you as a key employee.

HOW THE PROGRAM WORKS

Structurally similar to *domestic* non-qualified plans, this program simply uses an Irish-American treaty to eliminate risks traditionally associated with this very common strategy for wealth accumulation. The leased employee arrangement originated with highly compensated entertainers and is well suited for other affluent members of society with substantial income above their actual needs.

APPENDIX 2: CAPS SEMINAR MATERIALS (CONT.)

These concepts are well tested, and the contracts we put in place are based on court precedent.

Dublin is home to the prestigious International Financial Services Centre (IFSC) which boasts offices of 22 of the world's top 50 banks. Ireland's long-term commitment to the financial services sector has reduced inflation to one of the lowest in Europe, nearly eliminated public sector borrowing, and generated growth of the Gross Domestic Product to nearly 7 percent (7%). This environment represents a very stable platform for financial and business operations. The international leasing company operates The Program from Dublin in order to take advantage of the conservative environment rich in tradition and influence.

A Few Details:

The corporate entity you are leased to (your company) pays a U.S. based personnel leasing entity for your entire compensation AND deducts the entire amount as an expense.

The U.S. leasing company pays you your salary, and you pay your non-business bills. Your mandated expenses are paid with before-tax dollars in accordance with the Meals and Lodging Rules in IRC Section 119. The U.S. personnel leasing company pays your taxes and transfers the surplus to Ireland less the operating fee.

Both the U.S. and international companies promote your skills worldwide.

When you retire, you tell the international company via the U.S. personnel leasing company how much to send you and how often. Upon your death, the remaining amount is paid to your spouse and heirs at whatever frequency you express in your formal letter of wishes.

SUMMARY

- Your entire program is established and put into operation along with the mandated expense contracts for a one-time charge, generally funded from tax savings and deductible as a business expense. The setup fee is twenty five thousand dollars ($25,000).
- The total fees on all monies processed through The Program are ten percent (10%).
- You will enter into an employment agreement with a resident-owned Irish employee leasing entity. The Irish employee leasing entity will agree to pay you a salary designed to meet your needs, reimburse your business expenses, and establish a deferred compensation program for your benefit.
- The Irish entity does not and will not conduct business in the U.S., and therefore, it will "loan-out" the right to your U.S. services to a domestic employee leasing company who then leases you to your current employer for a substantial fee.

APPENDIX 2: CAPS SEMINAR MATERIALS (CONT.)

- The U.S. employee leasing entity assumes the international employee entity's obligation to pay you a salary designed to meet your needs.
- The Irish employee leasing entity can provide a variety of benefits.
- The Program is flexible enough to accommodate even extreme fluctuations in income. A participant may even skip several years in succession if necessary.
- You pay income tax only on the money that is repatriated. With sufficient contributions, you may never have to withdraw any of the pretax principal and would therefore never pay taxes on this portion.

In an effort to assist your understanding of how an **International Deferred Compensation Program** works, we have created a chart and Figure 1 (below). In this example, we have assumed the individual is establishing the International Deferred Compensation Plan, is currently working for a financial planning firm, and is earning $500,000 per year. Our example, James Client, needs an income of $200,000 per year (before tax) to maintain his family lifestyle and wants to defer the rest (minus the administrative fee). James Client works for ACME Financial Planners via a series of five contracts with an International Deferred Compensation Program and two firms that are owned and operated as separate entities, International Executive Leasing Services (IELS) and Domestic Executive Leasing Services (DELS). These two firms charge an administrative fee for the services that they provide. In this example, the combined charge is 10% or $50,000 (10% * $500,000). The relationships are described below.

> **Contract #1** – is for the worldwide services of James Client. This contract is between James Client and IELS. IELS is based in one of the countries that has a treaty with the U.S., e.g., Ireland. It is IELS's responsibility to market the services of James Client worldwide. This contract spells out the terms and conditions under which James Client renders services for IELS. No money is exchanged between James Client and IELS.

> **Contract #2** – is for the U.S. services of James Client. DELS contracts James Client from IELS to perform work in the United States at a rate of $250,000. This is the $500,000 of Contract #3 minus the $200,000 of Contract #4 less the $50,000 in Administrative Fees.

> **Contract #3** – is between DELS and ACME Financial Planners for the services of James Client to AMCE Financial Planners in the U.S. ACME pays DELS $500,000 per year, his current salary.

APPENDIX 2: CAPS SEMINAR MATERIALS (CONT.)

Contract #4 – is between DELS and James Client. This contract specifies James Client's annual salary as $200,000 for his services to ACME Financial Planners, Inc. This salary is subject to any and all federal and state taxes.

Contract #5 – is between IELS and the International Deferred Compensation Program. In this example, each year IELS would send $250,000 which is credited to James Client's deferred compensation account.

The following is a summary of James Client's Program.

	Prior to Plan	James Client's Program
Payment by ACME	$500,000	$500,000
Total Administrative Fee for DELS and IELS		($50,000)
U.S. Income Tax *	(-$175,000)	($56,000)
Net U.S. Income (consists of:)**	$325,000	$394,000
Deferred Income		$250,000
Disposable Income	$325,000	$144,000

*The tax bracket after the plan is implemented would be 28% since the gross income under our example is $200,000. ** This does not take into consideration payroll taxes and state taxes that may apply.

Figure 1 – Seminar Model

CASE STUDY 10:

Auditing a Private Third-Party Claims Processor for Medicare

Yan Xiong, Ph.D.
California State University Sacramento
Daniel W. Law, Ph.D.
Gonzaga University

LEARNING OBJECTIVES

After completing and discussing this case, you should be able to
- Understand IT issues associated with three-party processing of government-insured medical claims.
- Appreciate computer audit software.
- Identify and provide remedies for a number of internal control weaknesses.
- Learn to apply internal control concepts, common internal control activities, and control issues surrounding the information technology use.

INTRODUCTION

This case study involves the relevant audit, fraud, and information technology (IT) issues associated with the third-party processing of government-insured medical claims. A fictitious private contractor provides claim processing (paper and electronic) for the United States Department of Health and Human Services (HHS), the administrator of Medicare (U.S. funded medical insurance). You should take the perspective of an auditor for HHS in addressing the internal control and other audit and fraud-related issues found in the case.

I. RELEVANT INFORMATION

To keep pace with the explosive growth of information technology (IT) applications in the realm of financial reporting, audit procedures and techniques must be continually updated and improved. In turn, auditing and accounting information systems students need to learn these procedures and techniques to prepare themselves for challenging careers in these fields. The AICPA and other accounting professionals recommend that auditors acquire necessary knowledge on IT to effectively evaluate computerized internal controls (Bagranoff et al. 2004). This case study was developed to help you recognize key issues relative to auditing, fraud, and IT and then make appropriate recommendations to address these issues.

The case involves an audit of a fictitious, private, third-party processor of government-funded medical claims. The senior auditor, Bob, works for the United States Department of Health and Human Services (HHS), the administrator of Medicare (U.S. funded medical insurance). Bob is auditing Medicare Southwest (MSW), a small subsidiary of Acme Corporation, which represents one of the largest affiliations of health-care plans in the American southwest. Both Acme and MSW are private contractors and generate the bulk of their revenues by processing medical premiums and claims. Specifically, MSW processes Medicare claims from providers within four states in the American southwest. MSW relies heavily on Acme for both direct and indirect support in processing claims.

Upon review of MSW and Acme's claim processing procedures, Bob and his staff uncover a number of areas of concern. The auditors learn that physical and logical security of information is potentially problematic, especially as these relate to confidentiality and proper authorization. Further, a number of personnel issues surface including the separation of duties and the use of temporary employees. Finally, a possible fraudulent activity requires further investigation.

You are asked to take Bob's position and identify and address these areas of concern through a series of questions posed by the course instructor. Further, you should identify and/or recommend specific audit techniques and procedures that would be useful in addressing the areas of the concern and detecting potential fraud.

The objective of Part 1 is to help you understand internal controls in both manual and computerized environments. The objective of Part 2 is to introduce you to the scope and objectives of the information system audit and to familiarize them with different concurrent auditing and fraud-detection techniques.

Although the case utilizes a realistic scenario relevant to the United States, it has broad application internationally, as the key issues are not specific to any one country. Internationally, the case could be presented as is or modified slightly to reflect another country's reality relevant to third-party processing of government insurance claims.

II. STUDENT HANDOUT

Medicare is a federally funded program in the United States that covers the cost of medical care for the elderly and disabled. Medicare is divided into two parts: 1) Medicare Part A, which provides basic protection against the costs of inpatient hospital and other institutional providers, and 2) Medicare Part B, which covers the costs of doctors and other healthcare practitioners that are not covered under Medicare Part A.

Bob works as a senior auditor of Information Systems (IS) for the U.S. Department of Health and Human Services' (HHS), which administers the Medicare program. HHS maintains contracts with several private health care organizations across the country to process Medicare electronic and paper claims from health care providers, including individual physicians, clinics, and hospitals. The private processors are granted exclusive rights to process medical claims from providers within broad geographic regions, which consist of several states. One of these companies, Medicare Southwest (MSW), processes Medicare claims from providers within four states in the American southwest.

MSW is a relatively small organization with approximately 80 employees. However, its parent company, Acme Corporation, consists of one of the largest affiliations of health-care plans in the southwest. The vast majority of Acme's $5 billion in revenue is composed of private health care premiums that are collected and processed for other private subsidiary organizations. Only a relatively small portion of Acme's revenue (approximately $100 million/year) comes from MSW.

MSW is located on the campus of Acme's Houston, Texas facility. In addition to the 80 MSW employees, approximately 1,200 Acme employees work at the site. These Acme employees provide direct and indirect support for all of the subsidiaries, including MSW. Approximately 60 Acme employees are assigned to provide direct support for MSW. Most of these employees are data entry personnel and managers, although a few make up a small, dedicated Information Technology (IT) staff. Other Acme staff members who support the entire Acme facility provide indirect support, including some IT and building security.

Claims Processing

As the senior federal IS auditor, Bob and the three lower-level auditors have just started to examine the claims processing system. Bob has learned that Acme provides a wide variety of services related to claims processing for its subsidiaries, including MSW. For example, Acme maintains a large data center to process *all* electronic claims, including those from MSW. Acme's staff also processes paper claims.

During the initial tour of Acme's claims processing and data center areas, Acme's IT Security Officer and MSW's internal auditor provided Bob and his staff with an overview of MSW's entire claims process (see Figure 1). Health care providers, including individual doctors, clinics, and hospitals, submit MSW claims to the Houston facility either electronically, or through hard copies sent via U.S. mail. As electronic claims are received, they are automatically screened by Acme's computer system for errors and discrepancies, such as missing information and incorrect amounts claimed for particular medical procedures. If the claims do not contain any apparent errors, they are automatically processed by Acme's computer system, and a check is created and mailed to the health care provider. If errors are discovered, the claims are automatically forwarded to Acme's onsite adjudication department for further review. The adjudication staff attempts to correct the information by contacting the provider or by adjusting the amounts to match the procedure performed. After correction, the adjudication staff submits the claim back through the electronic processing system without further review.

Paper claims are received and sorted in the mailroom, along with all other mail for all subsidiaries. Paper claims are then delivered to Acme staff members who enter the claims data into the system. Prior to final submission, the data that is entered into the system is checked and approved by the single data entry manager on duty. The manager is able to correct any errors prior to submission. After submission, the claims are processed and paid.

All claims contain confidential data, including names, social security numbers (government identification numbers), and specific health care treatments provided to patients. Bob noticed that most of the Acme adjudication and data entry personnel are actually temporary employees hired through agencies. Acme prefers to use the services of temporary agencies to allow more flexibility and to reduce hiring costs in these high-turnover positions.

Bob also noticed that the data entry personnel who support MSW shared their facility with the data entry personnel from the other private subsidiaries. In fact, some of the data entry personnel who support MSW also work on claims from other private Acme subsidiaries. The manager of the claims processing staff explained that a separate facility was not available, and that a shared facility and workload allows for more flexibility to adjust for changes needed in staffing levels.

Since employees dedicated to several different subsidiaries share the data entry area for paper claims, the manager said that no one "owns" the space. Consequently, no single manager is responsible for approving, deleting, and reviewing all physical access to the data entry area. Instead, each individual manager is responsible for initiating requests to grant and delete physical access for their own temporary and permanent employees by notifying the facilities manager. The facilities manager can only print lists of everyone with access to the facility. Therefore, the lists are never reviewed, because individual managers are only familiar with their own employees. The facilities manager did state, however, that the individual managers of any employees who were terminated promptly notified him.

As part of the audit procedures, Bob and his staff examined a sample of twenty incoming electronic claims. The claim amounts were then compared with the amounts actually processed and paid by the computer system. Bob and his staff noted that the amount claimed exceeded the amount paid by the computer system by five cents for every third claim. They further observed that several of the lead programmers for the computer system had the ability to make changes to payment amounts.

PART I

Required:

- Address the following questions as they pertain to the noted areas of concern:

Physical Security

- What concerns might Bob have about the receipt of the paper claims with the regular mail?
- Why would Bob be worried about the sharing of the facility and staff members by several Acme subsidiaries (including MSW)?
- Why would Bob be concerned that no one reviews the physical access lists for everyone who may enter the processing facility?
- Related to physical security, Bob and his staff also requested a list of recently terminated employees and a current list of employees with physical access to the data entry and/or data center facilities. Using these lists, what types of tests could the auditors conduct to ensure that physical and logical access are properly controlled?

Logical Security

- In addition to the recently terminated employee list, Bob and his staff requested information related to logical security. Using the following requested information, what types of tests could the auditors conduct to ensure that logical access is properly controlled?

    - Current list of employees with logical (system) access privileges to the claims processing system, including users and administrators.
    - List of security software parameters, such as password length/type, number of logon attempts allowed; etc.
    - Procedures to control changes to claims processing and support software, along with logs or other records, which list recent changes.

Personnel

- What unique concerns might Bob have regarding the use of temporary employees?
- Why would Bob be concerned about the activities of the "single data entry manager"? What types of controls should be implemented?
- Why would Bob be worried that the adjudication staff can resubmit claims "without further review"?
- Bob learned that a single system programmer can write, test, and approve changes to the claims processing system software. Why is this a concern?

PART II

Required:

Address the following questions as they pertain to the noted areas of concern:

Audit Techniques

- Bob and his staff purposefully embedded 20 fictitious claims, which included the same type of data as a real claim, into the claims processing program. What is the name of this auditing technique, and what is its purpose?
- Bob also discovered that audit modules had been embedded within the claims processing program. These modules flag claims that exceed a specific dollar amount for a claimed procedure and records them in a special audit log. What is the name of this auditing technique, and what is its purpose?
- Bob and his staff decided to review the amounts submitted for payment for a particular sample of claims and then compare them with the actual amounts paid to the providers. Bob noticed that the amounts paid were consistently slightly lower than the amounts submitted. Since the difference only amounted to a few cents for each claim, why would Bob be concerned about this?
- Fraudulent claims have been a frequent concern in the Medicare program, including:

  - multiple claims for medical procedures that are usually not performed on the same patient more than once within a particular time period (e.g. organ transplants).
  - claims for medical procedures that cannot be performed for a particular patient (e.g. physical therapy coma patients).
  - claims for deceased individuals.

How can Computer Audit Software (CAS) assist auditors in identifying these types of fraudulent claims?

- To determine if the five-cent discrepancy for every third claim was fraudulent, what types of procedures might be used?

IV. SUMMARY/CONCLUSIONS

This case focuses on security and control procedures and relevant audit issues of both paper and electronic systems for the third-party processing of government-insured medical claims. As computerization of accounting information systems continues to accelerate, the accounting profession is undergoing radical change as it strives to provide value in today's automated society. In addition, to comply with Sarbanes-Oxley Section 404 requirements and SAS No. 94, auditors must assess internal financial controls and IT controls. Our first goal is to help you understand security and control issues in both manual and computerized environments.

As enterprise wide systems eliminate the traditional paper-based audit trails and environments become heavily automated, auditors are increasingly using concurrent audit techniques (Gelinas et al. 2001). Our second goal is to introduce you to the scope and objectives of the information system audit and to familiarize you with different concurrent auditing techniques.

This case provides an opportunity for you to take the perspective of an auditor for HHS in addressing the security and control and other audit and fraud-related issues in both the paper and computerized environments. The case has application in upper division information systems, auditing, fraud, and forensic accounting courses and has been useful in helping students identify and address complex issues involving fraud, auditing, and IT.

REFERENCES

Bagranoff, N., M.G. Simkin, and C.S. Norman. 2004. *Core Concepts of Accounting Information Systems*, 9th Edition. Hoboken, NJ: John Wiley & Sons, Inc. 448.

Gelinas, U.J., Jr. W.A. Levy, and J.C. Thibodeau. 2001. Ntorood Office Supplies, Inc.: A Teaching Case to Integrate Computer-assisted Auditing Techniques into the Auditing course. *Issues in Accounting Education*: 603-637.

Hall, J. A. 2001. *Accounting Information Systems*. 3rd Edition. Mason, OH: South Western College Publishing. 133.

Romney, M. B. and Steinbart, P.J. 2005. *Accounting Information Systems*. 10th Edition. Upper Saddle River, NJ: Prentice Hall. 324.

Figure 1: MSW's Claim Processing System

CASE STUDY 11:

The Misguided Bond

Seth C. Anderson, Ph.D., CFA

Kim Capriotti, Ph.D.
Jacksonville University
Vincent Shea, Ph.D., CPA
St. John's University

LEARNING OBJECTIVES

After completing and discussing this case, you should be able to

- Recognize retail broker account mismanagement.
- Compare conventional bonds with put-constrained bonds.
- Learn a five-step forensic accounting process.

INTRODUCTION

This case features a 78 year-old married retiree who is seeking to improve the income from a retirement portfolio. Although the client has substantial savings, the client is not a sophisticated investor. He had previously relied on his late financial advisor who had recently passed away, but currently he relies on a financial advisor in the same retail brokerage office who "inherited" the account. The new broker advised the client's purchase of a put-constrained bond of a very risky nature of which the client was not aware. Ultimately, the client lost a substantial portion of his assets with the new speculative bond. You are provided with the client's yearly summary investment account statements, as well as excerpts from the prospectus. A dialogue format is used to present the issues, facts, and terminology of the case.

RELEVANT FACTS

Late in 2001, Ralph Martin, a former clothes salesman, sat on his patio evaluating his current retirement portfolio. Ralph, a 78 year-old retiree, had little interest in investment and had previously depended on his long-term friend and financial advisor for investment advice. However, Fred had died almost two years earlier, and Blink Stowards, another advisor, had worked with Ralph since then. At the time of Fred's death, Ralph's $750,000 portfolio was split somewhat equally among intermediate term bonds paying income at approximately 6%, blue chip stocks yielding income of approximately 3%, and CDs paying income of approximately 5%. If it had been up to Ralph all of his money would have been in CDs because he was scared of stocks and bonds. Because of Fred's earlier guidance, the $35,000 portfolio income, along with their social security and his wife's teaching pension, allowed them to live comfortably and to lend some assistance to several college-age grandchildren.

Blink had been attentive of Ralph and had suggested several sells of "stodgy" equities such Heinz Foods, SCANA (Electric Utility), General Motors, and three natural gas utilities, in order to hopefully benefit the portfolio corpus, by investing in AT&T, Cisco, and a few other non-dividend paying telecommunications related stocks. The high-tech stocks had declined (although the old stodgy equities maintained their market values), but both Ralph and Blink were convinced that their long-term growth potential outweighed any other price risk. However, the CD component would be maturing very soon and then would need to be reinvested. Looking in his local paper's business section, Ralph saw CD rates at 2%, which would generate only $5,000 on the $250,000 principal in CDs.

Ralph mulled over the decline in income of their portfolio currently relative to the income generated earlier. He thought to himself that perhaps Blink might be able to make some suggestions which would supplement his annual income. He decided to call Blink the following Monday.

Meanwhile, in the Classroom

Susan Romano, a professor of accounting, was ending her afternoon forensic accounting class with a discussion of how to investigate the possible existence of broker account mismanagement. Earlier in the session she had discussed a generalized model for forensic accounting, which she and two other professors had earlier presented in an article.

The five-step process they used in the study entails:

I.   Defining the question(s) of interest.

      A forensic accountant hired as an expert must segment a broad legal question into inquiries that can be objectively measured.

II.   Employing benchmarks that are commonly accepted to address the question(s).

      Commonly accepted standards are selected for measuring the objective inquiries.

III. Cleaning data in a methodical fashion, which objectively allows the database to be compared to the benchmarks set forth. Data are purged of unreliable and unrepresentative observations in order to minimize the effects of data-entry error and increase the reliability of results.

IV. Comparing the data to the benchmarks.

The forensic accountant compiles observations into a format in order to compare the data set to the commonly accepted standards.

V. Providing conclusions that link question(s) to the benchmarks and then to the data. Conclusions are drawn which relate the forensic techniques employed to the questions of interest. (Waldrup et al, 2004).

Romano stated, "The two primary types of fraud usually involved in broker-age investment accounts include either "churning" (over-trading) of an account, or suitability/disclosure matters for securities in the account.

After answering a couple of questions, she continued, "In either instance, the forensic accountant needs to use the values on the client's investment account statement to determine the client's account profitability. There are two questions here. First, what calculations are required using these account values to reflect the amount of profits/losses incurred by the client? Second, are these profits/losses appropriate?"

A student queried, "Is there a formula that we should use to compute the amount of profits/losses?"

"In fact, there is a formula, and you probably are already familiar with it. Do you remember how you would compute the profit/losses on an investment account for the year?" She turned and wrote on the board the following formula:

"Total profits/losses = ending account equity value - beginning account equity value + total withdrawals - total deposits."

The Following Monday

Blink answered the first call of the day and heard Ralph Martin, with whom he hadn't spoken in several months. After a few perfunctory remarks Ralph began, "On Saturday I was looking at my portfolio and figured that my annual income now will only be about $21,000 if I renew my CDs at the 2% going rate. My stock income is significantly less than it was…"

"Yeah, that's right, but as we discussed the last time we talked, the potential growth from the telecommunications and other issues we bought probably outweighs any loss income."

"I agree. However, I'm pretty concerned about the extremely low rates on CDs now. What do you think about buying more bonds?" (See http://biz.yahoo.com/f/g/g.html for discussion of bond terminology.)

"It's good that you called at this time. Our research department has just put out a buy recommendation on some high-yield bonds that are backed by the stocks of several major companies. These bonds are short-term, only 12 months until maturity, and pay 12% annually. I haven't seen all of the details on them, but this really might be a good way to increase your total income and at the same time avoid the interest rate risk of intermediate-term and longer-term bonds."

"That certainly sounds good to me. What are the companies that back these bonds? You know that I don't like risky companies. This is all of the money that I have."

"Right off hand I remember that National Telecommunicating Data and Glorious Home Products are two of them. Both of these companies have done very well over the past five years and are certainly good companies for the long pull. Since these bonds are so short-term, I would be very comfortable for you to own them. Why don't you come down tomorrow and let me show you some information."

The Next Morning

Ralph sat across from Blink, who handed him a computer printout with statistics on three of the new "STRIDEs" offering by National Telecommunicating Data, Glorious Home Products, and Immediate Biotech. After briefly discussing the three companies, both Blink and Ralph agreed that the best company for Ralph would be National Telecommunicating Data (NTD), whose stock was trading at $20 per share. Each $1,000 unit face value of the offering had attached 50 shares of the NTD stock.

Ralph used a pencil to compute that the $250,000 currently in CDs would generate $30,000 of income, if invested in STRIDEs, which would give him a total of $46,000 on an annual basis.

"I like the increased income, but what are we going to do in a year from now when these things mature?"

"Well, our research department tells us that interest rates should go up in a year or two, and perhaps we can go back into CDs at that time. Anyway, the additional income from these high quality STRIDEs should help out over the next year."

"Yeah, that certainly will help."

Blink rose from his desk to shake hands as they concluded the meeting. "We don't yet have the prospectus for these STRIDEs available for distribution, but I'll get you one as soon as I get them." Blink had not read much about these new securities but was very attracted to selling them because of the commission. He trusted his manager's recommendation about the new STRIDEs and their safety.

"Great. You take care of it. You do what needs to be done."

Two weeks later Ralph received a thick packet of information and quickly flipped through the two documents filled with financial information. Before setting it aside, he thought, "Maybe I'll read this later, but I've never really understood this financial stuff anyway."

One Year Later

Blink stammered, "Ralph, I'm just as surprised as you. I never imagined that National Telecommunicating Data would be on the ropes now. This is unbelievable."

"Well, what about the principal amount? It was due last week and now your New York office says I've got to accept NTD stock because NTD stock price went down. I thought this was a bond where my money was safe."

Blink coughed nervously and responded, "I thought so, too!"

Over the next several days there were meetings between Ralph, Blink, and the brokerage office manager. Ralph was disgusted with the situation. They were no help.

The Lawyer

Upon the advice of his personal lawyer, Ralph met with another lawyer who specialized in complaints against brokerage offices. The lawyer carefully listened to what occurred with the STRIDEs at the brokerage office.

They agreed that the lawyer would contact a university professor of accounting who specialized in the area of forensic accounting.

Romano Gets a Call

Susan Romano entered the mailroom and noticed the pink telephone message slip awaiting her. Later that day she called Lynn Jinks, a lawyer with whom she had worked previously.

"Well, what do you have, Lynn?"

"I've got a potential client who lost a large portion of his retirement funds in something called a STRIDE, which is a new product of sorts sold by Big Brokerage Group."

"STRIDEs? What the heck are you talking about? I've never heard of STRIDEs in the financial world."

"I'm sending you all of the information on this case if you're willing to take a look at it."

The Information

Three days later Romano received a four-inch deep box containing a 321-page prospectus with an attached supplemental prospectus, year-end account statements, and numerous other papers pertaining to Martin's account. Among these papers was the opening account statement that showed the client's primary investment objectives in order as: (1) preservation of capital, (2) income, and (3) moderate growth. After reviewing the client's stated objectives, she turned to the year-end statements. The following table gives the values seen by her as reported on Martin's yearly statements for the last three years:

Statement Period January 1, 2000 – December 31, 2000		
	1/1/2000 Value	12/31/2000 Value
Bonds	$250,000	$250,000
CDs	250,000	250,000
Stocks	250,000	250,000
Total Portfolio Value	$750,000	$750,000
Income Source for the year:		
Dividends	7,500	
Bond Interest	15,000	
CD Interest	12,500	
Total Cash Disbursements for the year:		$35,000
Total Cash Received for the year:		0

Statement Period January 1, 2001 – December 31, 2001		
	1/1/2001 Value	12/31/2001 Value
Bonds	$250,000	$250,000
CDs	250,000	0
Stocks	250,000	175,000
STRIDEs	0	250,000
Total Portfolio Value	$750,000	$675,000
Income Source for the year:		
Dividends	1,000	
Bond Interest	15,000	
CD Interest	12,500	
Total Cash Disbursements for the year:		$28,500
Total Cash Received for the year:		0

Statement Period January 1, 2002 – December 31, 2002		
	1/1/2002 Value	12/31/2002 Value
Bonds	$250,000	$265,000
CDs	0	0
Stocks	175,000	175,000
STRIDEs	250,000	1,500 (NTD Stock)
Total Portfolio Value	$675,000	$4441,500
Income Source for the year:		
Dividends	1,000	
Bond Interest	15,000	
CD Interest	0	
STRIDE Interest	12,500	
Total Cash Disbursements for the year:		$28,500
Total Cash Received for the year:		0

Romano looked at the summary diagram from their article that was written on the chalkboard to her left.

She thought, "It's obvious that the question of interest is the financial impact incurred relative to the benchmark of a well-managed portfolio. It was pretty clear that Martin's portfolio had experienced significant losses. As to the data, the year-end statements are all that we need. The comparison will be easy."

However, Romano will need to evaluate all related information to conclude whether or not the account had been mismanaged. Susan began reading the statement of claim, which was prepared for the arbitration between Martin and Big Brokerage and saw:

"In December of 2001 Big Brokerage, through Blink, advised Martin that he reinvest maturing CD monies in safe shorter-term investment grade bonds. Toward that end, Big Brokerage, through Blink, advised Martin that he should purchase National Telecommunicating Data bonds called STRIDEs that were tied to National Telecommunicating Data stock. Big Brokerage advised Martin that: (1) investors would receive very high, double digit returns; (2) the bonds were investment grade and backed by National Telecommunicating Data stock that could be sold to protect the principal; and (3) the bonds were safer, short-term investments. Big Brokerage represented to Martin that this was a secure investment, that Big Brokerage stood behind the investment, and there was no way to lose his principal. Big Brokerage further told Martin that if the value of National Telecommunicating Data stock linked to the bonds fell to the value of the principal of the bonds, then the stock could be liquidated to repay the principal."

Romano then turned to the many-page prospectus issued by Big Brokerage for the issuance of bonds and could find nothing for the STRIDEs. She turned to the supplemental prospectus for the STRIDEs and began to determine what type of product these actually were. She read the following:

"A STRIDE combines a bond and a put option on a specific stock or index. When an investor purchases a STRIDE, he or she simultaneously purchases a bond and indirectly sells a put option on the underlying common shares or index. This simultaneous transaction provides STRIDE securities with a relatively higher coupon than would otherwise be paid on a traditional corporate bond. This is because the put premium received is combined with the normal coupon rate of interest to produce an enhanced coupon rate. In the case of this specific STRIDE, the coupon rate on the bonds is 5%, while the rest of the enhanced coupon rate of 12% is the put premium. The interest is paid every six months."

"If the share price for the underlying equity security or index is at or above the strike price of the STRIDE at maturity, the holder of the STRIDE will receive a cash repayment at par. However, if the underlying equity or index is below the strike price of the STRIDE at maturity, the holder will receive payment in the form of a predetermined numbers of shares. Thus, the holder bears the full downside risk of the common stock without protection of principal. It is also important to keep in mind that the STRIDE note is not an obligation of the company whose equity is used as the reference stock."

Romano later read in the supplemental prospectus that the holder would receive payment in the form of shares based on the market price per share of the underlying stock at the time the bonds are issued.

After reflecting on this, Romano realized that these STRIDEs were actually put-constrained bonds, which were quasi bonds, which paid interest in addition to a deferred put premium. (See http://biz.yahoo.com/opt/basics4.html for discussion on put and call options.)

After about an hour, Romano finished reading the prospectus and concluded, "What a squirrelly product – a misguided bond of sorts. All this investment did was open up the investor to huge potential losses and limited the potential on the upside. Big Brokerage has essentially protected itself from all risks when it sells these STRIDEs to investors. The put component added risk to this product because it required the owner to accept the underlying NTD shares at approximately $20 per share regardless of its current market price. In addition, Big Brokerage can immediately use the proceeds from issuing these STRIDEs to pay for operating costs." She thought about how STRIDEs differ from convertible bonds, which can be exchanged for a given number of shares at a specified price. Convertibles would allow people to have protection of the underlying bond while having potential stock appreciation. In contrast, the put component of the STRIDEs might well force the bond owner to buy the related stock at a distressed price and give up the bond value.

Romano finally thought to herself about the ethical implications of Big Brokerage selling these STRIDEs to Ralph Martin, a 78 year-old retiree. Did Blink Stowards give Ralph the "whole story" with respect to these STRIDEs and their risk level? Although all of this pertinent information is disclosed in the STRIDEs prospectus which Romano just finished reading, is it reasonable to think that "Joe Investor" would understand these put-constrained bonds?

Susan Romano needs your help on the following questions.

UNDERGRADUATE STUDENT QUESTIONS

1. What is the formula to calculate the profit or loss for Martin's investment account?

2. What is the formula to calculate the annual return for Martin's investment account?

3. What is Martin's actual return for 2000, 2001 and 2002?

4. What would have been Martin's return for years 2000, 2001 and 2002 if his portfolio had remained with its initial holdings? (Assume original stock holdings remain unchanged and did not decline, and renewal of the CD.)

5. Explain Martin's responsibilities as the writer of a put option. What are his potential losses if NTD stock declines?

6. Compare and contrast STRIDEs with conventional bonds. (Note: both pay conventional coupons, but STRIDEs have a deferred put premium payable to the owner.)

7. How appropriate were these STRIDEs for a 78 year-old with Martin's stated investment objectives? Search suitability information at "NASD Conduct Rule 2310"

8. Considering that the prospectus and accompanying supplemental prospectus exceeded 300 pages, is it reasonable to expect "Joe Investor" to digest this volume of information?

9. How does Blink's representation of the STRIDEs as reported in the statement of claims contrast with the actual nature of this product, as reported in the supplemental prospectus?

10. Assume you are an arbitration panel member. Would you order the brokerage firm to award Ralph any damages? If so, how much? Why?

GRADUATE STUDENT QUESTIONS

1. What is Martin's actual return for 2000, 2001 and 2002?

2. What would have been Martin's return for years 2000, 2001 and 2002 if his portfolio had remained with its initial holdings? (Assume original stock holdings remain unchanged and did not decline, and renewal of the CD.)

3. Compare and contrast STRIDEs with conventional bonds. (Note: both pay conventional coupons, but STRIDEs have a deferred put premium payable to the owner.)

4. How appropriate were these STRIDEs for a 78 year-old with Martin's stated investment objectives? Search suitability information at "NASD Conduct Rule 2310"

5. Considering that the prospectus and accompanying supplemental prospectus exceeded 300 pages, is it reasonable to expect "Joe Investor" to digest this volume of information?

6. How does Blink's representation of the STRIDEs as reported in the statement of claims contrast with the actual nature of this product, as reported in the supplemental prospectus?

7. Assume you are an arbitration panel member. Would you order the brokerage firm to award Ralph any damages? If so, how much? Why?

REFERENCES

Anderson, S. C. and D. A. Winslow. 1992-93., *Defining Suitability.* Kentucky Law Journal. Vol. 81, No. 1, 105-122

NASD Manual, July 2001, CCH Incorporated, Chicago.

Waldrup B., S. Anderson, and K. Capriotti. *Forensic Accounting Techniques: A Defensible Investigatory Process for Litigation.* Journal of Forensic Accounting, Vol. 5, No. 1, 1-16.

http://biz.yahoo.com/f/g/g.html

http://biz.yahoo.com/opt/basics4.html

CASE STUDY 12:

A Form of Money Laundering

D. Larry Crumbley, Ph.D., CPA, CFF, Cr.FA
Louisiana State University
G. Stevenson Smith, Ph.D., CPA, CMA
Southeastern Oklahoma State University

LEARNING OBJECTIVES

After completing and discussing this case, you should be able to

- Recognize legal and illegal money laundering.
- Ponder a form of money laundering from the ethical viewpoint.
- Learn about GASB No. 33 and restricted funds.
- Learn about the layering of transactions to clean money.

You are auditing a state university in Louisiana, and in the engineering department you find that a number of endowed professorships and endowed chairs are vacant. In fact, there are more of these endowed positions than qualified faculty.

Donors give monies to universities in the form of professorships and chairs to be given to specific faculty members. The professors then promote the endowed position by various activities (e.g., articles, grants, books, newspaper articles, etc.). If there is no designated professor for one of these positions, the earnings accumulate within the fund.

As an external auditor (or internal auditor) you find that the department is taking the earnings from the unassigned positions (a restricted fund) and using the monies for general uses. For example, a department head is assigned as many as five endowed professorships to be used in the department for various expenditures and those positions are unfilled. Thus, the department head is using endowment monies for discretionary purposes.

You read about money laundering in a fraud course while in college. You have read in the newspapers about how Stanford University and other universities were caught using Federal restricted funds for general use. Also, you know that certain parishes in Louisiana also were caught in a form of money laundering. Parish School Boards would collect sales taxes designed for teachers' salaries and use the funds for general use.

1. What would you do?
2. What should you do?
3. Is this a form of money laundering? Why or why not? Check out GASB No. 33. Federal and Louisiana laws should be consulted.
4. Suppose you tell your supervisor about the department's activities, and he/she tells you to forget about it. What would you do? What should you do?
5. Assume that you believe this activity is a form of money laundering and your firm will do nothing. Should you report this activity to the legislative auditors? Would you report it to anyone else?
6. If you assume this activity is not illegal, is the practice ethical for a university? Why or why not?

CASE STUDY 13:

Ponzi Scheme or Accounting Malpractice: Beware of Cowboys Wearing the White Hats

D. Larry Crumbley, Ph.D., CPA, CFF, Cr.FA
Louisiana State University
Nicholas G. Apostolou, DBA, MBA, CPA
West Virginia University

LEARNING OBJECTIVES

After completing and discussing this case, you should be able to

- Recognize signs of a Ponzi scheme.
- Learn a number of expert witness concepts.
- See that there are two or more different sides to a legal dispute.
- Learn the various stages of a courtroom battle.

INTRODUCTION

An external auditor is required to perform an assessment in accordance with generally accepted auditing standards for the purpose of rendering an opinion that the financial statements have been prepared in accordance with general accounting principles applied on a consistent basis. The audit is essentially intended to uncover significant deviations from standards and to verify that acceptable accounting and auditing practices have been used in the preparation of financial statements.

A forensic accountant takes a more proactive, skeptical approach to examining the books of a company. This specialist makes no assumption of management integrity and brings to the evaluation process less concern than an auditor with whether the reports conform to GAAP and more interest in exposing any possibility of fraud. Since a forensic accountant often faces legal issues, an accountant practicing in the forensic area needs to have an understanding of the legal environment in which businesses operate. For example, the evidence the forensic accountant derives from an investigation may require his/her testimony as an expert witness. Prosecutors, criminal, and civil attorneys often use forensic accountants before trial and as expert witnesses.

The techniques of forensic accounting and the legal environment that expert witnesses face are illustrated in this case using a real-world situation. This case highlights the importance of familiarity with the basic rules of accounting, SEC actions, litigation releases, Ponzi schemes, temporary restraining orders, law briefs, receivers, and knowledge of courtroom procedure.

JUST THE FACTS, MA'AM

Wilson Energy Resources was a Nevada corporation. Its principal place of business was located in Woodland Hills, California. Wilson Energy was managing general partner of a number of oil and gas offerings. As the Managing General Partner, Wilson through its owners, Mr. James Anders and Mr. Robert Sands, exercised exclusive authority over the operation of wells and properties in which interests were offered.

Mr. Robert Sands was the co-owner of M&M Company. As one of the owners of M&M, Mr. Sands operated and controlled the offerings made by M&M Company and controlled the operations, bank accounts, and other day-to-day operations of the companies. For example, Mr. Sands was the signatory on most of the M&M bank accounts into which investor monies were deposited as well as on the accounts from which distributions were made to investors.

TEMPORARY RESTRAINING ORDER

On September 22, 1997, Judge Dick Train, the Judge of the U.S. District Court of the Central District of California in the Eastern Division, issued a temporary restraining order (TRO) whereby the assets of the defendants and principals were frozen. A receiver, Jay Lane, was empowered and directed to conduct an investigation to locate and account for all of the assets of the companies – a fourteen-year business. He was to take custody and control of these assets, and take all actions necessary and appropriate to preserve these assets.

The TRO was based upon a declaration of Jeanne Neighbors, a certified public accountant employed by the Securities and Exchange Commission (SEC). She was the senior accountant in the Pacific Regional Office located in Los Angeles, California.

OFFSETTING CHECKS

The defendant, Wilson Energy, offered and sold securities to investors in the form of joint ventures and general partnership interests in oil and gas properties. Mountain Petroleum, Inc. served as the operator, on behalf of M&M Company, of most oil wells in North Dakota in which they had an interest. Mountain's primary duties were to present properties for acquisition to the defendants and to operate the oil and gas properties. Over a period of about two years, however, Mountain did not send Wilson approximately $2,234,824 of oil and gas revenues. Instead, Mountain merely offset this money against expenditures that Mountain incurred in the oil and gas fields. The amount of expenditures that Mountain incurred was in dispute, as well as the amount that the defendants should have received.

These offsets were memorialized by Mountain with voided checks in the correct amount. The SEC's accountant knew about the more than two million dollar offsets to cash receipts and revenues *before* she prepared her initial report which resulted in the TRO. She was at the deposition of Keith Cole (Mountain) on August 14, 1997, and Mr. Cole clearly told the SEC about huge offsets of cash receipts and revenues. Larry Luke, Wilson Energy's revenue accountant, described these massive offsets in his deposition on March 12, 1997, as did Barbara McLean (Mountain) in her deposition on August 15, 1997. The defendants themselves were even forced later to acquire these voided checks from the SEC.

In her first declaration filed in support of the SEC's motion for a TRO and appointment of a receiver, Jeanne Neighbors compared cash receipts of $120,004.39 (without about $1,253,286 of offsets) to the cash distributions of $1,313,925. The SEC accountant then made the inflammatory statement "that less than 10% of investor distributions were derived from oil and gas operations based on distribution checks issued during the relevant period." In other words, the SEC argued that Wilson Energy was operating a Ponzi-like scheme.

Where Did The Money Come From? (Receipts)		Where Did the Money Go? (Disbursements/Expenses)	
Beginning Balance	$268,439	Money Distributed to Investors	$2,281,255
Money Raised From Investors	6,704,320	Employees / Principals / Overhead	$2,332,066
Oil and Gas Production	394,575	Oil Field Operations	$1,616,000
Other	194,575		
		Attorney's Fees	1,027,984
		Other	158,626
		Ending Cash Balance	$145,978

The receiver, Jay Lane, hired a CPA, Jim Finn, from San Diego. The receiver's November 6, 1997 "cash receipt statement" prepared by Mr. Finn appeared as follows:

CASH RECEIPTS STATEMENT

The Receiver stated that the findings of the CPA support the conclusion that during 1996 and 1997, defendants used significant portions of investor money to make distributions on prior unrelated investments rather than for the purposes described in the offering memoranda. For example, in 1996, the defendants made distributions to investors of $819,740 in excess of the profits actually derived from the oil and gas operations. To make matters worse, according to Jay Lane, the defendants apparently failed to pay the up-front expenses related to the wells in excess of $430,000. Thus, even the funds characterized by defendants as "net income" were illusory.

Receiver Lane argued that by making distributions to investors, the impression was created that many wells were profitable when, as a result of the expenses for reworking and maintaining the wells, there were no profits. Moreover, according to the offering memoranda, the expenses for reworking the wells and the purchase of mineral rights were to be paid out of the initial investment, not from income from operations. Thus, by implication, the defendants were operating a Ponzi scheme. There were about 33 new investors over the two-year time period.

JUDGE'S ESCAPADES

In a hearing on November 21, 1997, and November 25, 1997, at the request of defendants to have the receiver removed, Judge Train stated that this "was one of the worst set of books that I have ever seen kept by an accountant." [During this hearing the judge stressed that he had previously worked for Arthur Andersen, and he knew accounting.] However, he seemed obsessed about the fact that the cash flow from investors was commingled into one single bank account.

QUESTIONS AND REQUIREMENTS

1.   What are some characteristics of a Ponzi scheme? Why is it called a Ponzi scheme?

2.   Was this situation a Ponzi scheme? Use the Internet to learn more about other Ponzi schemes. Is this like Bernie Madoff's scheme?

3.   Was there any improper professional conduct involved in this case study? Read SEC Rul. 102(e)(1).

4.   If you were the expert witness for the defendant, what would be your arguments?

5.   What should happen to the SEC accountant and plaintiff's expert witness?

CASE STUDY 14:

Remaining Skeptical and Firm

Dr. Donald L. Ariail, CPA, CGMA, CFF
Southern Polytechnic State University

LEARNING OBJECTIVES

After completing and discussing this case, you should be able to

- Appreciate the value of being skeptical.
- Understand the process of an inventory count.
- Observe the pressures placed upon an auditor.

A young staff accountant, Sam Adder, was assigned to observe a year-end inventory count. The client under audit was in the business of selling oil packaged in standard sized drums. On arriving for the inventory observation and counting as prescribed by Generally Accepted Auditing Standards (American Institute of Certified Public Accountants, 2011, AU Section, 331), the young accountant found a warehouse full of sealed drums stacked from floor to ceiling. The CPA firm's observation procedures specified that not only must the count be observed, but also that a spot check must be made of a small sample of the drums to verify that they actually contained an oil-like substance.

After observing the inventory count, Sam randomly selected a few easily reachable drums for the content check. The warehouse manager assigned to assist with the observation reluctantly broke the seals on the selected drums, and the accountant verified that they held a substance which appeared to be oil. The accountant then requested that a forklift be used to remove a stack of drums so that one close to the bottom of a stack could be opened and checked. The warehouse manager, who had worked for the client company for many years and was much older and more experienced than the accountant, refused to dismantle the stack and stated that he had already broken enough seals and that it was a waste of time and money for him to break any more. He declared that prior auditors from the accounting firm had never been so unreasonable, and he implied that the request was due to the accountant's inexperience. He told the accountant to "just go with what you have."

What should Sam do?

CASE STUDY 15:

The Use of Restructuring Reserves to Manipulate Reported Income at Moonstay Corporation

Alan A. Cherry, Ph.D.
Loyola Marymount University

LEARNING OBJECTIVES

After completing and discussing this case, you should be able to

- Use the FARS system and find an EITF abstract.
- Access the SEC web site and read a speech.
- Learn about contingent liabilities.
- Consider the ethical ramification of an audit failure.

INTRODUCTION

The main focus of this case is on the fraudulent inflating of a restructuring reserve at Moonstay Corporation in late 1996. This technique was actually just one of the many aspects of the massive financial reporting fraud that took place while Moonstay was being run by controversial CEO "Whipsaw" Bill Smith. The case also deals with Moonstay's unnecessary accrual of a contingent liability. You are asked to discuss the role played by Moonstay's external auditors.

This case illustrates how a company can manipulate its reported income for two or more years through the use of an accounting game called restructuring reserves. The game was played at a very high level at Moonstay Corporation during 1996 and 1997, during which time CEO Whipsaw Bill Smith was Moonstay's chief executive officer (CEO).

INTRODUCTION

After a spectacular though brief tenure as CEO of Stormish Paper Company, which ended with the sale of Stormish to Kinter Corporation for $9.4 billion, Bill Smith, known as Whipsaw for his fondness for firing people, took some time off and then agreed to become CEO of the troubled but respected consumer products company, Moonstay Corporation. The market capitalization of Stormish had increased by $6.3 billion during Smith's time there, with Smith's net worth increasing by about $100 million, and both Wall Street and Moonstay stockholders were thrilled at the prospect of another phenomenal turnaround at Moonstay. Indeed, on July 19, 1996, the day after Smith was hired, shares of Moonstay stock were bid up nearly 60 percent, the largest one-day increase to that point in time in the history of the New York Stock Exchange. Four months later, Whipsaw outlined a restructuring plan to the Moonstay board of directors. He told the Board that he would eliminate half of the company's 12,000 employees, stop producing 87 percent of existing products, close the majority of its factories and warehouses, and divest several lines of business. He informed the board that this downsizing would save the company $225 million per year but also result in a one-time pretax charge of $300 million.

According to the Notes to the Consolidated Financial Statements found in Moonstay's 1997 Form 10-K filed with the SEC, the total restructuring charge was actually $337.6 million. This charge, which helped produce a net loss for 1996 of over $228 million, was described in the Notes as having been allocated in the manner shown below:

Restructuring, impairment, and other costs	$154,900,000
Cost of goods sold (inventory write-downs)	92,300,000
Selling, general and administrative expenses (for increases in environmental and litigation reserves)	42,500,000
Estimated loss on sale of discontinued operations	47,900,000
Total restructuring charge to earnings	$337,600,000

CREATING THE ILLUSION OF A TURNAROUND

Ed Paul is considered one of the most successful stock investors in history, and he has written a series of letters to shareholders that are both informative and entertaining. There are usually a couple of pages devoted to accounting issues, and the 1998 letter focused on restructuring charges, which Paul described as a "distortion." He indicated that restructuring was frequently a device for manipulation. A part of costs for a number of years is typically dumped into a single quarter. The timing is designed to allow future quarters to exceed investor expectation.

Sure enough, Moonstay reported successively larger profits for each quarter of 1997, culminating in earnings before discontinued operations for the year of over $123 million and a bottom line of over $109 million. This result was an apparent turnaround of over $300 million from the year before, and Wall Street responded by bidding Moonstay shares up to a high of $52 per share in March 1998. Unfortunately for many investors, creditors, and other Moonstay stakeholders, much of the miraculous turnaround was the result of creative accounting. Moonstay's chief financial officer (CFO) Robert Kurt, who also worked with Smith at Stormish, liked to remind fellow executives that he was Moonstay's "biggest profit center," and Smith stated at meetings that, "if it wasn't for Robert and the accounting team, we'd be nowhere."

Things started to unravel quickly at Moonstay in early 1998, with the stock price going down fast in reaction to a series of disappointing revenue and profit reports and projections. After an article in *Forbes* by Matthew Toast questioned the accounting practices at Moonstay, the board of directors took the extreme action of firing both Smith and Kurt on June 13, 1998. Moonstay's external auditor, the CPA firm of CPA Pintrest, then refused to allow its unqualified opinion on the 1997 financial statements to be used in connection with any securities offerings by Moonstay. The Board and the newly appointed top management team ordered a review of the company's prior financial statements. Moonstay hired the CPA firm of CPA Capital to assist the audit committee of the board and CPA Pintrest with the review. The review led to the filing of an amended 10-K with the SEC in November 1998. Included in this 10-K/A were restated financial statements. When these are compared to the originally issued statements, it is apparent that Moonstay had purposely overstated its loss in 1996 (a big bath) and followed that with an vastly overstated net income in 1997. While much of the misstatements resulted from improper accounting for revenues and various expenses, along with the use of sham transactions, the manipulation of the restructuring reserves created by the CFO in 1996 played a significant role as well. Indeed, it seems likely that Ed Paul had Moonstay in mind when he wrote about restructurings.

Meanwhile, the SEC informed Moonstay in June 1998 that its Division of Enforcement was launching an investigation. It took almost three years to complete that investigation, which resulted in the filing on May 15, 2001, of civil fraud charges against Smith, Kurt, former Moonstay controller Ron Glue, two other Moonstay officers, and the partner in charge of the CPA Pintrest audit, Phil Hart. Among the many examples of improper accounting found by the SEC was the padding of the 1996 restructuring charge with at least $35 million of improper reserves and accruals, excessive write-downs, and prematurely recognized expenses. The improper reserves were then drawn into income in each quarter of 1997, including a remarkable $21.5 million in the fourth quarter. According to the SEC, the bulk of the inflated reserves were in two areas. First, there was almost $19 million of general restructuring reserves that were clearly not in conformity with GAAP. It appears that the Enforcement Division deemed that this amount of reserve did not meet criterion found in Emerging Issues Task Force Issue No. 94-3 for recognition of such liabilities. Second, at least $6 million of a $12 million litigation reserve for environmental problems was recognized in violation of the FASB's Statement No. 5 on contingencies.

The impact of Whipsaw Bill Smith and his friends on Moonstay Corporation and its stockholders and creditors has been devastating. In February 2001, Moonstay had to file for protection from creditors under Chapter 11 of the U.S. Bankruptcy Code. The company had seen its long-term debt go from about $200 million when Smith was hired to about $2.6 billion. Positive retained earnings have been replaced by a deficit of over a billion, as massive losses had been reported each year starting with 1998. At the time of the bankruptcy, the company had just $15 million in cash and its stock was selling for a mere 51 cents per share, just one percent of its peak price in 1998 of $52 per share.

A LOOK AT THE DETAILS

Upon completion of the review by the two CPA firms, restated financial statements and accompanying notes were prepared and filed with the SEC as part of Moonstay's Form 10-K/A for the fiscal year ended December 28, 1997. Among the many restatements was a $98.4 million reduction in the pre-tax amount of the total restructuring charge taken in 1996. The allocation of the restated charge, now totaling $239.2 million, is shown below.

Restructuring, impairment, and other costs	$110,100,000
Cost of goods sold (inventory write-downs)	60,800,000
Selling, general and administrative expenses (for outsourcing and packaging redesign)	10,100,000
Estimated loss on sale of discontinued operations	58,200,000
Total restructuring charge to earnings	$239,200,000

Although greatly reduced, the first component of the restructuring charge still had a significant effect on Moonstay's financial statements. The notes explained that included in this charge were both cash and non-cash items. The cash items consisted of severance and other employee costs ($24.7 million), along with the costs of closing factories and other facilities ($16.7 million). The non-cash portion of the charge ($68.7 million) related to write-downs to the net realizable value of buildings, equipment, and other assets that Moonstay planned to dispose of as part of its downsizing. When Moonstay originally recorded these charges, their accountants estimated the employee costs to be $43 million and they wrote the assets down by $91.8 million. It appears that here was some of the padding of the 1996 charge that the SEC alleges was fraudulent.

However, even the reduced amounts, although deemed to be reasonable estimates as of the end of 1996, proved to be too high. The review of what actually took place during 1997 led to a reversal of accruals no longer required in the amount of $14.6 million. This shows up as a positive amount in Moonstay's restated income statement for fiscal year 1997. Interestingly, no such benefit appears on the originally reported income statement. Perhaps Moonstay's accountants were too busy reversing some of the purposely overstated reserves and accruals in ways that would not draw attention that they missed a legitimate opportunity to increase the 1997 net income.

According to both the notes and the statement of cash flows found in the original 10-K filing, Moonstay paid $43.4 million in cash during 1997 for costs associated with the 1996 restructuring plan. Included in this amount was a supposed $18.6 million for severance and other employee termination costs. However, the review by the two CPA firms only managed to find $21.2 million paid during 1997 for restructuring costs, or less than half the originally reported amount. In fact, the restated amount for severance and other employee termination costs was only $10 million. So it appears that Moonstay had charged an extra $8.6 million to the restructuring reserve for payments to employees during 1997 for work done that year.

Before posing a few questions to which you are to respond, shown below are some of the most important items from Moonstay's income statement and balance sheet as they were originally reported and as restated.

Selected items from Moonstay Corporation=s Income Statements (Amounts in thousands, except for per share amounts)				
	For the Year Ended December 28, 1997		For the Year Ended December 29, 1996	
	As Originally Reported	As Restated	As Originally Reported	As Restated
Net sales	$1,168,182	$1,073,090	$984,236	$984,236
Cost of goods sold	837,683	830,956	900,573	896,938
Selling, general and administrative expense	131,056	152,653	214,029	221,655
Restructuring and asset impairment (benefit) charges	0	(14,582)	154,869	110,122
Operating earnings (loss)	199,443	104,063	(285,235)	(244,479)
Loss on sale of discontinued operations, net of taxes	(13,713)	(14,017)	(32,430)	(39,140)
Net earnings (loss)	109,415	38,301	(228,262)	(208,481)
Net earnings (loss) per share of common stock:				
Basic	$1.29	$0.45	($2.75)	($2.51)

When it comes to the balance sheet, the restatement process did not result in dramatic changes in the December 29, 1996 Balance Sheet of Moonstay. There were some interesting changes, however, in the December 28, 1997 Balance Sheet, as shown below.

Selected items from the December 28, 1997 Balance Sheet (Amounts in thousands, except for per share amounts)		
	As Originally Reported	As Restated
Receivables, net	$295,550	$228,460
Inventories	256,180	304,900
Total current assets	658,005	602,242
Property, plant and equipment, net	240,897	249,524
Trademarks, trade names, goodwill and other, net	221,382	207,162
Restructuring accrual	10,938	5,186
[Restructuring accrual at 12/29/96]	[63,834]	[51,725]
Other current liabilities	80,913	118,899
Total current liabilities	198,099	233,127
Other long-term liabilities	141,109	154,300
Total shareholders' equity	531,937	472,079

QUESTIONS

1. How is the term liability defined by the FASB (see SFAC No. 6 in FARS or on the FASB's web site)? Obtain and read the speech by Walter Schuetze, "Cookie Jar Reserves," April 22, 1999, U.S. Securities and Exchange Commission, and then write a brief summary of Schuetze's thoughts about restructuring reserves such as those recognized by Moonstay. (If you have access to it, you should also read EITF Abstract 94-3.) Do you think the restructuring reserves recognized by Moonstay in 1996 should have been accrued as a liability? Why or why not?

2. Describe an alternative way to communicate the potential financial impact of a corporate restructuring that would avoid giving fraudsters the opportunity to practice "creative" accounting.

3. Moonstay's accountants originally charged $43.4 million of cash expenditures made in 1997 to the restructuring accrual account established in late 1996. According to the review conducted by the two CPA firms, only $21.2 million of cash paid in 1997 actually related to the restructuring of Moonstay. What was the effect on the 1997 reported earnings of improperly charging (debiting) $22 million to the restructuring accrual account? What are some of the accounts that probably should have been debited instead? (Hint: some of the amounts charged to the restructuring reserve involved such routine items as employee compensation and maintenance.)

4. The SEC charged that Moonstay violated FASB Statement No. 5, which deals with contingencies, by overstating a litigation reserve account related to environmental problems. Read the discussion of loss contingencies found in any Intermediate Accounting textbook. What might be the nature of Moonstay's violation of FASB Statement No. 5? Why would Moonstay's management want to accrue at least $6 million more than necessary as a loss in 1996?

5. As always happens, when an accounting fraud comes to light, people ask, "where were the auditors?" Moonstay is no exception, especially with the SEC bringing civil fraud charges against the CPA Pintrest partner in charge of the audit engagement. The evidence seems to indicate that this partner was aware of various aspects of the accounting fraud, yet signed unqualified audit opinions for both 1996 and 1997. Identify the stakeholders who have been harmed by this auditor's failure. Whose interests do you think this auditor was trying to serve? Whipsaw Bill Smith and his management team or the stakeholders you have identified? Why might an auditor favor the interests of management over those of other stakeholders?

REFERENCES

Byme, John A. 1999. *Chainsaw: The Notorious Career of Al Dunlap in the Era of Profit-At-Any-Price.* New York, NY : Harper Business.

Buffett, Warren E. 1999. Chairman's Letter. *Berkshire Hathaway Inc., 1998 Annual Report:* 3-19.

Emerging Issues Task Force (EITF). 1995. *Liability Recognition for Certain Employee Termination Benefits and Other Costs to Exit an Activity (including Certain Costs Incurred in a Restructuring).* EITF Abstract 94-3. Norwalk, CT: FASB.

Financial Accounting Standards Board (FASB). *Accounting for Contingencies.* Statement No.5. Norwalk, CT: FASB.

Schifrin, Matthew. 1998. The unkindest cuts. *Forbes* (May 4): 44.

Schuetze, Walter P. 1999. Cookie Jar Reserves (Speech by SEC Staff). *Web Site of the U.S. Securities and Exchange Commission.* (April 22).

Spiceland, J. D., J. F. Sepe, and L. A. Tomassini. 2001. *Intermediate Accounting.* Second edition. Burr Ridge, IL: Irwin McGraw-Hill.

CASE STUDY 16:

The Obvious Fraud

David O'Bryan, Ph.D., CPA, CMA, CFE
Pittsburg State University
Jeffrey J. Quirin, Ph.D., CMA
Wichita State University

LEARNING OBJECTIVES

After completing and discussing this case, you should be able to

- The appropriate way to follow-up on a tip.
- The importance of being thoroughly prepared before confronting a fraudster.
- Obtaining a confession may require compelling evidence of guilt.

> Assume you are an internal auditor for a large, multinational, manufacturing organization with a division in Mexico. One of your responsibilities is to investigate allegations made on the company's fraud hotline. When you arrive at work one morning you learn an anonymous tip was left on the hotline that alleges fraud involving the division manager.

"Pat's significant other is a fraudulent vendor," was the anonymous tip left on your company's fraud hotline. Pat is a division manager at your company.

"Wow. I can't believe this guy is so blatant," you're thinking as you review some accounts payable invoices while following up on this anonymous tip. The invoice that caught your attention is shown in Table 1.

A quick search of the AP file reveals a total of three invoices like the one in Table 1, all for identical amounts but on different dates. The division manager, Pat, has the authority to approve payment of invoices for less than $10,000. It is obvious to you that the manager has a created a shell company. You happen to know that Pat's significant other is named Kim, hence the name Kimco Marketing. There is no documentation to support these transactions other than the invoices, all of which are purportedly for marketing services.

Table 1: Kimco Marketing Invoice

Kimco Marketing
Marketing Specialists for the Mexican Region
La Quemada 3909, Benito Juarez
03020 Ciudad de Mexico

INVOICE

February 20, 2011

Pat U. Lyonsack
E. Z. Pickens Conglomerate, S. A.
Andres Bello 29
Mexico City, Distrido Federal 11560 Mexico
+52 55 5519 4698

Invoice Number: 10001

DATE	DESCRIPTION	AMOUNT
1/10/2011	Marketing Fieldwork	3500.00
1/22/2011	Market Research	3000.00
2/1/2011	Marketing Support Services	3250.00
	TOTAL DUE	$ 9750.00

Please remit the total amount due within 10 days

Thank You,

[signature]

Holly Unlikely, Billing Clerk

The manager's office is not more than 30 feet away, and Pat can be seen at the desk. You throw the invoices in a file, grab your buddy in the next office, and head for Pat's office. After all, it doesn't take a brain surgeon to know what's going on here.

ASSIGNMENT

You or your team should assume you are the internal auditors going to interview Pat. After reading the scenario above, your initial task is to brainstorm about how you will confront Pat about the fraud allegation. Next, compile a written list of the questions you will ask in the interview with Pat and the sequence in which they will be asked. Ultimately, your objective is to determine whether a fraud has been committed and, if so, obtain a confession from Pat. At the conclusion of this planning session be prepared to interview Pat (who may be portrayed by your instructor).

CASE LEARNING OBJECTIVES AND IMPLEMENTATION GUIDANCE

Introduction and Objectives

This case is based upon an actual fraud investigation that was conducted at a Fortune 500 company. The mishandling of that investigation resulted in no punitive action against the fraudster and allowed the fraudster to recover damages from the victim company for wrongful termination. The primary objective of this case is to demonstrate what not to do when one suspects fraud or wrongdoing. A secondary objective is to illustrate how important it is to be prepared for an admission-seeking interview.

Problem-Based Learning

This case utilizes the innovative, problem-based learning (PBL) method introduced to the accounting discipline by Johnstone and Biggs (1998) and Milne and McConnell (2001), and illustrated in an accounting education context by Durtschi (2003, 2010). PBL approaches to instruction originated in medical schools but have application to a wide variety of other disciplines. PBL consists of giving either an individual or team of students a realistic, ill-defined problem set in a real-world context. It is an investigative approach to learning and therefore results in an active learning process recommended for accounting programs by the Association to Advance Collegiate Schools of Business (AACSB).

Within a typical PBL assignment, the students' initial task is to identify the additional information necessary in order to solve the case. Students must then ascertain where to find that information, which could require interviews with the appropriate parties. Finally, students are required to evaluate, analyze, and synthesize the information they obtain to develop a proposed solution, which generally takes the form of a supervisor-defined work product.

Consistent with AACSB proposed learning objectives, the aforementioned interview procedures and written solution requirements foster student growth from both oral and written communication perspectives. The context of the current case study further enhances AACSB accounting curriculum learning objectives by offering an environment whereby students must utilize critical thinking skills to ascertain a series of questions designed to obtain the necessary information during an admission-seeking interview.

PBL in Fraud Education

Most published fraud cases present the details of a scheme, who perpetrated the fraud, and how they were caught. The focus is on what can be learned from the case after-the-fact. We refer to these as "20-20 hindsight" cases and they play a valuable role in fraud education. They are especially useful to help students identify the red flags of fraud and to determine how the control environment could have been modified to prevent the fraud from occurring.

However, 20-20 hindsight cases suffer from several weaknesses. First, in many real-world fraud examinations the investigator does not know who is perpetrating a fraud or what scheme or schemes they are using. The critical role of the fraud examiner or forensic accountant is to determine who is actually perpetrating the fraud and how.

Second, 20-20 hindsight cases do not help students develop investigative or interviewing skills. By their very nature, these cases tell their reader what happened. Students do not get an opportunity to develop a fraud theory, collect evidence to test the theory, revise the theory as necessary in light of the evidence or lack thereof, and synthesize the results into a meaningful report.

The PBL approach puts students in the role of an investigator who does not know many of the facts related to a potential offense. The process is purposely unstructured and mirrors practice by being iterative when the evidence fails to support the fraud theory. Within the context of using PBL in fraud education, we refer to these types of cases as the "20-20 foresight" approach. They require students to develop their own vision of the fraud, not merely read another person's rendition of what happened.

Motivation

The current case study aims to illustrate the importance of interview preparation and following recommended protocol when conducting a fraud examination. In forensic investigations, the ACFE and others recommend working from the outside in. That is, gather documentary evidence, interview cooperative witnesses, build a case file, and then confront the alleged fraudster(s) near the conclusion of the investigation.

What seems like common sense to those of us in this field is not always so apparent to those not trained in fraud auditing. This case is primarily based on the experience of a Fortune 500 company. They discovered that their division manager at a foreign subsidiary was committing fraud. The company employees immediately confronted the fraudster and terminated him the same day. The fraudster denied the allegations, destroyed key evidence that could have proven the allegations, and sued the company for wrongful termination. Ultimately the company suffered a six figure loss from the embezzlement compounded by a six figure settlement of the wrongful termination suit.

The aforementioned case did not begin with an anonymous tip. We have added this element of the case based upon the recently reported situation at Renault (Jones and Lublin, 2011). Anonymous tips are often useful in fraud detection, but the Renault case provides additional motivation for the lesson we are striving to impart in this case; fraud investigations should be done in a careful, methodical manner:

"Renault is the poster child for why you want to approach these situations with a sense of balance, and not have people rush to judgment," according to Robert Fatovic, the chief legal officer at Ryder Systems, Inc. (Jones and Lublin, 2011).

In the Renault case the company fired three top executives based upon an anonymous tip and an incomplete investigation. The employees were steadfast in professing their innocence. Ultimately, the company learned it was apparently the victim of a hoax (Gauthier-Villars, 2011) and publicly apologized to the fired employees (Moffett and Pearson, 2011).

It is easy to tell students what to do and what not to do in a lecture format. This case study was written so that they can see what could happen if they do not follow the appropriate investigation process. In our experience, a short, simulated interview demonstrating the incorrect approach is much more engaging, and entertaining, than simply telling students the proper way to conduct an investigation; as a result, students are much more likely to attain, and retain, our learning objectives.

REFERENCES

Durtschi, C. 2003. The Tallahassee BeanCounters: A Problem-Based Learning Case in Forensic Auditing. *Issues in Accounting Education.* 18 (2): 137-173.

Durtschi, C. 2010. Return of the Tallahassee BeanCounters: A Case in Forensic Accounting. *Issues in Accounting Education.* 25 (2): 279-321.

Gauthier-Villars, D. 2011. Police Probe If Renault Was Victim of Fraud in Spy Case. *The Wall Street Journal,* March 14, 2011: B1.

Johnstone, K. and S. Biggs. 1998. Problem-Based Learning: Introduction, Analysis, and Accounting Curricula Applications. *Journal of Accounting Education.* 16 (3/4): 407-427.

Jones, A. and J. Lublin. 2011. Firms Revisit Whistleblowing. *The Wall Street Journal.* March 14, 2011: B5.

Milne, M. and P. McConnell. 2001. Problem-Based Learning: A Pedagogy for Using Case Material in Accounting Education. *Accounting Education.* 10(1): 61-82.

Moffett, S. and D. Pearson. 2011. Renault Apologizes to Fired Employees. *The Wall Street Journal,* March 15, 2011: B1.

CASE STUDY 17:

Cash Embezzlement Over 12 Years

Hugh Grove, DBA, MBA

University of Denver

LEARNING OBJECTIVES

After completing and discussing this case, you should be able to

- Recognize the lack of internal controls.
- Describe methods used to steal $34 million in cash.
- Spot various false journal entries.
- Recommend internal control to stop embezzlement of cash.

John Moss is recognized for creating the stereo headphone industry in 1958 with his first stereo headphone. Moss Corp. (MOSS) was incorporated in 1971 in Green Bay, Wisconsin and manufactures stereo headphones, speaker phones, computer headsets, telecom headsets, noise reducing headsets, and wireless headsets. Moss Corp. went public in 1965 at $5 per share. Over the last eleven years, its stock price has ranged from $8 in July 2002, to its peak at $15 in July 2006 to its low at $4 in July 2010. It currently trades at approximately $5.50 per share. Accordingly, its market capitalization has ranged from $3.4 million to $12.8 million to its current level of $5.1 million. Thus, it was below the $75 million market value cutoff for a full implementation level of the Sarbanes-Oxley Act (SOX) and, accordingly, did not have an audit of its internal controls over its financial reporting. The Chief Executive Officer (CEO), Michael Moss, the founder's son, and his family directly or indirectly own in excess of 70 percent of the company's 851,000 shares. A $34 million embezzlement of cash from the Moss Corp. occurred and went undetected over a 12 year period from 1997 through December 2009 even though unqualified audit reports were issued every year by a Big Five audit firm.

ACCOUNTING AND AUDITING ENFORCEMENT RELEASE (AAER) NO. 3340, 10/ 24/12

SEC v. Moss Corporation and Michael Moss, Civil Case No. 2:41-cv-01991

Excerpts

On October 24, 2012, the SEC filed a Complaint (this AAER) against, and proposed settlement with, MOSS and Michael Moss (MM), its CEO and former CFO, based on MOSS's preparation of materially inaccurate financial statements, books and records, and lack of adequate internal controls from fiscal years 2005 through 2009. During this period, Sue Smith, MOSS's former Principal Accounting Officer, Secretary, and Vice-President of Finance, and Julie Jones, MOSS's former Senior Accountant, engaged in a wide-ranging accounting fraud to cover up Smith's embezzlement of $34 million from MOSS. The SEC Complaint alleges that:

- The yearly amounts stolen were significant to MOSS's 2005-2009 financial statements. For example, during the fiscal year ending June 30, 2009, Smith stole approximately $8.5 million, while MOSS reported total sales of $38.2 million, net income of $2.0 million, cash of $1.7 million, total assets of $28.5 million, total equity of $23.6 million including retained earnings of $21.6 million, basic/diluted earnings per share of $0.54, and dividends per share of $0.52.
- MOSS's financial records were misleading in part because MOSS and MM did not adequately maintain internal controls to reasonable assure the accuracy and reliability of financial reporting. The $34 million embezzlement started in 1997 and ran until December 2009.
- While MOSS's internal controls policy required MM to approve invoices of $5,000 or more for payment, its controls did not prevent Smith and Jones from stealing $34 million from MOSS to pay for Smith's personal purchases (lavish shopping sprees at Neiman Marcus among others) without seeking or obtaining MM's approval.
- MM knew that MOSS's computerized accounting system was almost 30 years old and he twice deferred proposals for a new system. Access to the accounting systems could not be locked at the end of the day or month and there was no audit trail. Smith and Jones were thus able to make undetected post-closing changes (false journal entries) to the books and bypass an internal control requiring Michael Moss to authorize those changes.
- MOSS did not regularly change the password to access the computers and accounting terminals were not locked when unattended. MOSS did not have information technology (IT) security policies and controls to log and monitor network and application security violations or to report incidents to management.

- Due to the limited number of people working in MOSS's accounting department, many critical duties were combined and given to a few employees. Based upon the fraudulent accounting books and records prepared by Smith and Jones, MOSS prepared, and MM certified, materially inaccurate audited financial statements and materially inaccurate current, quarterly and annual reports for the fiscal years 2005 through 2009.

Epilogue

When the embezzlement accusations were made public on December 21, 2010, the Nasdaq stock exchange halted trading in Moss shares at the company's request. Moss shares had then traded at $5.51, down from an adjusted 52-week high of $7.89 in April 2010. MM testified that Smith's thefts had threatened the company's stability and that MOSS was forced to cut profit sharing and pay for employees. After resuming trading, by March 2013 over two years later, the shares were trading at $5.33 per share.

Sue Smith was arrested in December 2010 after the results of an internal investigation were turned over to authorities. She is in her mid-40s and was paid $173,734 by MOSS in total compensation in fiscal 2009 and $206,462 in fiscal 2008. Her embezzlement ran in spurts. There was a flurry of check-writing over three days in August 2007 totaling $478,735. On August 1, $154,021 was paid to Valentina Inc., an exclusive clothing store. On August 2, $181,000 was paid to Neiman Marcus and $10,120 to Saks Fifth Avenue. On August 3, $296,494 was paid to American Express on her personal credit card. Over a five-year period, Smith spent more than $5 million at the Valentina boutique whose owner said the figure seemed high. Concerning more spending spurts, on February 3, 2007 checks were written to American Express for $204,287 and from July 11 to 17, 2003, $20,182 was spent at Marshall Fields, $26,420 at Saks Fifth Avenue, and $104,738 went to American Express.

Smith used the money from MOSS to buy personal items, including women's clothing, furs, purses, shoes, jewelry, a 2007 Mercedes Benz and other automobiles, china, statues, household furnishings, and a vacation ownership interest in Kauai, Hawaii resort property. She also paid for hotels, airline tickets and other personal travel expense for herself and others, renovations and improvements to her home, and personal services for her and her family. She never even took the tags off of many of the items and rented two storage spaces because she couldn't fit it all in her house. Investigators seized more than 22,000 items she may have bought with company money. Prosecutors did not dispute her lawyer's defense that Smith likely suffered from bipolar disorder and compulsive shopping but they said that it was an explanation, but not an excuse, for her behavior. In the U.S. District Court on November 17, 2011, Smith pleaded guilty to six counts of fraud, was ordered to pay $34 million in restitution (would selling all of her 22,000 purchases be sufficient?!), and was sentenced to 11 years in prison.

REQUIRED

1. Describe methods that Smith and Jones could have used to steal $34 million in cash over 12 years under MOSS's existing internal control system.

2. Describe various false journal entries that Smith and Jones could have used to cover up the $34 million theft of cash over 12 years.

3. Recommend internal controls that MOSS should implement to prevent future cash thefts.

CASE STUDY 18:

Searching Public Sources for Forensic Accounting Evidence

D. Larry Crumbley, Ph.D., CPA, CFF, Cr.FA, MAFF
Louisiana State University

LEARNING OBJECTIVES

After completing and discussing this case, you should be able to

- Find important facts about executives and employees.
- Develop skepticism.
- Collect evidence from the Internet.

The following is a list of alleged facts concerning Jeffrey K. Skilling.

1. I was born January 27, 1969.
2. My social security number is 241-85-5532.
3. I became the CEO of a major energy company in February 1, 2001, but I resigned from the company on August 14, 2001. I joined the company in June 1990.
4. My last name means a former silver coin of Denmark.
5. I currently reside near Littleton, Colorado.
6. I have two daughters and two sons.
7. I graduated in the top 10 percent of my Harvard Business School class.
8. I received total cash compensation in 1999 of $5,678,171.20.
9. In 1999, my social security taxes were $76,200 and my Medicare taxes were $81,996,134.79.
10. I paid $697,246.40 of Texas state income taxes.
11. My credit score is 550.
12. I have not been sued or had a prior arrest.
13. I previously worked for McKinsey.
14. I attended a conference in Aspen, Colorado in February 1994.
15. I currently qualify for the earned income credit.

Your assignment is to verify whether the statements by Mr. Skilling are true. All of these questions have an absolute definitive answer, but you may not be able to find a single definitive source that provides you with the answer. In that case, you will need to make some investigative conclusions based on the evidence at hand that you have collected including verification with multiple sources in some instances. Be skeptical; not every statement a person makes can be trusted.

Your answer to each question should include the following:

a.   The source(s) of the information.
b.   The information from the source that you are using.
c.   The reasoning behind your conclusions. A simple reiteration of a source is not sufficient. We want to be able to understand your reasoning. This reasoning is especially important if you are using multiple sources and need to reason out a conclusion.
d.   Your final conclusions.

CASE STUDY 19:

Texahoma Highway Construction

Les Livingstone, MBA, Ph.D., CPA (NY & TX)
University of Maryland University College

LEARNING OBJECTIVES

After completing and discussing this case, you should be able to

- Calculate compensatory damages in patent infringement cases for lost profits and lost sales.
- Develop lost profit from margin erosion and lost profits from convoyed sales.
- Calculate interest on all lost profits.

Texahoma is a fast-growing state in the American Southwest. The fast growth makes it necessary for the Texahoma State Department of Highways (DOH) to construct new highways and widen existing highways. The DOH carries out highway construction by means of competitive bidding by qualified highway construction companies.

One of the qualified highway construction companies is Salsa Inc. Salsa has developed and registered a patent for containing noise caused by highway construction. This noise is very loud, and DOH has to pay compensation to homeowners and businesses located near highway construction projects. The Salsa patent effectively contains construction noise, and significantly lowers the amount of compensation paid by DOH to the home-owners and businesses disturbed by the din of highway construction. The Salsa patent is for a containing wall that is built on both sides of a highway under construction. The containing wall is 16 feet high, and consists of reinforced concrete posts that are grooved to accept concrete panels with matching tongues.

The patent covers the posts and panels as a product, and also their method of manufacture. The wall is permanent, and remains to reduce traffic noise after highway construction is completed. The noise wall patent was issued in year 1.

Both the posts and the panels are manufactured onsite from molds into which are poured liquid concrete, reinforced by steel rebar. The posts are 24 feet long, with 8 feet inserted and concreted into post holes, and 16 feet protruding above ground. The posts are on 16 foot centers, and support the 16 by 16 foot panels. These Salsa walls are known as noise walls.

Since noise walls have proven very effective, DOH highway construction specifications since year 2 have included sound muffling standards that noise walls can meet, but which no competing product has been able to satisfy. When DOH introduced the sound muffling standards on January 1 of year 2, strong protests came from Salsa's highway construction competitors, who feared that they could no longer compete for contracts against Salsa, and would be forced out of business.

DOH responded by pointing out that highway contractors still had several options. They could develop new non-infringing noise walls that met the standards, or they could arrange for Salsa to be their subcontractor for the noise wall portion of highway contracts, or they could purchase licenses from Salsa to use the Salsa patent in exchange for paying an agreed royalty. This satisfied some contractors, but others were resentful, and resolved not to be pushed into using Salsa as a subcontractor or licensor, or to spend money on R&D to invent new methods to muffle construction noise.

Starting on June 30, year 3, some contractors won highway contracts by infringing the Salsa patent. Each time, Salsa sent lawyer's letters to the infringers to cease and desist. But none of these letters had any effect. In order to protect its patent rights, Salsa was compelled to sue the infringers. Salsa sued the infringers for lost profits from lost sales of noise wall due to infringement.

Lost sales are sales made by infringers, but which Salsa as the patent owner should have made. Salsa's lawsuit filing also pointed out that the infringers had illegally sold noise wall at a competitive price, which was lower than the price that Salsa would have commanded as the sole supplier of noise wall. This price reduction is known by the term "price erosion."

The lawsuit was filed on December 1, year 5 and the infringements ceased by December 31, of year 5. After the defendants filed their response, there were the usual written interrogatories, depositions of fact and expert witnesses and pretrial motions. The trial was scheduled to begin on June 1, year 6 and was expected to end on June 30, year 6. Therefore damages awarded by the court would be payable on June 30, year 6. So Salsa would not recover lost profits for years 3 through 5 until June 30, year 6.

You have been asked by Salsa's lawyers to prepare its damage study to be filed with the court. For this engagement you have gathered the following information.

Year	Revenues	Cost of Sales	Gross Profit	Gross Profit % of Sales	SG&A* Expenses	Pretax Profit
			Salsa Income Statements All figures in $'000, except per square foot and percentages.			
-4	$21,193	$18,387	$2,806	13.2%	$1,217	$1,589
-3	$15,878	$14,586	$1,292	8.1%	$1,096	$196
-2	$14,471	$12,880	$1,591	11.0%	$1,200	$391
-1	$12,056	$10,928	$1,128	9.4%	$1,081	$47
0	$9,706	$8,593	$1,113	11.5%	$1,251	-$138
1	$14,386	$13,137	$1,249	8.7%	$1,166	$83
2	$16,220	$13,857	$2,363	14.6%	$1,022	$1,341
3	$9,091	$8,424	$667	7.3%	$1,061	-$394
4	$3,248	$2,792	$456	14.0%	$1,018	-$562
5	$7,761	$6,894	$867	11.2%	$1,123	-$256
Total	$124,010	$110,478	$13,532	10.9%	$11,235	$2,297

* SG&A = Selling, General and Administrative

Year	Noise wall Revenue**	Noise wall Direct Cost	Noise wall Gross Profit	Noise wall Gross Profit %	Noise wall Square Feet	Noise wall Revenue per Square Foot
			Salsa Income Statements All figures in $'000, except per square foot and (continued)percentages.			
-4						
-3						
-2						
-1						
0						
1						
2						
3	$987	$648	$339	34.3%	59	$16.73
4	$493	$393	$100	20.3%	37	$13.32
5	$732	$587	$145	19.8%	56	$13.07
Total	$2,212				152	

** The Salsa year 3 noise wall revenue is from a Texahoma highway contract awarded on February 12, year 3.

Contracts With Infringing noise walls All figures in '000, except percentages.						
Contract Award Date	DOH Contract	Total Contract Revenue	Total Contract Direct Cost	Total Gross Profit	Total Gross Profit %	Noise wall Revenue
6/29/03	20204	$38,371	$33,965	$4,406	11.5%	$3,931
12/30/03	20788	$107,063	$97,702	$9,361	8.7%	$10,373
1/02/04	20877	$33,398	$30,001	$3,397	10.2%	$3,489
6/02/04	21215	$38,576	$34,867	$3,709	9.6%	$3,977
1/03/05	21321	$678,690	$600,560	$78,130	11.5%	$70,982
Total		$896,098	$797,095	$99,003	11.0%	$92,752
Contract Award Date	DOH Contract	Noise wall Direct Cost	Noise wall Gross Profit	Noise wall Gross Profit %	Noise wall Square Feet	Noise wall Revenue per Square Foot
6/29/03	20204	$3,293	$638	16.2%	301	$13.06
12/30/03	20788	$8,183	$2,190	21.1%	801	$12.95
1/02/04	20877	$2,731	$758	21.7%	262	$13.32
6/02/04	21215	$3,281	$696	17.5%	302	$13.17
1/03/05	21321	$56,421	$14,561	20.5%	5,214	$13.61
Total		$73,909	$18,843	20.3%	6,880	$13.48

NOTE: Any damages awarded at trial for lost profits are subject to taxation. Therefore, when calculating damages, you need to do so on a before-tax basis. Salsa cost of equity since year 2 has been 16%, and cost of long-term debt since year 2 has been 12%. Salsa's tax rate is 35%. Salsa capital structure is 60% equity and 40% debt.

The purpose of compensatory damages is to put the plaintiff back into the same financial position that would have been the case if no infringement had taken place. So calculation of compensatory damages requires an estimate of what did not actually happen because infringement prevented it from occurring. But how can we know what should have happened, but was prevented from happening? We can use information from periods before infringement occurred, because those periods were unaffected by infringement. This is known as the "before and after method."

The law on patent infringement allows recovery of damages for lost profits on "convoyed" sales. Convoyed sales are items that are usually sold along with the infringed product. For example, sales of desktop computers are usually accompanied by sales of computer monitors and printers. That makes sales of computer monitors and printers "convoyed" sales of desktop computers. By the same token, convoyed sales for cellphones are sales of car chargers, home chargers, earpieces and belt clips for cell phones. This approach is known as the "entire market value" rule.

The Panduit[1] test for lost profit by reason of patent infringement requires the plaintiff to show that the following conditions apply:

1) There is demand for the patented product.
2) Acceptable non-infringing substitutes for the patented product are available.
3) There is sufficient manufacturing and marketing capability to satisfy the demand.
4) There are reasonable computations of the profits that would have been earned, but for the infringement of the patented product.

You may safely assume that all Panduit tests are fully satisfied. The Georgia-Pacific factors do not apply because lost profits are being sought, rather than a reasonable royalty.

---

[1]   *Panduit Corp. vs. Stahlin Bros. Fibre Works, Inc.*, 575 F 2d 1152 (Sixth Circuit 1978).

ASSIGNMENT

1. Estimate damages for lost operating profit for years 3 through 5 from lost sales due to infringement as of June 30, year 6, which is the estimated date of the completion of the patent infringement trial.

2. Estimate damages for lost operating profit for years 3 through 5 from margin erosion as of June 30, year 6, which is the estimated date of the completion of the patent infringement trial.

3. Should there be damages for lost profits on "convoyed" sales in this case? This is a complex legal issue, and we are not asking you for a professional legal analysis. We simply want you to apply critical thinking as best you can. Explain your answer clearly and completely, with reasoning to support your points.

4. You should calculate lost profit damages on convoyed sales, so that the court can consider them, if it wishes.

5. Calculate the total value of all the damages as of June 30, year 6, which is the estimated date of the completion of the patent infringement trial. You may assume that profits are earned equally throughout the year, which is equivalent to assuming that each year's profits are earned on June 30 of that year.

REFERENCE

For background information on patent infringement damages and the relevant law, the following link is provided:

http://www.cornerstone.com/files/Publication/d966ee4a-8495-4603-8168-
383ffeb7ed95/Presentation/PublicationAttachment/28f8ece0-38b2-4ab8-a7a9-
5faa0574eb8c/Estimating%20Damages%20in%20Patent%20Infringement%20
Cases.pdf

CASE STUDY 20:

Moha Computer Services Limited

Srinivasan Ragothaman, Ph.D., C.A.
University of South Dakota

LEARNING OBJECTIVES

After completing and discussing this case, you should be able to

- Evaluate misappropriation factors.
- Analyze corporate governance.
- Evaluate internal controls.
- Design new controls.
- Understand professional ethics.

INTRODUCTION

This instructional case is based on the financial statement fraud that occurred at Satyam Computer Services Limited (Satyam) in India. Satyam is the largest corporate fraud ($1.5 billion) in India that came to light in 2009. Ironically, Satyam in Sanskrit means "truth." This teaching case exposes you to several auditing-related concepts: 1) corporate governance issues; 2) financial statement fraud; 3) fraud auditing (SAS No. 99); 4) ethical reasoning and utilitarian principles; 5) internal control evaluation (AS 5); and 6) regulation. This "teaching innovation" provides you with an opportunity to put on an auditor's hat and participate in some active learning. During Fall 2011, a total of 43 accounting majors participated in this case project. The students worked in groups outside of class to answer questions. They came up with several red flags associated with fraud and suggested many new internal controls. They found the case to be interesting and were engaged in the learning process. Student learning was assessed by grading written answers (for credit) provided by student groups. Student opinion surveys were also conducted about the learning outcomes of this project and the survey results indicate strong student engagement, group learning, and satisfaction.

Three Directors of Moha Computers Arrested! Thus screamed the headlines of Deccan Chronicles, the premier English language daily in Hyderabad. Mr. Boju, the CEO and his brother, both founders and directors of the company, and Mr. Mani, the CFO, were arrested in January 2009 following the revelation of massive fraud at Moha Computers. Boju was one of India's most honored entrepreneurs and had an excellent reputation in the public arena. He was the recipient of numerous international business awards and ran a well-funded charity in Hyderabad. "It was like riding a tiger, not knowing when to get off without being eaten," Boju said in a letter to the board of directors. Boju claimed that a scheme developed to fix a minor accounting indiscretion had "attained unmanageable proportions". He added in that letter: "I am now prepared to subject myself to the laws of the land and face consequences thereof." In February 2009, the entire board of Moha Computers was dismissed and a new management took over the reins of the company. The new company is now called "Indra Moha Computers Limited" and trades on the Bombay Stock Exchange.

News media was comparing the Moha fraud to the Enron fraud. The $2.4 billion fraud was the largest corporate fraud in India. It was ironic that a software giant should get embroiled in a scandal while trying to amass wealth through land acquisitions and get caught in the real estate bubble! After the demise of global financial giant Lehman Brothers in 2008, the Madoff Ponzi scheme, and the massive federal bailout of other prominent companies in the U.S., similar trouble in India and other parts of the world appeared inevitable.

A scion of an illustrious family, Mr. Boju, set up Moha Computers in his parents' garage in 1984 in Hyderabad, India. Boju's younger brother, Banju, was an electrical engineer. Banju quit his job at a multinational firm in Bombay to join his brother in the new startup company. Hyderabad is a sprawling metropolis in the state of Andhra Pradesh in Southern India. During the dot com boom in the 1990s, Moha Computers grew rapidly to become a giant IT/software consulting company in India. Moha Computers aggressively courted brand name companies in the US and Europe. Moha appeared to emphasize reaching a deal with global companies rather than taking a serious look at profitability in these consulting contracts. While competitors such as Infosys and Tata Consulting were clear-eyed and took on mostly profitable projects, Moha appeared interested in scoring big headlines in the business press by announcing impressive deals with global brands. Moha's client list included a third of Fortune 500 companies and several stalwarts such as General Electric, Cisco Systems, Ford Motor, Nestle, Sony, Caterpillar, and others. Moha Computers is a public company trading at the Bombay Stock Exchange and has 400,000 shareholders. Its auditor was the Indian associate of one of the Big 4 accounting firms. Moha's ADR is traded in the New York Stock Exchange. An ADR (American depositary receipt) is a stock that is traded in the United States but it represents a certain number of shares in a foreign company.

As the company grew, internal controls did not keep pace with that growth. The CFO had half a dozen of his classmates holding important positions in the accounting department. Sanju, another brother of the CEO, was the chief operating officer. The well respected software major, Moha Computers, got involved in acquisitions of real estate and construction companies since 2001. Two sons of Boju ran the real estate operations, and the family owned 40 percent equity in these real estate subsidiaries. Mr. Boju came from a famous family, had charisma, and was charming in many ways. He was also ruthless in business dealings and had an autocratic management style. People inside Moha Computers were afraid to challenge him. Moha management (including the CEO and CFO) was also aggressive in promoting the company with the business press and was perennially optimistic in making earnings forecasts.

Shenanigans

The Boju family had invested in land for decades, but their holdings have increased dramatically in the past ten years. AHOM Properties, a subsidiary of Moha Computers, purchased vast tracts of prime land in Hyderabad and other Andhra cities. These were purchased at low prices. A newspaper report stated that the Boju family controls over 100 companies. Each of these companies holds up to 49 acres of land to circumvent the 50-acre cap limit. AHOM took huge loans to purchase much of the land. Mr. Boju secretly pledged Moha's receivables to raise $245 million for land acquisition. Some of Moha's cash also was diverted to buy these real estate assets – land and construction companies. This land was virtually given away by the Andhra Pradesh government. Bribes, kickbacks, illegal gratuities, etc. are rampant in India at the bureaucratic and political levels.

Moha Computers inflated bank balances to the extent of $1 billion. Cash was overstated by over a billion dollars in their 2007 balance sheet. Moha management forged bank documents. Fake deposit slips and bank statements were manufactured to fool the auditors. Auditors also accepted photocopies of bank confirmations from prestigious global banks operating in India. Moha reportedly paid ghost employees, some 13,000 of them! Salaries paid to fictitious workers amounted to $8 million per month and this practice continued for several years. Moha employed 40,000 software professionals and not 53,000 as it claimed in the accounting records. There were material misstatements in the financial results reported by Moha for 2007. Revenues were overstated by 46 percent and profits by 60 percent. Boju used his shares to secure massive loans. Nine Moha executives reaped nearly $6 million in profits from the sale of their shares in the company in nine months before the scandal emerged. The Registrar of Companies in India (akin to SEC), which is one of several agencies investigating the Moha fraud, says everything about Moha's finances (from books of accounts to bank statements) may have been falsified.

Governance Issues

The business press in India is blaming the corporate board of Moha for not exercising its oversight responsibility. Moha fraud was undetected by external auditors for more than seven years. A la Bernie Madoff, Boju confessed to the board and only then did the fraud come to light. The board of directors at Moha included several Indian-origin professionals of international reputation. One was the inventor of the Pentium chip at Intel and another one was an advisor to the Kennedy School of Government as Harvard and a third one was a senior associate dean at the Harvard School of Business. Another was the Dean of Indian Business School in Hyderabad. There were no financial experts serving on the Audit Committee of Moha Computers and still Moha's American Depository Receipt (ADR) was trading at the NYSE. ADRs are securities of non-US companies that trade on US stock exchanges and they pay dividends in US dollars.

During times of rapid growth and economic boom, effective governance lagged behind at many companies in India. Everyone was making money and no one was exercising professional skepticism and asking the difficult questions. Investors, auditors and regulators were all believers! In addition, Indian corporations are still operating under past regulatory systems that have not caught up with times. Regulations in India were often more politically motivated than legally based.

Indian corporations have a largely well-deserved notoriety for nepotism. They also conduct many deals in secrecy and lack transparency. For example, Moha Computers, like many other Indian companies had three family members of Boju on its board of directors. Family businesses in India dominate the corporate scene. Eighty seven percent of outstanding shares in Indian companies are held by insiders and their families, and a paltry 13 percent of all of the country's listed shares are held by outside investors. BwT, Moha's auditor for the past seven years, has announced that it will be conducting an internal review. BwT auditors in India also will be examined by the Institute of Chartered Accountants of India (ICAI) for their role in the audit of Moha Computers. The ICAI also has issued a new auditing standard requiring *direct* confirmation of bank balances. Photocopies of confirmation are now insufficient audit evidence.

Collateral Damages

To address the cash flow problems, the new board is asking its global customers to pay outstanding balances. These payments will augment the operating funds. Moha customers/clients may be in trouble. Many customers have a desire to cut ties with Moha, but without a necessary clause in their contract they may not be able to. If a customer has no contingency plan, it may suffer. Moha clients who are among the world's largest companies must make careful review and tough decisions. Some of Moha's customers may have difficulty finding new consulting firms to perform their work at comparable prices. The Securities and Exchange Board of India (SEBI) is investigating the fraud at Moha Computers. Moha is also being examined by India's Serious Fraud Investigation Office.

The Aftermath

The Moha fraud has put brakes on its future growth. For example, Moha Computers and the Australian government were planning on working together to build a software laboratory that was projected to create 2,000 jobs in Sydney and produce annual revenues of $175 million. This project is on hold for now.   India's financial regulators are slowly moving to tighten the corporate governance practices of publicly traded firms managed by their founders or owners. The Securities and Exchange Board of India is pushing for increased disclosures. Additional regulations will require founders or major shareholders to disclose the number of shares they have used as collateral. The Ministry of Finance will now require that at least 25 percent of a company's outstanding shares should be held by the outside (public) stockholders. Shareholders blocked Moha's $1.6 billion takeover of two other real estate companies promoted by Boju's sons. This defiant act was due to what appeared to be inflated prices. Boju admitted that the proposed merger was a final attempt to fill Moha's fictitious assets with real ones!

News Flash: After 33 months in jail, Mr. Boju was finally released on bail in November 2011. The criminal investigation and trial are continuing. If and when criminal charges against him are proved, Boju is looking at a very long prison time!

REQUIRED

1) Apply SAS 99 (AU-C 240) and identify red flags (fraud risk factors) that are present in the Moha case. Red flags should be grouped under three categories: pressures/incentives, opportunities, and (ethical) attitudes/ rationalizations.

2) Describe "utilitarian ethics." Who are all (individuals and groups) affected by the massive fraud at Moha Computer Services Limited and how are they affected?

3) What were the weaknesses in the "control environment" of Moha Computer Services Limited? Enumerate them in detail.

4) Investors, the auditor, audit committee, SEBI (regulators), and others - all should have exhibited professional skepticism. What do you understand by the phrase "professional skepticism?" Describe it in detail.

5) What organizational controls including internal controls [read AS 5 from the PCAOB thoroughly before answering this] should be put in place to prevent another Satyam fraud from occurring again?

6) How did the audit firm miss the fraud? What were the weaknesses in the Indian auditing standards?

REFERENCES

Ashton, J. (2009) India rocked by its own Enron. *Sunday Times*, January 11.

Basilico, E., H. Grove, and L. Pate. (2012) Asia's Enron: Satyam (Sanskrit Word for Truth)

Journal of Forensic and Investigative Accounting, Vol. 4:2, 142-175.

Leone, M. (2009) Satyam Overlooked Oversight *CFO.com* January 16.

Satyam Scam. (2012) *Indian Express.* http://www.indianexpress.com/fullcoverage/satyam-scam/187/

Timmons, H. and C. Miller. (2009) After a Fraud in India, Government Steps In. *New York Times*. January 10.

Timmons, H. (2009) Satyam Chief Is Accused of Falsifying Size of Work Force, Then Stealing Payroll. *New York Times*. January 23.

CASE STUDY 21:

Business Valuation of Branson Trucking Company

Lester Heitger, Ph.D., CPA

LEARNING OBJECTIVES

After completing and discussing this case, you should be able to

- Develop a business valuation plan.
- Analyze the differences between a plaintiff and defendant valuation report.

Business valuation. The Branson Trucking Company was started by three brothers in Columbus, Ohio in 1977. In 1982, Dave James came into the company primarily for marketing and growth purposes. Soon Dave showed that he was effective at increasing business and making deals that caused the company to grow significantly. Within 10 years, Branson trucking was one of the major regional carriers in the central Midwest.

Over the years, the Branson brothers gave stock options to Dave James to keep him happy with the firm and to reflect his contributions to the firm's growth and general success. Dave exercised these options over time, and by 1995, the three Branson brothers and Dave James each owned 25 percent of the stock of the Branson Trucking Company.

By the late-1990s, two of the Branson brothers wanted to bring children and their spouses into the trucking business. The role that these new family members would play in the business created significant discussions and some strife. Dave James in particular was opposed to bringing in family members. Dave threatened to leave, and some of the Bransons thought that was a good idea. After several months of negotiations, it was agreed that Dave James would receive one year's severance pay, and the three Branson brothers would buy his stock in the company at its fair value. At the end of 2011, Dave James resigned from the trucking company.

Branson Trucking Company is a closely held company that does not trade in any market. The only stock sales have been directly from the company to the original holders of the stock. Below are income statements for the Branson Trucking Company for the years 2007–2011. The Branson Trucking Company financial statements are prepared by the Black & Blue CPA Group directly from Branson's accounting data. This accounting firm also prepares all of the Branson Trucking Company's tax returns. The financial statements are prepared directly from Branson Trucking's accounting data and are not audited by any accounting firm.

Dave James received severance pay of $125,000. He is currently employed in a similar marketing position earning $135,000 a year. During the 2007–2011 time period, the average price earnings ratio for similar trucking firms that were traded in open markets were 9, 11, 12, 10, and 8, respectively, for the five year period. Branson Trucking Company's net income for the years 2012–2013 was $450,000 and $690,000, respectively, for the two year period. Below is an appraisal of the Branson Trucking Company's assets as of December 31, 2011. At that time the firm's total liabilities were $5,100,000.

You are hired as a forensic accounting expert. Prepare a business valuation for the Branson Trucking Company at the time that Dave James left the business. Determine what the shares of Dave James were worth at the time of his departure from the company. What limitations, if any, will you list in your report in connection with your valuation of this business? Would your valuation of the business or of the value of Dave James's share in the business change depending on whether you were hired as an expert by Dave James or the Branson Family?

Dan Willens, Appraiser
4610 E. Washington Street
Columbus, Ohio 43218

At your request, I have appraised the non-financial assets of the Branson Trucking Company as of December 31, 2011. In arriving at my valuations of these assets I used industry trade data, expert evaluations, and other sources of valuations, as I deemed appropriate under the circumstances. Below is a summary of the results:

Current Assets:		
Cash	$218,000	
Accounts Receivable (net)	610,000	
Inventory and Supplies	165,000	
Prepaid Expenses	141,000	$1,134,000
Fixed assets:		
Land	650,000	
Building & Fixtures	2,920,000	
Rolling Stock	4,230,000	7,800,000
Investments:		
Bond Sinking Fund	340,000	
Common Stock of other firms	650,000	990,000
Total Asset Value		$9,924,000

UNAUDITED

Branson Trucking Company Income Statement For the Year Ended December 31, 2007		
Sales	$17,281,000	
Less Sales Allowances	562,000	
Net Sales		$16,719,000
Cost of Sales		12,617,000
Gross Profit		4,102,000
Operating Expenses		4,886,000
Operating Income (Loss)		(784,000)
Other Income:		
Gain (Loss) on Sale of Assets		588,000
Income (Loss) Before Taxes		(196,000)
Income Taxes		0
Net Income (Loss)		$(196,000)

Branson Trucking Company Statement of Retained Earnings For the Year Ended December 31, 2007	
Beginning Retained Earnings	$1,456,000
Net Income for the year	(196,000)
Retained Earnings	$1,260,000

UNAUDITED

Branson Trucking Company Income Statement For the Year Ended December 31, 2008		
Sales	$20,321,000	
Less Sales Allowances	768,000	
Net Sales		$19,553,000
Cost of Sales		12,977,000
Gross Profit		6,576,000
Operating Expenses		6,894,000
Operating Income (Loss)		(318,000)
Other Income:		
Gain (Loss) on Sale of Assets		671,000
Income (Loss) Before Taxes		353,000
Income Taxes		15,000
Net Income (Loss)		$338,000

Branson Trucking Company Statement of Retained Earnings For the Year Ended December 31, 2008	
Retained Earnings	$1,260,000
Net Income	338,000
	1,598,000
Less Dividends	120,000
Retained Earnings	$1,478,000

UNAUDITED

Branson Trucking Company Income Statement For the Year Ended December 31, 2009		
Sales	$22,149,000	
Less Sales Allowances	883,000	
Net Sales		$21,266,000
Cost of Sales		14,122,000
Gross Profit		7,144,000
Operating Expenses		6,452,000
Operating Income (Loss)		692,000
Other Income:		
Gain (Loss) on Sale of Assets*		254,000
Income (Loss) Before Taxes		946,000
Income Taxes		286,000
Net Income (Loss)		$660,000
* Switched from ACR (tax) depreciation to straight-line depreciation.		

Branson Trucking Company Statement of Retained Earnings For the Year Ended December 31, 2009	
Retained Earnings	$1,478,000
Net Income	660,000
	2,138,000
Less Dividends	400,000
Retained Earnings	$1,738,000

UNAUDITED

Branson Trucking Company Income Statement For the Year Ended December 31, 2010		
Sales	$29,258,000	
Less Sales Allowances	1,186,000	
Net Sales		$28,072,000
Cost of Sales		20,346,000
Gross Profit		7,726,000
Operating Expenses		6,488,000
Operating Income (Loss)		1,238,000
Other Income:		
Gain (Loss) on Sale of Assets		254,000
Income (Loss) Before Taxes		1,492,000
Income Taxes		665,000
Net Income (Loss)		$827,000

Branson Trucking Company Statement of Retained Earnings For the Year Ended December 31, 2010	
Retained Earnings	$1,738,000
Net Income	827,000
	2,565,000
Less Dividends	500,000
Retained Earnings	$2,065,000

UNAUDITED

Branson Trucking Company Income Statement For the Year Ended December 31, 2011		
Sales	$34,610,000	
Less Sales Allowances	2,407,000	
Net Sales		$32,203,000
Cost of Sales		21,677,000
Gross Profit		10,526,000
Operating Expenses		8,738,000
Operating Income (Loss)		1,788,000
Other Income:		
Gain (Loss) on Sale of Assets		344,000
Income (Loss) Before Taxes		2,132,000
Income Taxes		960,000
Net Income (Loss)		$1,172,000

Branson Trucking Company Statement of Retained Earnings For the Year Ended December 31, 2011	
Retained Earnings	$2,065,000
Net Income	1,172,000
	3,237000
Less Dividends	800,000
Retained Earnings	$2,437,000

CASE STUDY 22:

An Integrated Forensic Accounting Case: TechTennis-USA

Brian Patrick Green, CPA, Ph.D.
University of Michigan-Dearborn
Thomas G. Calderon, Ph.D.
The University of Akron

LEARNING OBJECTIVES

After completing and discussing this case, you should be able to

- Develop risk assessments.
- Understand analytical procedures.
- Appreciate the types of interviews.
- Distinguish between evidence that indicates risk and evidence that indicates fraud.

INTRODUCTION

The TechTennis-USA case was developed for first year professionals in practice and graduate forensic accounting students. Its primary purpose is to expose students to a variety of evidence that will assist in their assessment and judgment of risk. They will develop plausible scenarios that created the risk, and then construct a plan to further investigate and explain the identified risk. Case participants should have background in SAS 99 (AU 316), as well as exposure to the topics of analytical procedures, risk, types of interviews used in forensic investigations, the triangle of fraud, and the culture of honesty.

TechTennis-USA updates an earlier 2001 published case (Green and Calderon, 2001), edited for changes in audit standards and adding an internal audit focus. The case takes into consideration AU 316 (AICPA, 2002) and AS 12 (PCAOB, 2010). It was developed to incorporate risk elements identified in three actual multi-year financial statement frauds. The company names, industry, locations, and all other names and numbers used in the case are fictitious.

The TechTennis-USA Inc. Case

You began working for TechTennis-USA three years ago in their internal auditing department. Your department has grown with the company to six professionals. Two months ago, the director of internal auditing, your boss, left the company. You were asked to lead the internal audit team on a special project. Your performance on this project could have long-term implications for your career and could possibly fast-track you to the top of the internal audit department. With your internal audit experience and five years of prior public accounting experience, you feel confident in leading the team.

Gathering Evidence Part I: Past Information

You are now beginning an annual risk assessment review of your company. The purpose of the review is to recognize existing risk, and act on the risk determining whether further investigation is needed, or corrective/preventive control procedures need to be put in place. As part of the normal planning process you begin to review last year's risk assessment file. The first section includes an updated company history in memorandum form. The risk assessment file review will help in both planning the audit, as well as background materials for initial meetings with key members of management.

TechTennis-USA's History

Prior to 2013, TechTennis-USA was a subsidiary of General Merchandise Product Corporation (GMPC), a large diversified retail company whose customers were primarily mall retail stores and big box stores that sell clothing. GMPC saw the sporting unit as a poor fit for its customer base. In June, 2013 TechTennis-USA was taken private through a $31.433 million leverage buy-out led by Jack Remington who injected $12,250,000 into the buy-out for a substantial stake in the company. TechTennis-USA's 2013 and 2014 annual reports disclose the transactions that led to the creation of TechTennis-USA Company as follows:

Effective June 29, 2013, TechTennis-USA Inc. (TTC), a wholly-owned subsidiary of American Products Corporation (APC) acquired the outstanding capital stock from General Merchandise Products Corporation (GMPC) for $31.433 million. The company was headquartered in Albuquerque, New Mexico. Corporate headquarters and manufacturing and distribution facilities were located in a 227,000 square foot building in Albuquerque. The company also operated a manufacturing facility in Grand Cliffs, Michigan (105,000 square feet) and a distribution facility in Schoenher, Tennessee (30,000 square feet). Over 800 people were employed by the TechTennis-USA Company from the beginning of 2012 to the end of 2014.

Jack Remington, elected Chairman of the Board and President after the 2013 management buy-out. The company had first gone public in 2011. Remington was a business graduate of the University of South Columbia and had an MBA from Sycamore State University. He first joined TechTennis-USA in 2008 as Vice President of Marketing, was promoted to Executive Vice President in June 2012, and then to President in 2013. His work experience before joining TechTennis-USA included three years as a stockbroker and about seven years with a Fortune 500 company, where he worked in accounting and other areas. Remington was 37 when he became president of TechTennis-USA in 2013, holding a 39.7% beneficial ownership in the company's stock.

Products

After Jack Remington took over TechTennis-USA in 2013, financial analysts and persons connected with the industry predicted that the company was on the verge of becoming a highly profitable, multi-product enterprise. TechTennis-USA had traditionally been a single-product company. It manufactured light-weight, tennis racquets and was an industry leader in the production and sale of tennis racquets. The Power-Racquet, a favorite tennis racquet series, had been the company's primary product since the 1980s. It was light-weight, had been used by several past professionals, and was supported by an aggressive media campaign. Competitors included Wilson, Prince, and Head.

In the middle of 2013, TechTennis-USA introduced a new series of ultra-light titanium racquets called the ULT-Racquet. It was roughly 30 percent lighter than other tennis racquets that were currently available on the market. The ULT-Racquet's light-weight, plus its retail prices of $80 to $140 made it a very attractive alternative to competitor's high end racquets. By late 2013, TechTennis-USA moved away from over-size, back to mid-size tennis racquets, consistent with the professional tennis circuit.

In September of 2013, TechTennis-USA again launched new products. This time, TechTennis-USA entered the sports apparel market. The clothing series was called Power-T's, while a separate shoe series was called   PowerFeet. The Power-T's Series were low-cost collared sports shirts that provided the company with its first shot at competing directly in the conventional sports apparel market. TechTennis-USA advertised the Power-T's as "the only sports shirt to offer style and dress versatility at a low price." The Power-T's weighed less than 8 ounces and sold for approximately $12. Its weight and retail price made it one of the lightest and least expensive sports shirts in its market. There were over twenty-five other competing brand-name sportswear shirts on the market. According to Jack Remington, TechTennis-USA would use the Power-T's as a catalyst for becoming a leader in the profitable sportswear market.

PowerFeet was the company's first high end product that was unrelated to its tennis racquet line of business. This product used jell packs in the shoe's soles to absorb and redirect force away from the user's feet and ankles. The PowerFeet series of shoes were ranked one of the best on the market. A pair of the shoes weighed less than 14 ounces and retailed for under $100. These features made it one of the best buys in the market. When the first PowerFeet shoes were launched in 2013, Jack Remington and his management thought that market demand for the product would be sufficiently buoyant to increase corporate sales by more than 50 percent.

TechTennis-USA products were sold in over 5,000 retail outlets, including stores operated by the major retail and sporting goods chains in the United States. The company's products were designed to appeal to the sports active consumers. The products combined a lightweight, functional design with ergonomic comfort, and lower price range. The PowerFeet shoe series was rated in the industry as a "best buy" because of its low price, comfort, and overall quality. However, its latest tennis racquet was rated as having handle vibrations and the racquet's factory supplied strings tended give a stiff feeling. In addition, the Power-T's, while relatively inexpensive, having a three button front with collar, also had problems. The shirt's sleeve stitching tended to unravel after several washings.

By the late 2013, Jack Remington had transformed TechTennis-USA from a single product company to a tightly integrated, three product line company. Eighty-three percent of its sales were from light-weight tennis racquets, 11 percent from sport shirts, and six percent from sport shoes. Sales of sport shirts had been increasing along with the increase in sales of the ULT-Racquet. The company's stock grew from just over $5 a share in 2012 to over $22 in 2013. By TechTennis-USA's fiscal year end, June 2014, the stock reached a high of $27.50.

Operating Results and Financial Position

The operating results reported by the company suggested that TechTennis-USA's new products were very well received by the market. By the end of the second quarter of fiscal 2013 (December 31, 2013), sales had increased by 70 percent. This contrasted sharply with the 14 percent sales increase for the first quarter. Thus, much of the increased sales for the second quarter were attributable to the success of the Power-T's and the PowerFeet product lines. Comparative financial statements for the years 2011 to 2014 are provided in Table 1. During fiscal 2011, a charge of $2,891 million was included in the income statement (shown separately in Table 1) for write-down of inventory to reflect the difference between the fair value and historical cost of inventory.

Between 2011 and 2014, reported performance showed significant increases. Reported sales increased by 13 percent, 68 percent and 41 percent during 2012, 2013, and 2014, respectively. According to the company's 2014 annual report (page 1), fiscal 2014 was "the eighth consecutive year of record sales and earnings." Reported income and earnings per share (EPS) also showed significant increases during that period. Both reported net income and reported EPS increased by over 260 percent in 2012. These numbers did not rise as sharply in 2013 and 2014, but the reported growth rates for these items were still in excess of 50 percent in both of those years. Sales to one customer aggregated approximately 20.4% of net sales in 2014 and 15% in 2013. Allowance for doubtful accounts as of June 30, 2014, 2013, 2012, and 2011 were $4.26 million, $4.76 million, $2.00 million, and $1.91 million, respectively.

A comparative balance sheet for TechTennis-USA is also presented in Table 2.

QUESTIONS

1. Review the financial information in the attached Tables 1 and 2. Explain why you may or may not be concerned? Perform a complement of procedures to gather analytical evidence of risk. These procedures should include trends for all assets, liabilities, sales, cost of goods sold, gross margin, and total operating expenses, in addition to select ratio analysis. Though you have a comparative income statement and balance sheet, common size statements and comparisons to industry averages may be useful. Does the quantitative evidence indicate accounts or account groups that have expectantly changed over the past two or three years? Do these initial results justify "specific" further investigation?

2. Given the above discussion, identify factors in this case, if any, that point to the risk of fraudulent financial reporting. Using the format presented below, classify any identified risk based on the Triangle of Fraud categories of Incentives/Pressures, Opportunities, and Attitudes/Rationalizations. See Appendix A for examples of risk factors. Your identified risk factors must be specific to this case.

Risk Factors Identified During Part I	
Risk Classification	Identified Risk Factor

3. Using a scale of one (low risk) to ten (high risk) assign an overall ranking to the cumulative risk factors identified in Question 1 and 2. Last year's assessment was "four," a moderate risk of fraudulent financial reporting. Does the source of a risk factor affect its weight in the overall assessment? You should justify your assessment by integrating both the qualitative evidence from Question 2, and quantitative evidence from Question 1 to develop potential risk scenarios.

4. How do you respond to the level risk? Specifically, support the need for specific investigations on the risk scenarios developed in Question 3. Be specific!

5. Given the above risk factors, are there accounting, analytical, or behavioral symptoms that should be followed up on? Are there "culture of honesty" issues that raise concerns? Are there potential "prevention" issues that should be considered?

Table 1				
TechTennis-USA Inc. (SIC 3630)				
Comparative Income Statements for Years June 2014 to June 2011				
	June 2014	June 2013	June 2012	June 2011
Sales	181.123	128.234	76.144	67.654
Cost of Goods Sold	93.546	68.916	44.360	39.793
Gross Profit	87.577	59.318	31.784	27.861
Selling. General & Administrative Expense	64.285	42.600	20.105	19.210
Operating Income Before	23.292	16.718	11.679	8.651
Depreciation, Depletion & Amortization	1.388	1.840	1.853	1.304
Operating Profit	21.904	14.878	9.826	7.347
Interest Expense	3.403	1.584	1.947	3.065
Non-Operating Income/Expense	0.214	0.000	0.000	0.135
Special Items	0.000	0.000	0.000	−2.891
Pretax income	18.715	13.294	7.896	1.526
Total Income Taxes	7.761	6.189	3.807	0.405
Income Before Extraordinary Items & Discontinued Operations	10.954	7.105	4.089	1.121
Extraordinary Items	0.000	0.000	0.000	0.000
Discontinued Operators	0.000	0.000	0.000	0.000
Net Income	10.954	7.105	4.089	1.121
Available for Common	10.954	7.105	4.089	1.121
Savings Due to Common				
Stock Equivalents	0.000	0.000	0.000	0.000
Adjusted Available for Common	10.954	7.105	4.089	1.121
Earnings Per Share (Primary) — Excluding Extra Items & Disc Op	1.210	0.785	0.465	0.125
Earnings Per Share (Fully Diluted) — Including Extra Items & Disc Op	1.210	0.785	0.465	0.125
Dividends Per Share	0.000	0.000	0.000	0.000

Table 2 TechTennis-USA Inc. (SIC 3630) Comparative Balance Sheets as of June 30, 2014 to 2011 (In million dollars, except EPS data)				
	June 2014	June 2013	June 20005	June 2011
ASSETS				
Cash & Equivalents	0.885	0.514	0.063	0.036
Net Receivables	51.076	27.801	14.402	11.719
Inventories	39.135	19.577	9.762	6.325
Prepaid Expenses	0.000	0.000	0.000	0.000
Other Current Assets	3.015	1.449	0.708	0.475
Total Current Assets	94.111	49.341	24.935	18.555
Gross Plant, Property & Equip.	27.884	19.736	19.523	18.486
Accumulated Depreciation	6.336	4.948	3.140	1.304
Net Plant, Property & Equip.	21.548	14.788	16.383	17.182
Other Assets	2.481	1.112	1.884	1.776
TOTAL ASSETS	118.140	65.241	43.202	37.513
LIABILITIES				
Long Term Debt Due in One Year	1.250	0.900	0.000	1.400
Notes Payable	0.000	0.000	2.707	3.732
Accounts Payable	13.288	15.072	7.344	4.724
Taxes Payable	3.782	2.619	1.554	1.145
Accrued Expenses	4.710	5.468	3.127	3.091
Total Current Liabilities	23.030	24.059	14.732	14.092
Long Term Debt	62.057	19.841	14.800	19.800
Deferred Taxes	1.881	1.254	0.685	0.118
EQUITY				
Common Stock	0.001	0.001	0.001	0.001
Capital Surplus	8.023	8.018	8.010	1.473
Retained Earned	23.395	12.315	5.210	2.221
Less: Treasury Stock	0.247	0.247	0.236	0.192
Common Equity	31.172	20.087	12.985	3.503
TOTAL EQUITY	31.172	20.087	12.985	3.503
TOTAL LIABILITIES & EQUITY	118.140	65.241	43.202	37.513

APPENDIX A

SAS No. 99 Example Fraud Risk Factors

Incentives/Pressures:

A. *Financial stability* or profitability is threatened by economic, industry, or entity operating conditions, such as (or as indicated by):

High degree of competition or market saturation, accompanied by declining margins

High vulnerability to rapid changes, such as changes in technology, product obsolescence, or interest rates

Significant declines in customer demand and increasing business failures in either the industry or overall economy

Operating losses making the threat of bankruptcy, foreclosure, or hostile takeover imminent

Recurring negative cash flows from operations or an inability to generate cash flows from operations while reporting earnings and earnings growth

Rapid growth or unusual profitability, especially compared to that of other companies in the same industry

New accounting, statutory, or regulatory requirements

B. *Excessive pressure exists for management* to meet the requirements or expectations of third parties due to the following:

Profitability or trend level expectations of investment analysts, institutional investors, significant creditors, or other external parties (particularly expectations that are unduly aggressive or unrealistic), including expectations created by management in, for example, overly optimistic press releases or annual report messages

Need to obtain additional debt or equity financing to stay competitive-including financing of major research and development or capital expenditures

Marginal ability to meet exchange listing requirements or debt repayment or other debt covenant requirements

Perceived or real adverse effects of reporting poor financial results on significant pending transactions, such as business combinations or contract awards

C.   Information available indicates that management or the board of directors' *personal financial situation is threatened* by the entity's financial performance arising from the following:

Significant financial interests in the entity

Significant portions of their compensation (for example, bonuses, stock options, and earn-out arrangements) being contingent upon achieving aggressive targets for stock price, operating results, financial position, or cash flow

Personal guarantees of debts of the entity

D.   There is *excessive pressure* on management or operating personnel *to meet financial targets* set up by the board of directors or management, including sales or profitability incentive goals.

Opportunities:

A.   The *nature of the industry or the entity's* operations provides opportunities to engage in fraudulent financial reporting that can arise from the following:

Significant related-party transactions not in the ordinary course of business or with related entities not audited or audited by another firm

A strong financial presence or ability to dominate a certain industry sector that allows the entity to dictate terms or conditions to suppliers or customers that may result in inappropriate or non-arm's-length transactions

Assets, liabilities, revenues, or expenses based on significant estimates that involve subjective judgments or uncertainties that are difficult to corroborate

Significant, unusual, or highly complex transactions, especially those close to period end that pose difficult "substance over form" questions

Significant operations located or conducted across international borders in jurisdictions where differing business environments and cultures exist

Significant bank accounts or subsidiary or branch operations in tax-haven jurisdictions for which there appears to be no clear business justification

B.   There is *ineffective monitoring* of management as a result of the following:

Domination of management by a single person or small group (in a non-owner, managed business) without compensating controls

Ineffective board of directors or audit committee oversight over the financial reporting process and internal control

C.   There is a *complex or unstable organizational structure*, as evidenced by the following:

Difficulty in determining the organization or individuals that have controlling interest in the entity

Overly complex organizational structure involving unusual legal entities or managerial lines of authority

High turnover of senior management, counsel, or board members

D.   *Internal control components are deficient* as a result of the following:

Inadequate monitoring of controls, including automated controls over interim financial reporting (where external reporting is required)

High turnover rates or employment of ineffective accounting, internal audit, or information technology staff

Ineffective accounting and information systems, including situations involving reportable conditions

Attitudes/Rationalizations:

A.   Risk factors reflective of *attitudes/rationalizations by board members, management, or employees*, that allow them to engage in and/or justify fraudulent financial reporting, may not be susceptible to observation by the auditor:

Ineffective communication, implementation, support, or enforcement of the entity's values or ethical standards by management or the communication of inappropriate values or ethical standards

Nonfinancial management's excessive participation in or preoccupation with the selection of accounting principles or the determination of significant estimates

Known history of violations of securities laws or other laws and regulations, or claims against the entity, its senior management, or board members alleging fraud or violations of laws and regulations

Excessive interest by management in maintaining or increasing the entity's stock price or earnings trend

A practice by management of committing to analysts, creditors, and other third parties to achieve aggressive or unrealistic forecasts

Management failing to correct known reportable conditions on a timely basis

An interest by management in employing inappropriate means to minimize reported earnings for tax-motivated reasons

Recurring attempts by management to justify marginal or inappropriate accounting on the basis of materiality

B.   The *relationship between management and* the current or predecessor *auditor* is strained, as exhibited by the following:

Frequent disputes with the current or predecessor auditor on accounting, auditing, or reporting matters

Unreasonable demands on the auditor, such as unreasonable time constraints regarding the completion of the audit or the issuance of the auditor's report

Formal or informal restrictions on the auditor that inappropriately limit access to people or information or the ability to communicate effectively with the board of directors or audit committee

Domineering management behavior in dealing with the auditor, especially involving attempts to influence the scope of the auditor's work or the selection or continuance of personnel assigned to or consulted on the audit engagement

Adapted from: Appendix: "Examples of Fraud Risk Factors." American Institute of Certified Public Accountants (AICPA), Statement on Auditing Standards No. 99, (AU 316.85) *Consideration of Fraud in a Financial Statement Audit*, AICPA, December 15th, 2002.

GATHERING EVIDENCE PART II: OTHER INFORMATION

Jack Remington stood well over six feet tall. He had a highly competitive and winner-take-all approach to business. He was an ambitious, hard-working executive who worked long hours and bragged publicly about his and his family's successes. He brought some brilliant ideas to TechTennis-USA, and aggressively implemented many of them. He often stated in public that his primary management goal was to be the leading seller of tennis rackets in the U.S. and global markets. Fiscal 2016 was his unofficial target date for achieving the number one spot in the industry. He systematically and aggressively pursued that goal. He monitored internal operating performance closely, followed the stock price performance with the eye of an eagle, and was always eager to take direct action to keep his stock buoyant. Remington subscribed to the principle that in order to maintain investor confidence and keep the stock buoyant, earnings must always be moving upward. The company's budgets reflected this principle and Remington assertively monitored performance to ensure that profit targets were always met. In his first annual report to the stockholders (2012), Remington wrote the following:

> The "TechTennis-USA Personality" is one characterized by our basic approach to business—Commitment to ambitious goals and an aggressive pursuit of those goals. We set ambitious goals fully expecting to achieve them. We establish high performance standards for our employees and reward them based on their contributions. "Trying your best" is not enough at TechTennis-USA: you must make a contribution to the achievement of company goals.

> Commitment to goals, however, must be accompanied by an aggressive approach to problems and opportunities. We are not afraid to take calculated gambles or to make mistakes. We believe we have set up controls and systems to minimize the downside. We also believe that the highest rewards go to those companies that recognize opportunities and take well thought out chances.

People who worked directly with Remington often complained that his drive to succeed intimidated and alienated them. During his tenure at TechTennis-USA, particularly in his capacity as CEO, he always let people know that he was in charge. He developed a reputation among his subordinates for going after and eventually getting exactly what he wants. Turnover in the management ranks, and in departments headed by the CEO were high. Table 3 lists the officers and directors of the company from 2011 to 2014 and provides some insight into the levels of turnover among their ranks.

Management Compensation

The ratio of senior management compensation to sales in their industry averaged between 3% and 8% of net sales. TechTennis-USA's executive compensation statistics are provided in Table 3. Executive compensation at TechTennis-USA included both a cash and deferred component. The deferred component included a savings plan, a retirement plan, and a stock option plan.

Over 40% of the cash compensation paid to senior officers came from bonuses that were directly tied to reported sales and earnings. The stock option plan, established in July 2011 and before TechTennis-USA was formed, provided for the issuance of up to 200,000 shares of common stock to qualified senior officers and employees. A 2:1 stock split in August 2011 increased the number of shares committed to the plan to 400,000. The option plan was administered by a three-member committee of the board of directors. Largely as a result of the 2011 stock option plan, over 93% of salaried employees and more than 50% of non-unionized employees held stock in the company. All senior officers and directors listed in Table 3 had beneficial ownership of the company's stock at the time of their tenure.

Senior management at TechTennis-USA, and in particular Jack Remington (who had a 39.7% interest), had significant holdings in the stock of the company. As a group, the directors and officers held a 51.1% beneficial ownership of the company. Thus, their wealth and compensation were directly affected by the company's reported sales and profit performance.

The company advertised extensively. The advertising budget for the fiscal year 2014 was approximately $25 million, up from approximately $9 million in each of the previous two previous years. Actual advertising expense for 2014, 2013, and 2012 was $26.4 million, $18.56 million, and $9.42 million, respectively. The 44.18% increase in advertising expense between 2013 and 2014 resulted from new campaigns to promote domestic sales and from costs incurred to expand into Canada, Great Britain and Italy. Growth in research and development (R&D) averaged over $400,000 between 2011 and 2013. R&D expenses grew from $673,000 in 2011 to $1.18 million, $1.53 million, and $2.4 million in 2012, 2013, and 2014, respectively. The company had a reliable and stable source of raw materials. Significant raw material purchases included titanium mesh for the racquets, ultra-light cloth for the shirts, leather for the shoes and racquet handles, and corrugated containers for shipping. As of 2012, management expected no significant increases in the cost of raw material for the foreseeable future, and no raw material procurement problems were expected.

In the 2014 Remington stated:

> I feel especially good about the significant change in the company's product mix over the past four years. As early as 2011, virtually 100% of earnings came from just one line--Power-Racquets. Now, four years later, we have a broad base with three major lines contributing to our growth. TechTennis-USA is no longer the 'runt' of the tennis racquet and apparel industry in the United States. We have now positioned ourselves as a leader in the industry, as we continue our drive to become "the leader."

Significant portions of the company's assets were pledged to secure long-term financing. Various loan agreements contained several restrictive covenants, including restrictions on the incurrence of debt, declaration of cash dividends, maintenance of working capital, tangible net worth, retained earnings, and many revenue and operating income based ratios.

Internal Audit

For efficiency, TechTennis-USA internal audit department was an integral part of the accounting department. The audit committee, which met once a year to hire the external auditor, had three outside directors and two other members of the standing board of directors.

QUESTIONS

6. Identify and classify any additional risk factors that came to light through the information in Part II of the case. Do not repeat factors already identified in Part I. Document the new risk factors using the same Triangle of Fraud format found in Part I, Question 2.

7. Risk assessment is a cumulative process. Does the information in Question 6 change your risk assessment in Question 3?

8. Are risks due to control issues different from risk due to non-control issues?

9. Discuss your specific response, if any, to the newly identified risk factors. Use Question 4 as a guideline.

10. List three individuals you would like to interview to obtain more information. Discuss all parameters of each interview…purpose of interview, types of questions, and strategies when facing a difficult interviewee.

11. Do you have enough evidence to determine if fraud occurred?

Table 3 TechTennis-USA Company—Officers, Directors and Executive Compensation				
Position	2011	2012	2013	2014
Chairman/CEO	J.D. Remington	J. D. Remington $262,500 Salary $131,250 Bonus	J. D. Remington $288,144 Salary $288,750 Bonus	J.D. Remington $288,750 Salary $288,750 Bonus
Vice Chairman/ Exec VP	M. Harkness	M. Harkness $153,000 Salary $76,500 Bonus	M. Harkness $168,147 Salary $168,300 Bonus	M. Harkness $168,300 Salary $168,950 Bonus
Vice President/ CFO	K. Green	K. Green $79544 Salary $45,000 bonus	K. Green $22,231* Salary M. Bocade $23,538* Salary	M. Bocade $89,083 Salary $42,500 Bonus
Vice Presidents— Operations		G. Calderon	G. Calderon $111,269 Salary $78,750 Bonus	G. Calderon $143,000 Salary $108,750 Bonus
Other Vice Presidents	M. Green J. Helmuth B. Bublitz	J. Helmuth, Sales $74,904 Salary $22,219 Bonus A. Montgomery HR $62,590 Salary $17,000 Bonus		
Total cash compensation to executives Salary Bonus		$725,711 $291,969	$613,329 $535,800	$689,088 $608,950
Directors	Remington K. Green McHugh	Remington K. Green McHugh M. Green B. Bublitz	Remington K. Green Jamison Murphy M. Green B. Bublitz	Remington K. Green Jamison Murphy M. Green B. Bublitz Bocade

CASE STUDY 23:

Janet Janitorial and the Case of the Serious Service Business: A Financial Statement Analysis Case

David C. Hayes, Ph.D., CPA
James Madison University
Sarah Bee, MBA, CIA
Seattle University

LEARNING OBJECTIVES

After completing and discussing this case, you should be able to

- Find financial irregularities in financial statements.
- Analyze trends in account balances.
- Perform horizontal, vertical, and trend analysis.
- Compare financial ratios to industry averages.
- Gain a better understanding of the accuracy/effort trade off.
- Analyze the statement of cash flows.

As an accountant you are frequently asked to solve business or tax problems your friends encounter. Once again your accounting skills are called upon as a friend of yours, Janet Janitorial, asks you to look over her financial statements and advise her on them. She shares the following information:

After 20 years of service at her prior job, Janet was tired of the same old, daily routine and looking for a career change. At a New Year's party, she was talking with an old high school friend who had started an office cleaning business ten years prior. This friend enthusiastically described the excellent earnings potential in the industry with substantially more demand than supply of janitorial companies in the market.

In January, Janet decided to embrace the opportunity by quitting her job and starting a janitorial service, Acme Office Cleaning Services. She was fortunate that her friend from the New Year's party had more business than she could handle and was kind enough to refer this extra business to Janet. Janet's initial client was an office complex that she billed $20,000 per month.

Janet purchased three vans, cleaning equipment, office furniture and office equipment for $200,000. She made subsequent purchases of equipment as reflected in the changes in the balance sheet accounts. A local bank loaned her $120,000 at 6% for 6 years and Janet used her personal savings to pay the remaining $80,000.

Since she is the sole owner of the small business, she has been operating it as a sole proprietorship and has not issued any stock. She draws money out as needed rather than taking a salary. Janet lived off her savings and withdrew nothing for herself in the first year, using all her profits to grow the business. In Years 2 and 3, she withdrew about $5,000 a month. In Year 4 she only withdrew about $2,000 a month as things started looking bad. As the business seemed to recover in Year 5, she withdrew about $4,000 a month.

Janet's main duties are to sell janitorial services to office buildings as well as oversee the completion of the office cleaning jobs. She has a full-time administrative assistant who handles all of the accounting functions. Janet started her administrative assistant at a salary of $35,000 per year and has given her a small raise (2%) every year. Additionally, there are four full-time janitorial staff that help clean the office buildings. All four of these employees have been working for Janet since day one. Each janitorial employee is paid $15 per hour and all employees are paid every two weeks. Additionally, if the company has a good year, she rewards the employees and administrative assistant by letting them split a bonus of 1% of the net income amount. The bonuses are paid in the following year when the compiled annual financial statements are made available and the bonus amounts can be calculated. She supplements the janitorial staff with temporary workers to eliminate any overtime when business increases.

For Years 1 and 2, Janet had external accountants prepare a compilation report. For Years 3 through 5, she had a different set of external accountants prepare the compilation reports. The books are kept on an accrual basis of accounting in accordance with GAAP and that Property & Equipment is capitalized at cost and depreciated using the straight-line method over the useful life of the property (Janitorial Equipment and Vans 3 years and Office Equipment and Furniture 5 years).

REQUIRED

Go to http://www.cchgroup.com/Resources and download the "Janet Janitoral Spreadsheet.xls" file. Review Janet's financial statements and identify accounts that indicate potential irregularities. Consider simultaneously evaluating accounts that have relationships, for example, consider analyzing accounts receivable with sales and bad debt expense. Analyze the trends in related accounts to determine which accounts do not follow an expected pattern. Utilize analytical techniques including horizontal trend analysis, i.e. dollar and percentage change in accounts from year-to-year. Also, conduct vertical trend analysis, i.e. balance sheet accounts as a percentage of total assets and expense accounts as a percentage of sales. Review industry standard financial statements and compare Janet Janitorial Services financial ratios to industry averages (Janitorial Services – NAIC code 561720, SIC code – 7349).

Three financial ratio books are: "Industry Norms & Key Business Ratios" by Dun & Bradstreet, "Almanac of Business & Industrial Financial Ratios" ("Troy Almanac") and "RMA (Risk Management Association) Annual Statement Studies." Your university library should carry at least one of these reference books.

As you perform your analysis, be aware of the cost and benefit of your time, do not spend time investigating accounts that have minor trend deviations. Once your analysis is completed, identify accounts that suggest further investigation. by using the drop-down selections for each cell and placing a "Y" (Yes – Investigate the account) in the cell related to the questionable account for the specific year in the "Students Answers" tab. Select an "N" (No – Account appears to be OK) in the cells related to accounts that appear OK and do not require further investigation. Be prepared to explain why you would request further information for questionable accounts. When finished, enter your name or team # in cell B8 and print out the completed "Student Answers" tab in the spreadsheet or electronically submit your file – whichever is required by the instructor.

Janet Janitorial's Balance Sheets:					
ACME Office Cleaning Services **Balance Sheet** **As of 12/31**					
	Year 1	Year 2	Year 3	Year 4	Year 5
Current Assets:					
Cash	26,058	22,100	40,647	78,995	57,879
Accounts Receivable	15,212	18,406	38,532	37,888	33,759
Investments — Marketable securities	20,000	20,000	20,000	–	–
Supplies Inventory	34,430	11,822	29,350	38,039	77,368
Prepaid Rent	7,403	8,059	8,735	9,273	9,985
Total current Assets	103,103	80,387	137,264	164,195	178,991
Property:					
Cleaning Equipment	43,000	43,000	41,000	62,000	80,000
Vans	130,000	130,000	130,000	145,000	160,000
Office Furniture	15,000	16,000	16,000	17,000	17,000
Office Equipment	12,000	12,000	12,500	13,000	13,200
Total Property, Plant & Equipment	200,000	201,000	199,500	237,000	270,200
Less Accumulated Depreciation	(60,067)	(120,334)	(180,034)	(194,267)	(219,500)
Net Property, Plant & Equipment	139,933	80,666	19,466	42,733	50,700
Other Assets:					
Rent Deposit	5,000	5,000	5,000	7,000	7,000
Long term investments	–	30,000	50,000	–	–
Total Other Assets	5,000	35,000	55,000	7,000	7,000
Total Assets	248,036	196,053	211,730	213,928	236,691
Current Liabilities:					
Accounts Payable	42,377	5,123	38,050	52,215	77,128
Accrued Wages Payable	1,641	952	2,350	2,672	2,755
Short-Term portion of L.T. Debt	18,188	19,309	20,500	21,765	23,107
Total Current Liabilities	62,206	25,384	60,900	76,652	102,990
Long-Term Liabilities:					
Long-Term Note Payable	84,681	65,372	44,872	44,872	–
Total Long-term Liabilities	84,681	65,372	44,872	44,872	–
Total Liabilities	146,887	90,756	105,772	121,524	102,990
Equity:					
Retained Earnings	21,149	25,297	25,958	34,169	70,701
Janet Janitorial, Equity	80,000	80,000	80,000	80,000	80,000
Total Equity	101,149	105,297	105,958	114,169	150,701
Total Liabilities & Equity	248,036	196,053	211,730	235,693	253,691

Janet Janitorial's Income Statements:					
ACME Office Cleaning Services Income Statement Year ended 12/31					
	Year 1	Year 2	Year 3	Year 4	Year 5
Revenues:					
Sales	398,769	489,112	540,493	471,837	572,544
Expenses:					
Cleaning Supplies	57,812	62,005	69,542	67,900	82,150
Advertising & Promotion	13,567	8,554	10,381	12,888	7,391
Bad Debt Expense (write offs)	542	1,855	203	3,511	5,184
Bank Charges	1,822	2,650	2,001	3,225	1,881
Depreciation	60,067	60,267	59,700	14,233	25,233
Insurance	4,851	5,387	5,911	6,744	6,399
Interest Expense	6,734	5,677	8,500	3,365	2,100
Legal & Professional	3,200	7,988	9,433	10,573	5,544
Miscellaneous	451	826	155	2,736	3,928
Office Supplies	6,100	4,722	9,025	9,487	7,711
Payroll Taxes	19,176	24,517	26,875	26,151	32,887
Rent Expense	26,400	27,600	28,800	30,000	33,600
Repairs & Maintenance	6,712	12,542	10,615	15,228	7,000
Administrative labor	35,000	35,700	36,414	40,055	44,061
Direct Labor	124,800	151,625	187,542	177,872	206,853
Telephone	2,216	3,344	3,575	7,392	5,000
Travel	2,378	2,568	3,157	3,508	3,028
Utilities	5,792	7,137	8,003	4,758	8,062
Total Expenses	377,620	424,964	479,832	439,626	488,012
Net Income (Loss)	21,149	64,148	60,661	32,211	84,532

CASE STUDY 24:

The Escheat Cheat: A Short Story

Caitlin Mohs, M.S.
Louisiana State University

LEARNING OBJECTIVES

After completing and discussing this case, you should be able to

- Understand why financial needs can cause someone to rationalize fraud.
- Appreciate the use of QuickBooks to reconcile transactions.
- Increase your understanding of accounting work in a business.
- Recognize the need to be skeptical, especially with trusted employees.
- Appreciate the need for internal controls.
- Learn about escheat property, otherwise known as unclaimed property.
- Identify how IRS agents catch taxpayers.
- Learn how HRS Pro can allow a person to alter reports.

Cecilia Brighton awoke abruptly to the sound of her iPhone alarm and glanced at the time, 5:30 a.m., as she swiped the task bar to turn off the alarm and the reverberating notes of the song 'Chop and Chain' by The Black Keys. She groaned as she rolled out of bed and proceeded to dress for her morning run before work. Cecilia thought of her boyfriend, Landon Knight, as she laced up her sneaker and began stretching. It was 2013 and they had been dating seriously for three years. They had even discussed the possibility of marriage. However, Landon was waiting to officially pop the question until Cecilia had paid off all of her student loan debt. He did not want to be tied down to her debt and have it prevent them from making bigger purchases such as a home in the future due to a bad credit score. Cecilia knew Landon had valid points, and she didn't want to start their financial future together on a bad foot. But it was frustrating! It would be ages before she actually paid off her student loans in their entirety.

So far, Cecilia had managed to pay $5,000 of her $45,000 student loans during her first six months as an entry-level accountant at First Choice Human Resource Management. First Choice Human Resource was a company that primarily served as the human resources department for companies that outsourced their own human resources department. She grimaced as she started jogging down Rock Springs Ridge Road. Saving that $5,000 had been difficult enough. Unfortunately, her job was only paying $15.00 an hour and, after taxes, her total earnings per month ended up at around $1,930. Once Cecilia factored in rent, electricity, gas, groceries, and other utilities, she barely had enough left for entertainment while she was trying to pay off her student loans. Cecilia couldn't imagine spending another two years living off the bare minimum to pay off her loans. Also, that would be an additional two years of delaying her marriage to Landon.

Cecilia had considered going back to school to earn a Masters in Accountancy and earn the remaining thirty hours she needed to meet the 150-hour requirement to sit for the Certified Public Accountant examination. If she could pass the CPA exam, then she could attain a higher paying job and that would certainly help her pay back her loans. But she would rack up even more student loan debt in order to pay for the classes, books, and relative expenses which would further delay the complete repayment of her loans and her marriage to Landon.

One of Cecilia's more unreasonable ideas was to try her hand at gambling. However, common sense prevailed before she actually went through with her foolish gambling plan. Logically, she decided that she would rather not risk the little money she already had, especially since the taxes on gambling winnings would be around 25%. She would rather be guaranteed her current paycheck less her payroll taxes taken out. "Besides," she thought reproachfully, 'it's not like she could ever have a hope of counting cards as well as those students from M.I.T. Let's not go there again," Cecilia thought with a slight trace of embarrassment. Ultimately, Cecilia knew that she would have to figure out some other plan to accelerate her loan payment process and continue working at First Choice Human Resource Management in the meantime. Could she find a second job?

As she rounded the corner of N. Fairway Drive and Hiawassee Road at the end of her jog, Cecilia sped up and pulled out her keys to the front door. Now, it was time to shower and get ready for work at 8:00 a.m. She glanced at her clock again. 6:15 a.m. Perfect. Just enough time to get ready and arrive on time for work.

Cecilia turned her black Nissan Maxima into the parking lot of First Choice Management and made her way up the stairs to the main office. Once she entered the office she made her way over to the hand scanner to clock in for work. Cecilia entered her office that she shared with her fellow accountant, Julie, and her accounting manager, Laura.

"Good morning! How was your weekend?" Cecilia asked both ladies.

"It flew by way too fast as always. The boys had a band competition in Fort Lauderdale that lasted the entire weekend. Their band ended up placing second in the competition though, so they were pretty excited," said Laura.

"I had to go to another wedding this weekend. It was a beautiful ceremony and the food was great! Speaking of weddings, when are you and Landon going to finally tie the knot?" asked Julie.

"Oh, who knows! Hopefully soon though! I think Landon is just trying to save up for a nice ring, and we both plan on paying for anything related to wedding ourselves, said Cecilia.

Cecilia didn't like lying to Julie and Laura. Quite honestly, she really liked the ladies and had become good friends with them in her short time at First Choice Management. However, she was wary about telling them about her financial woes being the true reason she and Landon were delaying their future marriage. First of all, talking about money in such a way can make people feel uncomfortable. Also, she had read several articles about employers who didn't want to hire people who were in debt since they had a higher perceived risk of stealing from the company.

Cecilia settled into her desk and printed out the bank statement from the previous month and the appropriate reports from QuickBooks to reconcile the monetary transactions the company had entered into. Typically, the monthly bank reconciliations for their various accounts were fairly easy to verify and only took a short amount of time. However, the payroll account reconciliation could take days when there weren't any errors and sometimes over a week when there were errors.

Most of the errors came from checks being cleared for the wrong amount. Even though it was tedious to search through the thousands of checks, it was relatively easy to correct. The most painful errors to correct were the ones where the payroll department issued a new check or direct deposit and backdated it for a prior month without informing the accounting department. The change in amounts from a prior month would throw off all the account balances and require a lot of searching through the different clients' records to find the exact amount and the employee to whom it corresponded.

The work involved a lot of responsibilities and duties, and she likened it to detective work that was focused on numbers and transactions. Maybe it was forensic accounting, but she was not being paid for the detective work. She needed to sit for the CPA exam and then get the AICPA's CFF certification.

She was constantly reconciling or balancing different accounts, assets, and expenses, and if anything didn't match she had to search for what was causing her numbers not to match. Typically, her investigations began with determining to which client the error applied and whether the transaction related to taxes, wages, 401K benefits, or FSA/HRA. Next, she would pull the appropriate folder to confirm the amount, determine if she needed to call the bank, or investigate further. Several of the errors that Cecilia had discovered were due to other departments not processing reports properly, and thus, entering incorrect payment amounts.

Cecilia felt fulfilled by her job for the most part. She enjoyed being able to pinpoint a problem. She liked being a detective. She would then help solve the problem by identifying the issues, determining actions to undergo to fix it, and establishing procedures to prevent it from happening in the future. Honestly, Cecilia had a great many ideas on how these problems could be prevented in the future through internal controls. Currently, First Choice Management had a serious lack of internal controls in place. She understood that the growing company didn't exactly have the resources to engage in all the necessary internal controls. However, if First Choice Management ever decided to go public and register with the Securities and Exchange Commission, they would need to completely revamp their internal control procedures themselves or hire a professional accounting firm before the auditors could even begin to express an opinion on the company.

Just as Cecilia began to print out the forty-page check detail report to reconcile with the bank statement a notification on her Microsoft Outlook program popped up.

"Unclaimed Wages and Other Property Types Training in the Conference Room at 9:00 a.m." She read as it flashed across her computer screen.

"Another training!" Cecilia thought with irritation. Cecilia had undergone various types of training since she had begun working with First Choice Management, and she always looked forward to learning something new. However, Cecilia also began to realize that any type of new training meant she was going to be assigned a new, lengthy, and tedious project.

Apparently, for the past ten years, First Choice Management had encountered high turnover within their accounting department and never employed a Chief Financial Officer (CFO) before now. Due to the turnover and lack of a CFO, the company was, unbeknownst to them, in violation of several state and federal regulations relating to their accounting records. Now that Laura was finally in charge, she was determined to ensure that the company was in compliance with these regulations, and this damage control was typically where Cecilia came in.

Cecilia had been assigned with everything relating to researching the various reporting requirements, finding the proper documentation to support any of their claims regarding the reporting requirements, and presenting her findings to Laura. One of the more tedious and surprisingly hazardous assignments had been on fixed assets taxes. Laura had simply printed out a report from Quick-Books that detailed the type of assets, date acquired, and asset supplier and had let Cecilia go from there.

First, Cecilia had to research the state of Louisiana's rules for taxes on fixed assets. Then came the fun part of her research, traveling to the various storage buildings and acquiring documentation regarding the purchase and payment of these assets, some of which dated back ten years. Based on how unorganized the accounting department was prior to Laura's arrival, Cecilia had dreaded searching through the earlier years' records, and she was worried there would be a severe lack of evidence to support their asset records.

As Cecilia was searching through the storage boxes, she began collecting order confirmations, invoices, check stubs, and credit card bills to support the acquired assets' values and to compile them into a giant binder as evidence in the future. Unfortunately for Cecilia, most of the boxes she needed access to were at the bottom of large stacks of boxes. As she was removing boxes from one stack, another tower of boxes came crashing down beside her. She screamed as she avoided being hit and then mumbled about how she hated stupid, tall interns. She proceeded to clean up the files scattered all over the storage building floor.

Once Cecilia had collected all the necessary data, she began compiling a spreadsheet to organize the information and match it to the QuickBooks records.

For some of the items that were depreciable, such as the company cars, Cecilia had to go back to prior years' tax returns and determine if the numbers agreed. She was none too pleased when she realized some of the assets had been depreciated under Code Sec. 179. Now, she had to determine if those assets had actually qualified under Section 179 as new or used capital assets. Software also was included in the tax definition, and there was plenty of that stuff in the records she had collected. She remembered abhorring Code Sec. 179 in school due to its complex and confusing applications. Cecilia groaned as she realized she also would have to consider bonus depreciation too.

The fixed assets project had taken Cecilia about a month to finish. She presented her findings to Laura, who then signed the necessary forms that Cecilia had prepared. Cecilia then sent them to the proper state department and the noncompliance with fixed assets was solved. Hopefully, there would never be a problem again with the procedures Cecilia had typed up in regards to the acquisition or purchase of any additional assets.

Now, at the meeting Cecilia could start on a new venture of cleaning up another First Choice Management neglected issue. She settled into one of the oversized, comfortable conference chairs and poised her pen over her notepad as Laura began her presentation.

After the conclusion of the presentation, Laura assigned the entire unclaimed property project to Cecilia as she had predicted. Cecilia had a great deal of work ahead of her. During the presentation, Cecilia learned that unclaimed property, more formally known as escheat property, was property that had either been abandoned or was titled to a deceased person with no known heirs. It was the responsibility of the holder of the abandoned property to tell the state to whom it rightfully belonged. Also, escheat property included numerous items from unclaimed checks to safety deposit boxes to pieces of land.

Luckily for Cecilia, the only escheat properties she would be dealing with were unclaimed checks. Unfortunately, Cecilia also had to contend with the possibility that the rightful owners might live in different states, which meant entirely different rules and regulations regarding the reporting of unclaimed property. Laura's presentation had stressed the point that there was a severe lack of uniformity among the states in regards to the rules of reporting unclaimed property and to ensure that you followed the correct guidelines.

"Even worse," thought Cecilia, "I'll have to dig through ten years' worth of unclaimed checks before I even figure out to which states the company will have to report."

Cecilia commenced her new project by exporting the entire 'Un-cashed Checks' account from QuickBooks to Excel. As she scrolled through the report she couldn't believe how many un-cashed items there were. "Over 5,000 items worth a total of $257,894.32!" Cecilia thought exasperatedly in her head. A majority of these items were over five years old and for amounts of over $500. She didn't understand how people could have the luxury of working and just forgetting to cash their checks. It just didn't make any sense to her! "Didn't these people compare their W-2 forms, which displayed their total wages earned during the year, to their check stubs to determine that there weren't any errors?" She questioned. "Goodness," Cecilia continued to think, "people really are stupid."

After a month of identifying the proper owners of the unclaimed checks, while maintaining her typical day-to-day responsibilities, Cecilia had finally completed the spreadsheet of unclaimed property. Thankfully, all of the unclaimed checks belong to residents of Louisiana, which meant Cecilia only had to research Louisiana escheat property reporting requirements.

Cecilia began her research by visiting the Louisiana Department of the Treasury webpage for unclaimed property holder reporting. She discovered that she would have to go through a great deal more work before this project was complete. The holding reporting requirements page revealed that First Choice Management should do the following:

1. Mail out due diligence letters to owners to notify them of their unclaimed property, and inform them that if they fail to claim the property by a certain date, the property will be transferred to the state.
2. Create a report in the National Association of Unclaimed Property Administrators format to file electronically.
3. The property included in the report must be categorized correctly according to property type and dormancy periods.
4. A dormancy period is the amount of time a property can be unclaimed before it is considered abandoned and must be remitted to the state. Unclaimed wages have a year dormancy period after the date of original issue.
5. Calculate the total amount due for the reportable year plus any penalties for late reported property.
6. Upload the electronic file via the Department of the Treasury website and mail the payment to the Department of the Treasury Unclaimed Checks Division.

Despite the amount of work ahead of her, Cecilia was worried about the inevitable taxes and penalties that the company would surely be subject to. Cecilia estimated that about 90% of the unclaimed wages were past due. Instead of completing steps 1–4 as recommended, she focused on determining what the potential taxes and penalties First Choice Management might be subject to.

"Oh my goodness," thought Cecilia after she finished reading Louisiana's Unclaimed Property Act. According to Section 176 of the Act, First Choice Management could be subject to one of two huge penalties, depending on what the state determined. The least severe penalty stated that a late report, payment, or both would be subject to a $200 fine for each day that the report or payment was late, up to a maximum of $5,000. The most severe penalty stated that a knowingly late report, payment, or both would be subject to a $1,000 fine for each day that the report or payment was purposefully late, up to a maximum of $25,000.

Cecilia couldn't believe this penalty. The penalties were assessed based on each report. First Choice Management had eight years' worth of reports that would be considered late. Depending on the judgment of the state, Cecilia calculated that the potential penalties could range from $40,000 to $200,000. Cecilia knew the company wouldn't be able to survive the higher end of the possible penalty spectrum.

Thankfully, there was an additional clause that stated the entire amount of penalties could be waived if the holder acted in good faith and without negligence. Cecilia was certain the company might meet this condition. The company had just learned of their noncompliance with unclaimed property law and were attempting to follow the rules by getting all their unclaimed wages in order, which was proof of their intention to comply with the standards in good faith. But she remembered the saying ignorance of a law is no excuse. Cecilia immediately brought this information to Laura, who then conveyed the message to their CFO. While the CFO contacted First Choice Management's lawyers, Laura instructed Cecilia to continue with the other steps to properly complete the reporting requirements of unclaimed property in Louisiana.

Several weeks passed before Cecilia notified Laura of the potential penalties and had finished sending out the due diligence letters. Even though she had received several responses to the letters and was able to void the old checks and reissue new checks to the appropriate owners, her list of unclaimed wages was still substantially long. Cecilia and Laura decided that it would be best to start creating the reports the company would file with the state in order to have the report ready once they heard back from the lawyers.

One week later the lawyers informed the CFO that the Louisiana Department of the Treasury decided to waive all penalties since First Choice Management had acted in good faith and without negligence by recognizing their noncompliance and attempting to correct it. The Treasury requested that the past and current years' reports and payments be turned in on November 1, 2013 when the current year report was due.

Cecilia was shocked by the decision to waive all penalties, but still pleased with the outcome. She came to the conclusion that the Treasury probably preferred the more likely receipt of over $250,000 in unclaimed property instead of pursuing up to $200,000 in penalties that First Choice Management would fight against paying in court. Honestly, she wasn't surprised by this logic. The Department of the Treasury Unclaimed Property Division collected the unclaimed property and invested the money to earn interest. In essence, these amounts were in a fiduciary fund, which is where a governmental entity collects funds on behalf of a third party and then passes them on. In this case, the Treasury was holding the unclaimed property until the rightful owners claimed it. However, in the meantime, the Treasury was using the interest earned on the investment of the principal unclaimed property amounts to fund other activities. "In the end, it all comes down to money," thought Cecilia sadly.

Cecilia's thoughts turned gloomy as she began entering in the data about the various owners of the unclaimed wages to be reported to the state. Almost three months had gone by since she had started this project, and during that time she had only managed to pay off an additional $2,500 of her student loan debt. "Frustrating," she thought, "that I am trying to contact these people to give them money they were too lazy to claim in the first place. Now, it's going to go to the government, where it will probably remain unclaimed, while the State Treasury makes money off the interest."

Finally, after a few more hours of entering data into the specialized software for escheat property titled 'HRS Pro,' Cecilia was ready to generate the specific formatted files and fill out the corresponding Louisiana forms for her manager and CFO to review before handing the reports and money over the state. Cecilia organized the unclaimed property in the reports alphabetically by owner's last name. As she was double checking the information to ensure that there were no spelling or numerical mistakes, she noticed that across the span of three years a woman named Sarah Crawford was listed numerous times. Cecilia couldn't believe it. Sarah Crawford had amounts totaling almost $18,000. How in the world could someone have missed all that money?

Since Cecilia's curiosity was piqued, she decided to investigate by looking into Sarah Crawford's employee records. She glanced at Mrs. Crawford's salary and immediately knew why $18,000 was easily forgettable. The woman had made a half a million a year in salary. Cecilia still didn't understand why she would let that $18,000 in checks just remain un-cashed. Did Mrs. Crawford not cash any of her checks? Was she even a real person?

Cecilia then looked into Mrs. Crawford's earnings history, and the problem was solved. Apparently, Mrs. Crawford did exist, but she received her salary via direct deposit to her bank account. However, unbeknownst to Mrs. Crawford, whenever First Choice Management issued bonuses they were only in the form of checks. Over the years of 2006-2008, Mrs. Crawford had been issued a $3,000 bonus check semiannually each year. Cecilia realized that this woman had probably just thrown the checks away thinking they were simply her semi-weekly check stubs that First Choice Management sent to all employees for their income records.

Also, Cecilia realized that this unclaimed money of Mrs. Crawford could be the answer to her student loan debt problems. "Clearly," Cecilia rationalized; "Mrs. Crawford doesn't need the money if she hasn't been missing it for the past five years. I could use that $18,000 to pay off my student loan debt and have $500 left over. Also, there would be no excuse for Landon and me not to get married in the near future! All I have to do is figure out how to get my hands on that unclaimed money."

Once Cecilia arrived home that evening she powered on her laptop and began searching the Louisiana rules for how to claim unclaimed property found in their database. She found that anyone who wanted to claim property had to provide general identifying information, including proof of maintaining a residence at the address the holder reported as the true owner's last living address. Cecilia knew that she couldn't just swap out her name with Sarah Crawford's. She would have to find someone else that would be willing to go along with her scheme and act as a mule for Cecilia, and she knew just the person to do it.

Cecilia's mom, Claudia, had remarried several times over Cecilia's childhood. Currently, her mom went by Claudia Kennedy. Cecilia figured that since her mom didn't share the same last name as her, no one would become suspicious of her drawing out the money on Cecilia's behalf. She was confident that her mother would agree to the scheme, since she had co-signed on all of Cecilia's student loans and was just as indebted as Cecilia was in this whole mess.

That night Cecilia called her mom to outline the scheme.

"Hi sweetie! How are you? How's your job? Did they give you a raise yet?" Claudia answered the phone and immediately started shooting questions out at a rapid fire pace.

"Hi Mom. I'm doing well. Work is work, nothing new going on there. They haven't given me a raise, unfortunately." answered Cecilia.

"Honey, you really should think of getting a job elsewhere. They pay you next to nothing. How are you ever going to pay off your student debts? I certainly don't want any creditors banging down my door because you've defaulted on the payments. I never should have co-signed those stupid loans in the first place." said Claudia.

"Actually, Mom, I think I've come up with a way to pay off the remaining debt in less than a year's time," replied Cecilia.

"Dear, I thought we already agreed on this. Even though you are smart as a bean counter, you can't count cards as well as the M.I.T. students and make millions of dollars in a casino." Claudia said.

"I KNOW, MOM!" Cecilia shouted. That whole phase was kind of a sore subject with Cecilia. She liked to think of herself as above average intelligence, and that she had super mathematical abilities. Unfortunately, that had proved not to be the case when she had been kicked out of a casino for badly attempting to count cards.

"Sorry, Mom. You know that's a touchy subject for me. I've never been more embarrassed in my life. My new idea is somewhat unorthodox, but just hear me out." responded Cecilia as she explained to her mom about the unclaimed property project and Mrs. Crawford's $18,000 in unclaimed wages.

"How would you be able to replace Mrs. Crawford's name with my own? Wouldn't your bosses be able to see my name on the report, determine I'm not in the employee database, and eventually link me to you?" Claudia asked.

"The software we use, HRS Pro, allows me to alter reports after they've already been printed. All I have to do is switch out Mrs. Crawford's information with yours and then upload the file to the Louisiana holder-reporting page for unclaimed property. I'm the only one who knows how the program operates at work. All I have to do is give the reports to my manager and CFO to check over and sign. They trust me and the CFO honestly just wants the whole project off the company's hands. No one would ever be the wiser to it," explained Cecilia. "I'll even give you the extra $500 for helping me." Cecilia bargained with Claudia.

"I don't know, Cecilia, this doesn't seem very foolproof to me," said Claudia. "Wouldn't I have to pay taxes on all those reclaimed wages?" asked Claudia. "It seems like this will end up costing me money instead of me making $500." Claudia stated.

"I've already thought that through, Mom. Those wages can't be taxed since they were already taxed and paid for by Mrs. Crawford. You see, when Mrs. Crawford filed her tax returns for the tax years 2008-2010 she received a W-2 and her bonuses were included in Box 1, which contains your total taxable wages including bonuses. So, basically, Mrs. Crawford has already paid the taxes on her bonuses, but she just never claimed them," explained Cecilia.

"Ok, Cecilia, this sounds like a good idea. I'll do it. The sooner I cut my ties from that debt the better. Just tell me what to do when the time comes." responded Claudia.

"Thanks, Mom. I'll let you know when the money is available for you to claim. It shouldn't be too long from now," Cecilia said gratefully.

The following day at work Cecilia turned in the completed report, forms, and check to the CFO to sign. He returned it to her shortly thereafter and instructed her to go ahead and upload the file, and then deliver the confirmation page of the file upload, signed forms, and check to the lawyers for them to deliver to the Department of the Treasury. Cecilia smiled as she got to work on uploading the electronic report to the Louisiana Unclaimed Property Holder Reporting webpage. Before she set about uploading the report, she quickly changed the name and other identifying information to that of her mother, Claudia Kennedy. Once she received the confirmation page of her report being successfully filed electronically, Cecilia left First Choice Management and drove to the lawyers' office.

After Cecilia had arrived back at the office, her manager informed her that the lawyers had dropped off everything relating to the unclaimed property to the Department of the Treasury. Cecilia smiled and thought, "Step one is complete. Now, I just have to wait for the property to show up on the unclaimed property search engine online."

A few weeks later, after checking the unclaimed property website daily, 'Claudia Kennedy" finally popped up on the screen with six separate items totaling $18,000. 'Finally!' Cecilia thought excitedly. She immediately began to print out the proper paperwork and stuffed it into her briefcase to bring to her mom that evening.

Cecilia showed her mom the necessary paperwork over Claudia's kitchen table and helped her fill it out. Once the form was completed, Cecilia placed it in the mail. Now, all they had to do was wait for the reimbursement check to arrive in the mail. Cecilia couldn't keep the smile off her face. In a few weeks, all her financial woes would be solved.

'Ring! Ring!' Cecilia picked up her ringing iPhone to see 'Mom' flashing up the screen. She swiped the task bar to answer. "Hello Mom! I hope you're calling with good news!" she said.

"Yes, Cecilia, the money came! I just deposited the check and transferred $17,500 to your bank account. It should be showing up in your account in about a week." said Claudia excitedly.

"Thank you so much, Mom! Words can't explain how much this means to me. I love you!" exclaimed Cecilia.

"I love you too, honey. Now go pay off your student loans and start living happily ever after!" said Claudia upon ending the conversation.

A week later, Cecilia logged into her Capital One bank account online. The balance in her checking account read $17,500 more than the previous week. Cecilia, immediately make her last and final payment on her student loans by logging onto the student loan website. She submitted her payment of $17,500 and whooped for joy when the confirmation page popped up. She was finally done! Her student loans were paid off in full, and she could start focusing on other things in her life like her now impending marriage to Landon.

Unfortunately, seven months later after filing her tax return, Cecilia received a letter from an IRS agent. Her heart stopped as she began reading the letter. She was certain they had uncovered her scheme with her mother to steal the unclaimed wages from Sarah Crawford to pay off her student loan debt. Cecilia sat down at her kitchen table and began to read the letter.

It turned out her 2013 tax return had been selected for an audit. The results of the investigation led to her and her mother being charged additional taxes and penalties. In the contents of the letter the IRS agent informed Cecilia of how they had uncovered her attempted tax evasion.

REQUIRED

Outline how the IRS was able to catch Cecilia and her mother. What was the amount of taxes and penalties? Was the eventual outcome favorable or unfavorable?

CASE STUDY 25:

Finding the Missing $6,000 Theft

D. Larry Crumbley, Ph.D., CPA, CFF, Cr.FA, MAFF
Louisiana State University

LEARNING OBJECTIVES

After completing and discussing this case, you should be able to

- Develop an interviewing set of questions.
- Learn how to interview a possible fraudster.
- Determine what is a baseline and UpJohn warning.
- Learn 7 magic questions to ask suspects.

You own a small, solely-owned service corporation in a southern, mid-sized town. During one weekend $6,000 becomes missing from the business safe. Most of your employees have worked for you for a number of years. You trust them. The four suspects are:

- Sally, mother of two, age 29, divorced. Worked for you for 5 years. Quiet person. Has accounting knowledge.
- Vance, single. Smokes. Age 23. Has been known to gamble. Hard worker. Worked for you for 6 years. About to get married.
- Velvia, worked for you 7 years. Age 51. Husband died 2 years ago. Comes to work early and stays late. Two grown children.
- Howard. Worked for you for 3 years. 25 years old. Has a college degree. Single. Religious. Marketing background. Likes sports.

The office was not broken into by an outside person. You have not called the police, and you plan to interview each of the four individuals on Tuesday afternoon. Your wife, who is a lawyer, works with you in the company. You do not suspect her.

1. How would you go about interviewing each of the individual?
2. What is meant by a baseline?
3. What is an UpJohn warning?
4. What questions would you ask each of the employees?

CASE STUDY 26:

Is the Current Use of Impression Management by Professors in the Classroom Similar to Earnings Management by Corporate Executives?

D. Larry Crumbley, Ph.D., CPA, CFF, Cr.FA, MAFF, FCPA
Kenneth J. Reichelt, Ph.D., CA, CPA (Canada)
Louisiana State University

LEARNING OBJECTIVES

After completing and discussing this case, you should be able to

- Determine whether an accounting technique is legal or aggressive earnings management.
- Learn about our dysfunctional accounting control system in higher education.
- Divide SET management techniques into harmful and good classroom teaching practices.
- Develop capital market, contracting, and regulatory incentives to manage earnings.

Higher education is experiencing the simultaneous phenomena of widespread use of student evaluation of teachers (SETs), student use of publisher test banks, grade inflation, course work deflation, student moral decline (resulting in widespread cheating and plagiarism), and increasing lower student motivation. SAT scores declined from 1972 until 1997, started increasing in 1998, and began another decline in 2006 to the present. Rosovsky and Hartley (2002) identified the beginning of grade inflation and the drop in SATs with the introduction of SETs.[1]

This decline in higher education is clearly explained by agency theory (e.g., Jensen and Meckling 1976),[2] a popular economic theory used by accounting researchers. Agency theory posits that because the actions of the agents (professors) are too costly to be observed by the principal (administrators, board of trustees, and legislators), agents are more likely to shirk/cheat. In higher education, professors manage the impressions of students to favorably rate their SET scores (Crumbley and Reichelt 2009), knowing that doing so is not easily observable

---

[1] Rosovsky, H., and M. Hartley. 2002. *Evaluation and the Academy: Are We Doing the Right Thing?* American Academy of Arts & Sciences. Available at: http://www.amacad.org/publications/monographs/Evaluation_and_the_Academy.pdf.

[2] Jensen, M. C., and W. H. Meckling. 1976. Theory of the Firm - Managerial Behavior, Agency Costs and Ownership Structure. *Journal of Financial Economics* 3 (4):305-360.

by their superiors or other faculty, and, in turn, it will lead to promotion, tenure, and improved compensation, all with much less effort.[3]

To elaborate, legislators for public universities and Board of Trustees in private universities tell administrators to increase retention rates and to evaluate the teaching effectiveness of university professors. Administrators then hire the inventory (students) to evaluate (e.g., audit) the professors. While using students in this manner may be an inexpensive and quick way to evaluate professors, this method does not measure learning. In fact, this dysfunctional system has actually reduced respect for professors and the higher education process. Administrators prefer higher SET scores, which lead to higher grades, higher student retention rates, and more tuition and tax revenues. As the chart in Figure 1 illustrates, professors will focus on pecuniary benefits and inflate grades and decrease their course work to survive because they are caught between a rock and a hard place.[4]

Figure 1

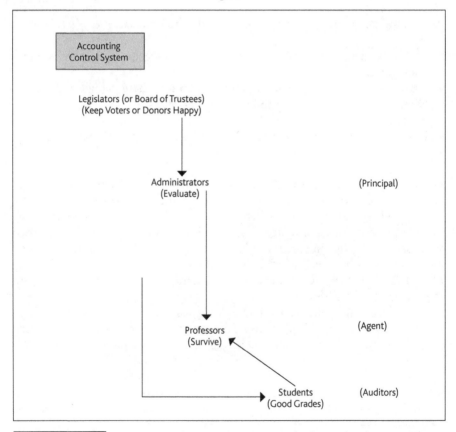

3   Crumbley, D.L., and K.J. Reichelt, "Teaching Effectiveness, Impression Management, and Dysfunctional Behavior: Student Evaluation of Teaching Control Data," *Quality Assurance in Education*, Vol. 17, No. 4, 2009, p. 378.
4   Flinn, R.E., and D.L. Crumbley, *Measure Learning Rather Than Satisfaction in Higher Education*, Sarasota, FL: AAA, 2009, Preface, xiv.

Professors today may be hired, rewarded, promoted, tenured, punished, and fired largely based on student opinions at the end of each semester about their classroom teaching.[5]

As an example of this dysfunctional system, a Dean at Louisiana State University gave the following instructions to her professors:

> Please know that your eligibility for future multiyear contracts will be contingent on satisfactory performance through a review of your annual performance reviews, instructor evaluations, and rate of student success as measured by the percentage of students receiving a D, F, or withdrawing from your course.

Apparently, this college was experiencing a reduction of incoming students, so "hard" professors and "hard" courses will now be penalized even when students drop the course. Here is more than subtle pressure on the professors to give higher grades and deflate course content.

Faculty promotion, tenure, and merit decisions typically are based on some combination of research, teaching, and service. Research normally is based on quality and quantity, while teaching effectiveness is based on peer evaluations, grade distribution, drop rates, and SET scores. The SET questionnaire is a control device used to audit professors and to measure their performance by students. As an analogy, where stakeholders rely on financial and other statistical information, they are deeply concerned with the relevance, reliability, comparability, transparency, and neutrality of the data. In fact, the rise of the accounting profession occurred primarily because of the desire for better financial reporting. Both public and private educational institutions utilize external or internal audits, but many administrators seem unconcerned with the relevance, reliability, comparability, and neutrality of the student data used to evaluate teaching. Because administrative decisions are often irreversible, positions and even careers may be at stake, data on which such decisions are made should be of proven validity.[6]

Suppose external auditors' performance was based solely on satisfied clients. Soon auditors would only be consultants, and there would be many more Enrons, WorldComs, and HealthSouths. Suppose prison guards' performance evaluations were based upon their prisoners' anonymous questionnaire evaluations? As Dr. Mike Davis often said, in education the inmates are in charge of the system, and they are clearly aware of their power over professors. This dysfunctional system in higher education causes professors to inflate grades and reduce course work content.[7]

The various pressures from administrators, legislators, peers, parents, alumni, and students upon professors are illustrated in Figure 2:[8]

---

[5]   *Ibid.*

[6]   Crumbley, D.L., and K.J. Reichelt *supra note 3.*

[7]   Crumbley, D.L., and G.S. Smith, "The Games Professors Play in the Dysfunctional Performance Evaluation System Used in Higher Education: Brainstorming Some Recommendations," in *Measure Learning Rather Than Satisfaction in Higher Education*, Sarasota, FL: AAA, 2009, p. 45.

[8]   Crumbley, D.L., and K.J. Reichelt *supra note 3.*

Figure 2

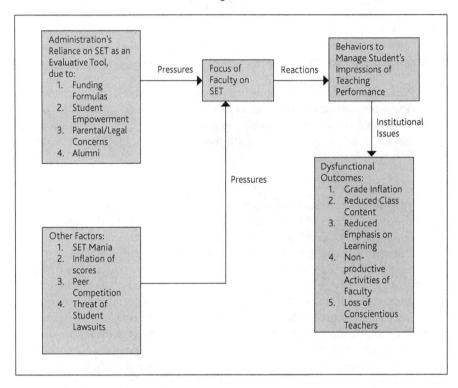

The pressures to increase their SET scores force professors to engage in impression management and dysfunctional behavior. An evaluation system based on SET scores causes professors to present themselves in a defensive manner in order to control the impressions students have of them.

Quite logically professors will try to manage their SET score, just as many executives manage their earnings. Massaging SET scores can be beneficial (or neutral) to learning or aggressive SET management (harmful to learning). But by definition one-half of all professors are below average, so many professors engage in aggressive SET management or pander pollution. Pander pollution may be defined as purposeful intervention by an instructor inside and outside the classroom with the intention of increasing SET scores, which is counterproductive to the learning process. The best approach is to give really high grades to the really poor students and induce the Santa Claus effect. Snyder and Clair found that students who received higher grades than they expected tended to give a "very positive teacher evaluation" (a happy birthday effect).[9] Worthington and Wong came to the same conclusion.[10] There is little adverse effect on a professor who inflates grades and deflates their course work.

---

[9]   Snyder, C.R., and M. Clair. 1976. Effects of expected and obtained grades on teacher evaluation and attribution of performance. *Journal of Educational Psychology* 68 (1): 75-82.

[10]   Worthington, A.G., and P.T. Wong. 1979. Effects of earned and assigned grades on student evaluations of an instructor. *Journal of Educational Psychology* 71 (6): 764-775.

Schipper defines earnings management as the "purposeful intervention in the external financial reporting process, with the intent of obtaining some private gain."[11] Healy and Wahlen state that "earnings management occurs when managers use judgment in financial reporting and in structuring transactions to alter financial reports to either mislead some stakeholders about the underlying economic performance of the company or to influence contractual outcomes that depend on reported accounting numbers."[12] Thus, SET management occurs when a professor grade-inflates or reduces coursework content with the intention of obtaining some financial gain, promotion, or tenure, which can have negative repercussions.

There are capital market, contracting, and regulatory incentives to manage earnings. Of course, there is both legal and aggressive earnings management. But the difference between legal earnings management and financial statement fraud can be the thickness of a prison wall. Although there have been thousands of accounting articles written about earnings management, little has been written about SET management. Further, an executive can go to prison for earnings management, but a professor is often rewarded or promoted for SET management.

W.R. Scott in his *Financial Accounting Theory* textbook outlines these "good" or legal earnings management techniques used by General Electric to "smooth earnings" from 1993 to 2007.[13]

- *Changes to the expected rate of return on pension plan assets.*
- *Sales of divisions.* Such sales generally lead to large special item gains.
- *Restructuring charges.* These are charges to current earnings to provide for expected costs of restructuring the operations of one or more of its many divisions. Apparently, GE managed the amounts and timing of these charges to offset large special item gains (e.g., sales of divisions). GE's objective was to avoid reporting higher earnings than could be sustained in future years.
- *Buying profitable businesses.* GE was constantly acquiring new subsidiary companies. If needed to prevent reporting an earnings decrease, managing the timing and identity of such acquisitions could achieve an immediate contribution to consolidated reported earnings in the year of acquisition.
- *Conservative accounting.* For example, rapid amortization of leased aircraft by GE's commercial finance division enabled large profits to be recorded when the aircraft are eventually sold. The timing of such sales can be managed by GE.
- *Allocation of purchased goodwill upon acquisition of subsidiary companies.* When GE acquires a subsidiary, it may decide, or be required, to dispose of segments of the acquired business. The flexibility under U.S. generally accepted accounting principles of allocation of the excess of amount paid for a subsidiary company over the fair value of assets acquired (i.e., purchased goodwill) enabled GE to record a gain on such dispositions, by allocating a relatively small amount of the excess amount paid to any subsidiary segments that is intended to be disposed of.

---

[11] Katherine Schipper. 1989. "Commentary on Earnings Management." *Accounting Horizons* 3 (4): 92.

[12] Healy, P. and J. Wahlen. 1999. "A Review of the Earnings Management Literature and Its Implications for Standard Setting." *Accounting Horizons* 13 (4): 368.

[13] W.R. Scott, *Financial Accounting Theory*, 7th Edition, Pearson: Toronto, 2015, pp. 476-477.

QUESTIONS

1. Decide whether these accounting practices would be considered aggressive earnings management by the SEC.

    a. Improper revenue recognition (e.g., bill and hold sales).

    b. Improper expense recognition.

    c. Using reserves to inflate earnings in years with falling revenues (cookie jar accounting).

    d. Shifting debt to special purposes entities.

    e. Channel stuffing.

    f. Careful timing of capital gains and losses.

    g. Use of conferencing technology to reduce travel costs.

    h. Postponement of repair and maintenance activities when faced with unexpected cash flow declines.

    i. Capitalizing marketing costs rather than expensing.

    j. Extending useful lives and inflating salvage values.

    k. Accelerating revenue from leasing equipment.

    l. Special purpose entities that are not consolidated.

2. What would have happened to university football or other sports teams if, starting in the 1960s and 1970s, coaches were hired and fired based on anonymous SET questionnaires of their players (such as professors)? What would happen if airline pilots were fired and hired based on passengers' anonymous questionnaires? What would happen if Internal Revenue Service agents were rewarded and fired by anonymous questionnaires of the taxpayers they audited?

3. If grades in universities and colleges continue to climb, what will happen to these institutions? What will employers be forced to do?

4. Faced with SET questionnaires each semester, using the classic prisoner's dilemma, what should a young professor do?

5. What are some capital market incentives to manage earnings?

6. Determine whether these steps that raise SET scores are aggressive SET management (harmful to learning), neutral, unclear, or "good" SET management (helpful to learning).[14]

   a. First and foremost, inflate your student's grades.

   b. Reduce the course material covered and drop the most difficult material first.

   c. Give easy examinations (e.g., true-false; broad, open-ended discussion questions; take-home exams; open-book exams).

   d. Join the college party environment by giving classroom parties on SET day. Sponsor student's officially approved class skipping days to, say, ball games or other events, as a means to increase student satisfaction. One Oregon professor prepares cupcakes on the day the SET questionnaires are distributed.

   e. Give financial rewards, such as establishing connections to potential employers.

   f. Spoon-feed watered-down material to the students.

   g. Give answers to exam questions beforehand. Either pass them out in class or, if the students are to work harder, put them on reserve in the library or on the Internet.

   h. Do not risk embarrassing students by calling on them in the classroom.

   i. Hand out sample exams, or take examination questions from the students' online exercises provided by the textbook publisher.

   j. Grade on a wide curve.

   k. Give SET as early as possible in the semester and then give hard final exams after SET questionnaires are given to students.

   l. Keep telling students how much they are learning and that they are intelligent.

---

[14] Crumbley, D.L., and G.S. Smith *supra note 7*.

m.   Delete grading exams, projects, and other material. If they turn in work, give them credit. The correctness of the work is not an issue.

n.   Teach during bankers' hours (9:00 – 3:00) favored by the students.

o.   Give the same exams each semester, allowing the answers to spread among students and grades to increase each semester.

p.   Avoid the effort of trying to teach students to think (e.g., avoid the Socratic Method).

q.   Provide more free time (e.g., cancel classes on or near holidays, Mondays, and Fridays).

r.   Avoid giving a cumulative final exam.

s.   Do not give a final exam and dismiss the class on the last class day. Even if the final exam is administratively required, try to find methods to avoid the final exam.

t.   Use simple slides so the students do not need to read the book and post the slides to the course website from which test questions will be taken.

u.   Where multiple classes are taught by different instructors, always ensure that your classes have the highest grade point average.

v.   Allow the students to participate in determining material coverage and the number of points assigned to difficult test questions.

w.   When possible, teach classes where common exams are used; then help students pass "this bad exam" for which you are not responsible.

x.   Allow students to re-take exams until they pass. It helps to put a page reference next to each question so the students can find the answer during an open-book examination.

y.   Give significant above-the-curve extra or bonus credit.

7.   In your opinion, is aggressive earnings management similar to harmful SET management? Explain your answer. Which is worse?

8.   How does U. S. higher education rank versus the rest of the world? How can this be measured?

CASE STUDY 27:

Is the Widespread Use of Test Banks by Students Fraud?

D. Larry Crumbley, Ph.D., CPA, CFF, Cr.FA, MAFF, FCPA
Christine Cheng, Ph.D.
Louisiana State University

LEARNING OBJECTIVES

After completing and discussing this case, you should be able to:

- Learn of the widespread availability of publisher test banks.
- Understand how use of publisher test banks is akin to fraud.
- Recognize the analogy to cheating on taxes and piracy of movies.
- Understand the negative impact of using publisher test banks and brain dumps on students and society.
- Learn how to develop a forensic technique to uncover students using publisher test banks.

INTRODUCTION

The Internet has given students widespread and anonymous access (either free or paid) to publisher test banks. Furthermore, the widespread access students have to publisher test banks is unlikely to diminish. Publishers are frustrated over legal attempts to have Internet providers cease infringing on their copyrights by publishing test banks and solution manuals or providing them for sale to students. Publishers' representatives indicate that legal victories are often met with a website being shuttered, only to have a new one pop up. In addition, the publishers' representatives indicate that their legal battles are confounded by websites hosted in overseas locations where copyright enforcement is limited. As such, it appears that students will continue to have ample opportunity to obtain publishers test banks from various Internet sources. Thus, the opportunity factor of the Fraud Triangle is clearly present.

One of the earlier examples of the mass test bank cheating occurred at the University of North Florida in 2010. A professor received 200 confessions from students using the test bank (one-third of the class).[1] Research by Ruedy *et al.*

---

[1]   Joyner, James. "Professor Gets 200 Confessions for Cheating." *Outside the Beltway*, November 22, 2010, http://www.outsidethebeltway.com/professor-gets-200-confessions-to-cheating/.

found that as many as 68 percent of students will cheat.[2] Thus, the percentage of accounting students who use publisher test banks range from 33 percent to 68 percent.

QUESTIONS

1. Is the use of a publisher test bank by a student cheating and/or fraud? Consider the Legal.com definition of fraud as the intentional use of deceit, a trick, or some dishonest means to deprive another of his/her/its money, property, or a legal right.

2. Compare this practice to a taxpayer cheating on his or her taxes.

3. Does the use of test banks positively impact a student's in-class exam grades?

4. Is the use of test banks a victimless phenomenon?

5. Design a forensic technique to detect students' use of publisher test banks.

---

[2]   Ruedy, N. E., C. Moore, F. Gino, and M. Schweitzer. 2013. "The Cheater's High: The Unexpected Affective Benefits of Unethical Behavior" *Journal of Personality and Social Psychology*, 105:531-548.

CASE STUDY 28:

Fighting International Fraud with the FCPA

Priscilla Burnaby, Ph.D., CPA
Bentley University
Susan Hass, MBA, CPA, CGMA
Simmons College
Brigitte W. Muehlmann, Ph.D., MST, CPA, CFM, CVA
Suffolk University

LEARNING OBJECTIVES

After completing and discussing this case, you should be able to

- Find financial irregularities in financial statements.
- Analyze trends in account balances.
- Perform horizontal, vertical, and trend analysis.
- Compare financial ratios to industry averages.
- Gain a better understanding of the accuracy/effort trade off.
- Analyze the statement of cash flows.

HEWLETT-PACKARD'S CURRENT PROBLEMS
WITH INTERNATIONAL KICKBACKS

Andrew and Susie were on a Midwest college campus discussing current events over lunch. Susie found an article about one of the topics they were studying in law and fraud class and brought it to Andrew's attention, "Andrew I just read in the *Wall Street Journal* (Crawford, 2012) that the Hewlett-Packard (HP) criminal bribery case we studied in class last semester is finally heating up. Remember the case was about a German branch of HP bribing a Russian official. The article says that German prosecutors filed bribery, tax evasion and embezzlement charges against Hilmar Lorenz, a German and former H-P marketing executive in Russia; Ken Willett, a Germany-based American H-P manager; and Päivi Tiippana, a Finn and former manager at the company. Prosecutors also indicted Ralf Krippner, a local German politician and businessman as an accessory.

The indictment alleges that Krippner billed an H-P subsidiary for services that were never performed and helped relay the funds." Susie noted, "This case has not yet been brought to a U.S. court. The Securities and Exchange Commission (SEC) is still investigating. If I remember correctly from articles we read (Yannet and Fuhr, 2010), the investigation began in 2007 after a German tax auditor became suspicious of payments totaling €22 million that a German HP subsidiary made to a small computer hardware firm near Leipzig from 2004 to 2006. They suspect Russian officials received €7.5 million in kickbacks for a € 35 million dollar contract to sell computer gear to Russia's Prosecutor General Office, the very office responsible to stop bribes. (Crawford, 2012)"

Susie continued, "The HP subsidiary recorded the payments as having been made for services rendered in Moscow. The investigation also identified three payment intermediaries (shell companies in multiple jurisdictions) and a Moscow-based computer supplier with foreign bank accounts as having conspired with HP to perpetrate the alleged bribery scheme. Using HP funds, the intermediaries, based in the former East Germany, allegedly paid fake invoices for equipment to the shell companies. The illicit funds then flowed through bank accounts all over the world, including the U.K., the U.S., New Zealand, the British Virgin Islands, Latvia, Lithuania, Belize, Austria, and Switzerland before making their way to Russia. (Yannet, and Fuhr, 2010)

This story is an international intrigue. The SEC has yet to file charges using the Foreign Corrupt Practices (FCPA) Act of 1977. It amazes me how long it takes to bring these people and companies to justice. And, it seems like the HP employees did not even benefit from the fraud except for getting credit for the sale.[1] I am looking forward to studying more international FCPA violations in our fraud and forensics course. It really takes a lot of information gathering and drilling down into the details to be able to bring a case like this to court. Andrew, what I don't get is that I thought all these U.S. companies have a code of conduct and policies to prohibit their employees from offering bribes to foreign officials. I thought the FCPA required that U.S. companies have accounting systems with adequate controls to prevent these fraudulent kickbacks. It has been years since the law was passed. How can this still be happening?"

STUDENT ASSIGNMENTS

Individual Assignments

Although the FCPA has been around since 1977, it is not until the last 12 years that the SEC has annually indicted multiple U.S. companies doing business in foreign countries using the FCPA. To gain an understanding of the FCPA, go to the SEC's website *http://www.sec.gov/spotlight/fcpa.shtml* and click on the FCPA (Securities and Exchange Commission, 2012b) hyperlink on the bottom left.

---

[1]   Although the employees did not take any cash directly, the sale earned the employees commissions or bonuses, led to potential salary increases and helped fulfill expectations in order to get promoted.

Then, answer the following questions.

1. Download the document, *A Resource Guide to the U.S. Foreign Corrupt Practices Act* (Criminal Division of the U.S. Department of Justice and the Enforcement Division of the U.S. Securities and Exchange Commission).

    a. Read Chapter 1, "Introduction," which describes the scope of the FCPA, discusses the costs of corruption, and covers the evolution of the law as well as how the SEC partners with the Department of Justice to fine companies and imprison those that break the law. It also provides an introduction to the efforts of the Commerce and State Departments to assist U.S. companies by advancing anti-corruption and good governance initiatives as well as an introduction to the international landscape.

    b. Read Chapter 2, "The FCPA: Anti-bribery Provisions," which explains the anti-bribery provisions.

    c. How can a law that was enacted more than 35 years ago still be relevant today?

2. Review the annual list of enforcement actions by calendar year for the past five years. From the SEC website, select a sample of five companies to read about in more detail. What strikes you about the companies you reviewed and their crimes?

    Go to *www.cbsnews.com/8301-18560_162-4080920.html* and view *The Price of Bananas* video. You will also find the transcript of the video at that link. Be ready to discuss the video in class.

    a. Chiquita Banana was making payments to a militant group. How does this action fall under the FCPA?

    b. What would you have done if you were faced with threats of deadly action against those that worked at the Chiquita Banana facilities under your supervision?

    c. What has been some of the fallout for Chiquita Banana?

3. Answer the questions in the FCPA Survey in the Appendix. Be ready to defend your choice based on your understanding of the FCPA and your personal beliefs.

4. To learn about codes of conduct, read the article, "Up To Code," by Paine, L., Deshpandé, R., Margolis, J., and Bettcher, K. (2005). *Harvard Business Review*, 83 (12), 122-133. Then answer the following questions:

a.   Should a company have a uniform global code of conduct policy? Why or why not?

b.   Should these policies be implemented globally, or at a regional, country, or local level?

c.   Should companies have specific global policies regarding gifts, gratuities, payments, entertainment, conflicts of interest, and related matters? Why?

d.   Who should be responsible for communicating, monitoring, and enforcing the company's policy?

Team Assignments

Based on what you have learned above by completing the individual assignment questions, work with your team to complete the following:

1.   On the SEC website, select a company from the SEC FCPA enforcement actions list from the two most recent years. Click on the case on the SEC's website for additional information about the company, situation, and issues.

2.   Research the company to find their Code of Conduct. After reading their Code, do you believe that management breached their duty to the company? Explain your answer.

3.   Find at least three other references (e.g., documents, articles, web links) about the company's problems with the SEC.

4.   Was the case you identified a civil or criminal proceeding? Explain the difference between the two types of indictments.

5.   Were the parties involved fined and/or served jail time? Where are guilty parties today?

6.   Write a five-page memo to the Board of Directors and create a 10-minute PowerPoint presentation to explain the fraud to the class. Include a listing of who was involved in the fraud and their home country, how the fraud was perpetrated, how that led the company to be indicted by the SEC, and subsequent conviction or fines. Also explain the financial and nonfinancial costs to the company. Include the information you found in questions 2 to 5.

Investigate the website below and the latest Corruption Perceptions Index (CPI). How should this index raise concerns about doing business in countries that have the higher corruption ratings?

http://www.transparency.org/research/cpi/overview. Note the U.S. (or your home country) ranking.

Was the company your group researched doing business in countries included in the CPI? If yes, what were the countries' scores and rankings in the latest published CPI?

CASE STUDY 29:

Consideration of Fraud in a Financial Statement Audit

Charles J. Russo, Ph.D., CPA, CVA, CMA

Amber Stone, M.S., CPA

Charles L. Martin Jr., DBA, CPA

Towson University

LEARNING OBJECTIVES

After completing and discussing this case, you should be able to

- Apply the Fraud Triangle.
- Understand the auditor's role in the case.
- Evaluate related party transactions.
- Understand the Sarbanes Oxley Act, Section 404.

INTRODUCTION OF KEY DECISIONS
AND DECISION MAKERS

INTRODUCTION

This case is based on actual fraud and the litigation that followed the discovery of the fraud. The Securities and Exchange Commission (SEC) filed suit against Insignia, Inc. in U.S. District Court in 2011. This court case involves falsified journal entries, misappropriation of assets, securities fraud, violation of the Sarbanes-Oxley Act (SOX), and responsibilities of the independent auditor. The key decisions and key decision makers are outlined below.

KEY DECISIONS

Falsified Journal Entries
- Alan Nixon, CEO and shareholder
- Bobbie Grant, Controller and shareholder

Misappropriation of Assets

- Alan Nixon, CEO and shareholder

Securities Fraud

- Alan Nixon, CEO and shareholder
- Charles Hoover, Former CEO and shareholder
- Bobbie Grant, Controller and shareholder
- David Polk, Company Attorney and shareholder

KEY DECISION MAKERS

Alan Nixon — CEO

The CEO, Alan Nixon, was falsifying journal entries and diverting money from the company into personal accounts. The journal entries debited payroll tax liabilities on the balance sheet and credited shareholder loans. Insignia, Inc. then made payments on the shareholder loans by paying Nixon. Securities fraud was the result when the falsified financial statements were filed with the SEC. Nixon also misappropriated additional cash by directing purchasers of newly issued stock to transfer funds to accounts controlled by Nixon. The FBI website had the background information on the CEO as reported by the U.S. Attorney's Office in 2014 including the following:

1. Nixon had transferred funds to his personal bank account and other accounts under his control.
2. Nixon manipulated the financial statements by understating the amount of payroll tax liabilities.
3. Nixon overstated the amount of loans made to him by the company.
4. Nixon directed purchasers of newly issued shares to transfer funds to accounts under the CEO's control.
5. Nixon stole $6 million and spent it on himself.

The city newspaper reported that in federal court, Nixon's family and supporters presented Nixon as a man who works hard at maintaining a small farm that he leased, as well as being a good father to his 18-month old son. The SEC countered that Nixon lied, cheated, and stole from the company for over two years and that this was a side of Nixon that family members have never seen.

Charles Hoover — Former CEO

The former CEO Charles Hoover was also associated with the Insignia fraud activities. Hoover appeared to have been motivated by his need for an over-the-top upper class lifestyle. An online business newspaper had the following description of the Hoover's rather extraordinary life style that included a vacation home in the Caribbean, a large brokerage account, and other personal assets.

The Hoovers later agreed to turn over $5.5 million in assets to the SEC. The SEC asked a federal judge to appoint a receiver to sell the former CEO's assets, including the vacation home in the Caribbean, a brokerage account, a custom motorcycle, Rolex watches, and upscale jewelry.

Bobbie Grant — Controller

Based on Grant's 2012 SEC Administrative Hearing the controller, age 35, was a certified public accountant. The SEC alleged that the controller, at the direction of Alan Nixon and on her own accord, was engaged in the fraud scheme. The result was false and misleading financial statements for 2006 and 2007. The SEC Administrative Hearing cited falsified journal entries, understating expenses, understating liabilities, and providing false information to Insignia's independent auditors. As a result of this SEC Administrative Hearing, Grant was suspended from appearing or practicing before the SEC as an accountant.

David Polk — Company Attorney

Based on the company attorney's 2012 SEC Administrative Hearing, David Polk, age 50, was an experienced attorney licensed to practice in multiple states. He served the company as an attorney to assist with SEC filings and other corporate matters. The SEC alleged first that Polk drafted two post-effective amendments and a supporting legal opinion that he knew or should have known contained false statements regarding the registration of millions of shares of Insignia stock; and second that Polk sold Insignia securities without a filed registration statement. The SEC suspended him from appearing or practicing before the SEC as an attorney. He can apply for reinstatement with the SEC after two years.

Insignia Auditors — Rigby Stevens., LLP

As the independent outside auditor, Rigby Stevens, LLP certified:

1. "That it had audited Insignia's financial statements in accordance with generally accepted auditing standards;
2. That it had planned and performed its audits "to obtain reasonable assurance about whether the financial statements are free of material misstatements";
3. That, in its opinion, the company's financial statements "present fairly, in all material respects, the financial position" of Insignia in conformity with generally accepted accounting principles; and that its audits provided "a reasonable basis for (its) opinions" (Sarbanes-Oxley Act of 2002, Sec. 302).

Rigby Stevens, LLP was named as a defendant in the class action claim filed against certain of Insignia's former officers and directors, its then external auditor, Rigby Stevens, LLP, and its stock transfer agent, Stock Registration, Inc., for violations of the SEC Act of 1934.

COMPANY BACKGROUND AND FORENSIC INFORMATION

COMPANY HISTORY

Alan Nixon, CEO, and Charles Hoover, former CEO, formed Health Care Staffing, Inc. in 2001. In 2004, a shell company called Insignia, Inc. (Insignia) was formed that never earned revenue or did business. In February 2005, Health Care Staffing, Inc. and Insignia performed a reverse merger. As a result, the new entity kept the name Insignia, Inc., and Health Care Staffing, Inc. became its subsidiary. Insignia then started operating exclusively in the health care staffing industry. Insignia was a publicly traded company and therefore was subject to SEC regulations.

When Nixon joined Insignia in 2005, Insignia's annual revenue was $3.5 million. By 2006, Nixon had managed to increase the company's revenue to over $40 million. One of the ways Nixon increased revenue was through acquiring small companies. The acquisitions were financed through a combination of Insignia stock, promissory notes, and cash. According to Form 8-K, Nixon held a Bachelor of Science (1998) in Business Administration degree from a large state university, and a Master's degree (2002) and a Doctoral degree (2003) from an Internet-based university. However, it was later confirmed that Nixon did attend the large state university but did not graduate with a Bachelor of Science degree. Nixon claimed to hold masters and doctoral degrees, but this online university is a known diploma mill, offering degrees over the Internet with no substantial work to be completed. According to the class action complaint filed in Federal District Court, Nixon owned 6,000,000 shares, or 22.5% of all common stock as of April 2006. Nixon became CEO in 2006.

Charles Hoover, former CEO, held the position from 2005 to 2006 while also serving as a Board member. Hoover never attended any of the Board meetings. As the CEO of a public company, there are certain burdens and responsibilities placed on CEOs, such as reviewing and verifying certain documents and signing them before they are filed. Hoover signed many documents without even reading them, let alone reviewing for accuracy. Additionally, Hoover's lack of understanding as to how the accounting system at Insignia worked made it extremely difficult to verify anything related to Insignia's finances.

Bobbie Grant served as controller for Insignia from 2005 through 2007. In 2006, she became a licensed CPA in the jurisdiction where Insignia's central office was located. Grant made false journal entries under the direction of Alan Nixon. As a CPA, she knew that the entries she made were incorrect and misleading. Her motivations were unclear, but the 2012 SEC Administrative Hearing stated that Grant not only made false journal entries at the request of the president and CEO, but that she also made false journal entries on her own initiative. The result was Insignia filing materially false and misleading financial statements in the company's annual and quarterly reports from 2005 through the first quarter of 2007. The company attorney, David Polk, was not an employee of Insignia, but provided services to Insignia from April 2006 to June 2007. Polk had been practicing law for nearly ten years prior to his services for Insignia. Polk also had credentials in securities regulation and his practice centered on financial securities. He filed forms for Insignia with the SEC that were later determined to be false. Polk was fined and enjoined from further violating Sections of the Securities Act of 1933 and ordered to pay disgorgement and prejudgment interest and a civil penalty while also suspending him from appearing or practicing before the Commission as an attorney for two years.

David Polk's involvement with Insignia began when the company needed to file post-effective amendments to some of its SEC filings. They intended to use the amendments as a way to register a new issue of stock, but regulations stated that the amendments could not be used for that purpose. They also reported the number of outstanding shares at $1 million less than it actually was. Additionally, the company attorney attached a legal opinion to the filings, which stated that he performed due diligence in preparing the forms. The class action complaint alleges that he was reckless in filing the forms because he knew, or should have known based on his title and experience, that what he was doing was wrong.

Ultimately, David Polk consented to an order permanently enjoining him from violating Sections 5(a), 5(c), 17(a)(2) and 17 (a)(3) of the Securities Act of 1933 as well as requiring him to pay disgorgement and prejudgment interest of $160,000 and a $20,000 civil penalty. He also agreed to settle a related administrative proceeding by consenting to the entry of an order suspending him from appearing or practicing before the Commission as an attorney for two years.

CEO Resignation and Class Action Lawsuit

Insignia appeared to be profitable and successful until August 2007 when Nixon suddenly announced his resignation. One day after Nixon announced his resignation, Insignia's stock price dropped by nearly 48%. A few days later, Insignia announced that it would be launching an investigation into a variety of accounts and transactions that seemed unusual. The stock price kept decreasing and subsequently led Insignia to file Chapter 7 bankruptcy. The SEC then filed civil charges against Nixon, Hoover, Grant, and Polk in 2011.

The Insignia Board of Directors generally consisted of three members after the merger: Alan Nixon, CEO/chairman, and two other individuals, Michael Shaw and Frank Young. Board members Shaw and Young were appointed by Nixon in 2006. The board held no annual meetings in 2005 or 2006, and public shareholders did not elect any directors.

According to the 2010 federal bankruptcy case for Insignia, as CEO and board chairman, Nixon had general authority to execute Shaw's signature on board-related documents. Therefore, Nixon had the power to execute documents on behalf of the majority of the board (two board members out of three). Nixon was directly involved in the fraud and served as board chairman during his entire time with Insignia. Bobbie Grant and David Polk, who were not board members, were also named as defendants. In the 2006 Proxy Statement, Shaw was discussed as having financial expertise in asset structuring, corporate structure finance, and multi-location profit centers.

A class action suit was filed in the United States District Court that alleged:

1. manipulations that enriched Nixon at the expense of the company ;
2. manipulations that artificially inflated Insignia's operating income and reported margins; and
3. manipulations that enabled Insignia to increase its borrowing, thus postponing the time when the company would run out of cash. This resulted in investors in Insignia common stock losing their investments.

The board members named as defendants in the class action suit included Nixon; Frank Young, member of the board of directors and chair of the Audit Committee; and Michael Shaw member of the board of directors and the Audit Committee. Others named in the suit included Jamie West, chief operating officer and acting CEO after the departure of Nixon; Rigby Stevens, LLP, the independent auditing firm; and Stock Registration, Inc., who failed to keep a proper accounting of the number of shares of stock issued by Insignia.

The class action complaint also noted that during 2005 and 2006, Insignia acquired six healthcare staffing companies as subsidiaries financed as follows:

- Subsidiary 1: December 2005, for $4 million cash, 300,000 shares of common stock, and assumption of $400,000 debt.
- Subsidiary 2: April 2006, for $13 million cash and 100,000 shares of common stock.
- Subsidiary 3: May 2006, for $250,000 and additional contingent payments.
- Subsidiary 4: June 2006, for $2 million cash, 700,000 shares of common stock , and additional contingent payments.
- Subsidiary 5: October 2006, for $6 million cash and 750,000 shares of common stock, with additional contingent payments to be made in stock.
- Subsidiary 6: November 2006, for $7 million cash, 200,000 shares of common stock, and assumption of $250,000 debt.

According to the class action suit, Insignia's reported revenue grew to over $40 million in 2006 from $3.5 million in 2005, and its disclosed market capitalization quintupled from $21 million on March 25, 2006, to $120 million on March 31, 2007. By the end of 2006, Insignia had over 300 corporate employees and 1,000 full time equivalent healthcare staffing professionals.

Nixon exercised immense power over the company as president of Insignia from February 2005 until his resignation in August 2007. He also served as CFO for the majority of his time as president, as well as CEO and board chairman from June 2006 until his resignation. Nixon was in complete control of Insignia during his employment. This control allowed him to direct funds out of Insignia for his personal benefit, improperly issue Insignia stock, and make false journal entries, which led to incorrect financial statements and SEC filings. Because of his control over the company, Nixon's actions constituted the largest part of the fraud and are discussed in greater detail below. Because Insignia was under $75 million in sales, it did not need an internal control report from its external auditors per SOX regulations. However, the external auditors still had to review internal control in order to determine the appropriate audit procedures needed to support the client's financial statements when rendering their audit opinion on this publicly-held company. This issue will be explored in a discussion question involving the auditor's role.

KEY ISSUES

FALSIFIED JOURNAL ENTRIES

During his time as CEO period, Nixon personally made entries for payroll accounts into the Insignia's computer system. Nixon also had administrative access to the computers of all employees at company headquarters, giving Nixon the opportunity to alter or delete employees' documents, without their knowledge. The suit claims that the other defendants were aware that Nixon served as the only internal control at the company, and no one made any effort to determine whether his reports to the other defendants were verified independently.

Insignia payroll software correctly recorded the amount withheld from each paycheck as a liability of Insignia and the entries included a credit to a payroll tax liability account. However, the payroll tax liability was later reduced by an offsetting entry to the "Alan Nixon loan" account. The effect of this misclassifying journal entry was to eliminate the payroll taxes payable balance by reclassifying them as amounts owed to Nixon. These reclassified amounts originating as payroll liabilities, appeared in Insignia's published financial statements for the quarter ended June 30, 2006, as a related party loan of $1.5 million without further explanation. By September 30, 2006, the related party loan to Nixon was $3.5 million and was $3 million at December 31, 2006, with this reduction in loan amount in the fourth quarter due to payments to Nixon. The loans were undocumented and had no interest.

Nixon made, and directed the controller to make, a number of fraudulent journal entries to Insignia's books. Rather than debiting the proper expense account, Nixon would debit a liability account called Loan Related Party. This account represented the loan from Nixon to Insignia. Due to the false entries, Insignia's financial statements led the reader to believe that Insignia was paying down a liability when it was actually incurring expenses by debiting a liability instead of debiting an expense. These entries made both the balance sheet and income statement appear healthier than they actually were. The pair also ran expenses through the Additional Paid-In Capital (APIC) account decreasing APIC. Although Nixon decided to book a lot of expenses to the wrong accounts, there were also expenses that were not placed on the books at all. These missing entries related mainly to the expenses of issuing stock to employees. All of the expense-related false journal entries led the annual reports to understate expenses by up to 1,500 percent during the years Nixon was in control.

When Insignia encountered a liability, such as payroll taxes, Nixon would record the liability into the Loan Related Party account rather than the correct liability account. When Insignia's external auditors, Rigby Stevens, LLP, questioned the large balance in a liability account titled Payroll Clearing, Nixon made a back-dated entry to move $1 million from the Payroll Clearing account to the Loan Related Party account. After making that entry, Nixon and the controller still signed a Management Representation Letter stating, among other things, they did not know of any fraud in the financial statements.

MISAPPROPRIATION OF ASSETS

Nixon also used false journal entries to allow him to pull money out of Insignia for himself. The entries to the Loan Related Party account that were discussed above made it appear that Insignia owed Nixon $3.1 million more than it actually did. He also pocketed $3.3 million by personally selling stock to investors and keeping the money for himself. Nixon also appeared to be selling his own stock in Insignia to a hedge fund, but he was actually issuing new stock to the hedge fund. This allowed payments from the hedge fund to be deposited to his personal bank account. In total, Nixon was able to steal $6.5 million dollars from Insignia over a period of approximately two and half years.

SECURITIES FRAUD

Form S-8 is required to be filed with the SEC to register newly issued shares of a company but no audit of an S-8 is required. When filing Form S-8, a stock issuer incorporates by reference, the audited financial statements of its Form 10K. The issuer may include the accountant's consent to use the accountant's report either directly or indirectly in the registration statement as an exhibit or via incorporation by reference to a consent filed with the Form 10K.

When Insignia issued new shares, Nixon provided false information on the forms regarding the number of shares and to whom the shares were being issued. Nixon and Hoover both signed off on these forms asserting that the information being provided was accurate, although they knew the information was incorrect. They also signed off on the quarterly and annual forms, which grossly misrepresented the number of shares outstanding.

The independent auditing firm of Rigby Stevens, LLP had accepted Nixon's verbal explanation. Rigby Stevens did not review the reclassifying journal entries in detail. If they had, they would have seen adjustments to the payroll tax liability account on the same day there were adjustments to the loan account.

Insignia paid over $2.5 million to Nixon during the first quarter of 2007. The ending balance of the loan account dropped to $1 million by March 31, 2007. There were over $4.5 million of unpaid payroll tax liability assessments from the IRS found in Nixon's office when he resigned. In the February 2008 federal bankruptcy filing, Insignia cited tax liabilities, penalties, and interest of $7 million.

IMPROPER ACCOUNTING FOR ISSUED SHARES

Insignia, Inc. December 31, 2006 annual report stated that Insignia had 45,000,000 shares outstanding. Stock Registration, Inc. was responsible for the stockholder registration list. The Stock Registration list stated that there were several million additional shares outstanding. Stock Registration, Inc. sent Nixon the correct registration list in an Excel file. Nixon edited the Excel file, and reduced the number of shares outstanding. Nixon then provided the edited list to the independent auditors. Rigby Stevens, LLP did not independently verify the number of shares outstanding by obtaining the official list from Stock Registration, Inc., as required by AU Section 326.21(a). Rigby Stevens, LLP should have obtained the official registration list and compared it with the data provided for the Insignia financial statements. Not doing so was a serious departure from generally accepted auditing standards.

The plaintiffs in the class action suit believed that the unreported shares were sold by Nixon on the open market. Under AU Section 316.85, inadequate segregation of duties should have alerted the auditor to the opportunity for the misappropriation of assets.

SOX SECTION 302 FALSE FINANCIAL STATEMENTS AND FALSE CERTIFICATIONS

There were multiple instances of securities fraud including:

1. Booking $1,000,000 in additional revenue by debiting accounts receivable and crediting revenue from a nonexistent reality television show.
2. In the first quarter 2007, inappropriately reporting income from operations from the exercise of stock warrants.
3. Increasing the debt borrowing limit with Cap Source by providing false certification of income. Insignia then borrowed close to the maximum new debt borrowing limit.
4. Filing false Form 8-K, Form 10-QSB, and Form IO-KSB with the SEC, and misleading the investing public.

5.   Nixon signing false financial statement certifications under SOX, including Form 8-K, Form 10-QSB, and Form IO-KSB.

Based on AU Section 316.85 A.2, "Opportunities," subsection b, Rigby Stevens, LLP should have been alerted to the risk associated with the lack of separation of duties and the consolidation of authority in one individual. The class action law suit alleges that Rigby Stevens knew of misrepresentations in Nixon's educational history and that the certifications included misrepresentations. The class action suit states that the auditing firm was reckless in failing to make themselves aware of clear deficiencies in Insignia's internal controls, especially related to Nixon.

Information released to the public on August 16, 2007, caused an immediate drop in the price of Insignia stock from $3.50 per share to $2.35 per share on volume of over 20,000,000 shares. Investors who contacted Insignia between August 16 and 19, received false reassurances that the company was financially stable despite the resignation of Nixon. However, Nixon, at the time of his resignation, had a personal brokerage account worth over $40 million with more than half of it in Insignia stock.

SOX SECTION 404 INTERNAL CONTROLS

SOX Section 404 states that each annual report required by the SEC must contain an internal control report. Each public accounting firm that prepares or issues the audit report shall attest to, and report on, the required internal control assessment made by management. The standards for performing the attest function shall be made in accordance with standards of attestation adopted by the Public Company Accounting oversight board (PCAOB). The text of Section 404 is as follows:

SEC. 404. MANAGEMENT ASSESSMENT OF INTERNAL CONTROLS

(a) Rules REQUIRED

.—The Commission shall prescribe rules requiring each annual report required by section 13(a) or 15(d) of the Securities Exchange Act of 1934 (15 U.S.C. 78m or 78o(d)) to contain an internal control report, which shall—

(1) state the responsibility of management for establishing and maintaining an adequate internal control structure and procedures for financial reporting; and

(2) contain an assessment, as of the end of the most recent fiscal year of the issuer, of the effectiveness of the internal control structure and procedures of the issuer for financial reporting.

(b) INTERNAL CONTROL EVALUATION AND REPORTING.—With respect to the internal control assessment required by subsection (a), each registered public accounting firm that prepares or issues the audit report for the issuer shall attest to, and report on, the assessment made by the management of the issuer. An attestation made under this subsection shall be made in accordance with standards for attestation engagements issued or adopted by the Board. Any such attestation shall not be the subject of a separate engagement

AUDITOR RESPONSIBILITIES

The auditor of Insignia was Rigby Stevens, LLP. In the April 21, 2008, class action complaint filed in U.S. District Court Rigby Stevens, LLP was named as a defendant along with Insignia former officers for misrepresenting the financial condition of Insignia through the SEC filings. There were three general categories of fraud identified in the class action complaint as interconnected frauds that ultimately resulted in Insignia common stock investors losing their investments:

1. Manipulation that enriched former CEO Andy Nixon at the expense of the company.
2. Manipulation that artificially inflated Insignia's operating income and reported margins; and
3. Manipulation that enabled Insignia to increase its borrowing, thus postponing the time when the company would run out of cash.

The Rigby Stevens CPA firm provides tax, audit, and consulting services on a regional basis in Florida. The audit fees charged by Rigby Stevens, LLP to Insignia were not disclosed at the time of publication of this case study.

In a Form 8-K/A filed with the SEC on August 30, 2005, the company announced that its former auditors, Rigby Stevens, LLP discussed audit difficulties with the Audit Committee of Insignia. Rigby Stevens, LLP informed the Audit Committee of difficulties it had encountered in performing the audit of Insignia's financial statements for the year ended December 31, 2006, regarding the untimely receipt of documents, including asset acquisition documents, board of directors' resolutions, and confirmations from management. The filed Form 8-K/A stated that despite encountering these difficulties, Rigby Stevens' reports on Insignia's financial statements did not contain an adverse opinion or a disclaimer of opinion.

FINAL THOUGHTS

The four defendants all agreed to settlements for their civil charges that involved repaying the amount of money that they received from their involvement in the fraud. Nixon's settlement included a ban from being an officer or director of a public company and to pay back the $6.5 million of funds he stole from the company plus interest. Hoover's settlement included paying $5.5 million plus interest and a $100,000 civil penalty, as well as a ban from being an officer or director of a public company. Grant's settlement included a permanent injunction and paying $400,000 plus interest. Polk agreed to pay $160,000 plus interest and a $20,000 civil penalty, as well as settling an action banning him from appearing before the SEC as counsel for two years. Based on their individual financial positions at the time of settlement, Nixon's and Grant's payments were waived. Thus, the financial penalty was reduced based on inability to pay.

However, Nixon still had to pay $40,000 to one former Insignia shareholder. This shareholder was the only person who took action seeking repayment of his losses. Once the civil charges were settled, some of the defendants still had pending criminal charges. In April 2014, Grant was sentenced to five years' probation for her role in the fraud. On December 4, 2014, Nixon was sentenced to 130 months in prison, beginning January 1, 2014. Upon his release, he will have to serve three years' probation. Although this fraud was estimated to have cost investors well over $200 million, the court reduced this amount to $40 million based on inability to repay. One of the reasons for Nixon's reduced sentence is that he cooperated with prosecutors and aided the bankruptcy trustees in reinventing Insignia under a new name. When asked why he committed the fraud, Nixon's response was simply that he wanted to appear successful.

DISCUSSION QUESTIONS

1. Describe Nixon's actions in terms of the fraud triangle.

2. Discuss the requirements of AU Section 316, "Consideration of Fraud in a Financial Statement Audit." Discuss the role of the auditor in the case of Insignia, Inc. under AU Section 316.

3. A lot of the fraudulent transactions were run through the Loan Related Party account. What audit procedures under AU Section 334 should have been performed in evaluating related party transactions? In your opinion, should the external auditors have discovered the fraud through the Loan Related Party account?

4. One reason that the Insignia fraud could occur was due to nearly nonexistent internal controls. SOX was passed in 2003, and companies were required to be in compliance for fiscal year 2005, which is when the Insignia fraud ended. What constitutes an effective system of internal control as it relates to the requirements of Section 404? Who is responsible for establishing internal controls?

CASE STUDY 30:

The Valuation of Economic Damages*

James A. DiGabriele, Ph.D., CPA, CVA, CFF, ABV, CFE
Peter L. Lohrey, Ph.D., CVA, CDBV
Montclair State University

LEARNING OBJECTIVES

After completing and discussing this case, you should be able to understand:

- Learn how to calculate economic damages.
- Appreciate the importance of litigation services.
- Understand how to gather personal injury information.
- Defend a fundamental valuation of economic damages.

INTRODUCTION

A litigation support service that forensic accountants provide is estimating economic damages due to an injury. Preparing a valuation of economics damages embraces a unique confluence of accounting, economics, and finance. The analysis of the loss of earning capacity for individuals arises from a variety of legal cases involving the need to estimate financial damages due to personal injury, employment discrimination, wrongful termination, and wrongful death. The different types of economic damages cases share common fundamental elements in estimating an individual's loss of earnings, but they are differentiated by methodological variations in the damage estimate itself.

For example, economic damages due to a personal injury would most likely include estimated lost earnings, lost fringe benefits, lost household services, and medical expenses. Wrongful death calculations, however, would be reduced by the decedent's personal consumption over their projected lifetime – and this would reduce the residual damages for the heirs. On the other hand, employment discrimination or wrongful termination proceedings valuation of damages would include the estimated time a plaintiff would need to catch up to the previous earnings.

The most common approach to gathering the necessary information to calculate these losses is through a fact-finding questionnaire, interview, or a letter of request. The needed information usually includes:

- Personal information such as the date of injury, level of education, marital status, race, age, and dependents.
- Pre-injury/death employment and earnings.
- Fringe benefits received.
- Post injury earnings and the likelihood of future employment.
- Household services provided before the injury/death and after the injury/death.

The objective of this case study is to illustrate the application of how to estimate personal economic damage calculations. This case estimates the value of economic damages due to a personal injury. The next section introduce the facts of the case.

CASE SUMMARY

The focus of this case is to provide a fundamental valuation of economic damages due to a personal injury. The aim is to restore the injured party to the position he or she would have otherwise been in had the injury not occurred.

The facts of the case are as follows: Jane Doe suffered an injury on 06/30/X1 at the age of 44.50. Due to the gravity of her injuries she had to quit her job at *Company A* immediately. She remained out of work until six months later when she was able to secure a new job that accommodated her disability at *Company B* on 01/01/X2.

Prior to Jane Doe's injury, her annual salary at *Company A* was $30,000, and her wages were growing annually at the average rate of inflation (3.35%). In addition to Jane Doe's base salary, she also received fringe benefits (e.g., health insurance, social security) in the amount of 14.50% of her base salary.

During the six months that Jane Doe was unemployed she did not receive any remuneration (i.e., short-term disability, unemployment). Jane Doe secured an alternate job at *Company B* on 01/01/X2 that catered to her permanent physical limitations. Her annual salary at *Company B* was $19,500. Her salary at *Company B* was expected to grow at the average rate of inflation (3.35%). In addition to her base salary at *Company B* she received limited benefits in the amount of 10.50% of her base salary.

ASSIGNMENT

A law firm has hired you as the forensic accountant to prepare a calculation of economic damages due to the injury that Jane Doe sustained. For purposes of this assignment, the following guidance and assumptions have been provided:

1. Despite Jane Doe's injury, she expects to continue working until the age of 65. Your objective is to calculate the economic damages that Jane Doe will experience over her work-life expectancy (age 65) due to lost wages and benefits.

2. Published statistics illustrate that Jane Doe's life expectancy, based on her age and education, is 85 years of age.

3. As a result of Jane Doe's injury, she can no longer perform household services. Legal counsel has asked you to calculate the amount of economic damages needed to replace the loss of household services over Jane Doe's remaining life expectancy.

4. Jane Doe's trial date is scheduled on the two-year anniversary of her injury. Economic damages calculated from that date forward will need to be discounted to present value.

Enclosure A - Economic Damage Assumptions	
Name of Injured	Jane Doe
Sex	Female
Date of Personal Injury	June 30, XXX1
Age at Date of Personal Injury	Age - 44.50
Age at Date of Trial	Age - 46.50
Worklife Expectancy	Age - 65.00
Life Expectancy	Age - 85.00
Growth Rate	3.35%
Tax Rate	25.65%
Benefits as a % of Annual Salary	
Company A	14.50%
Company B	10.50%
Risk of Unemployment	4.80%
Discount Rate (Risk-Free Rate of Return)	4.50%
Income	
Wages: Annual Salary at Company A (Pre-Injury)	$ 30,000.00
Wages: Annual Salary at Company B (Post-Injury)	$ 19,500.00
Household Replacement (Average per/hr)	
Food Preparation / Housekeeping Workers (Average per/hr)	$ 14.50
Replacement Hours per year (10 hours p/week x 52 weeks)	520 Hours
Annual Household Replacement Cost (520 x $14.50)	$ 7,540.00
Present Value Formula:	$\dfrac{Net\ Economic\ Damages}{(1 + Discount\ Rate)^{Time\ From\ Date\ of\ Trial}}$

ENCLOSURE B - PROJECTED INCOME
PRE INJURY EARNING CAPACITY BEFORE DISCOUNTING

Period by Age		(a) Projected Gross Wages	(b) Taxes	(c) Fringe Benefits	(d) Net Economic Benefit	(e) Risk of Unemployment	(f) Projected Income Age 44.50 - 65.00 *Before Discounting*
From	To						
44.50	45.00	$ -	$ -	$ -	$ -	$ -	$ -
45.00	46.00	-	-	-	-	-	-
46.00	46.50	-	-	-	-	-	-
46.50	47.00	-	-	-	-	-	-
47.00	48.00	-	-	-	-	-	-
48.00	49.00	-	-	-	-	-	-
49.00	50.00	-	-	-	-	-	-
50.00	51.00	-	-	-	-	-	-
51.00	52.00	-	-	-	-	-	-
52.00	53.00	-	-	-	-	-	-
53.00	54.00	-	-	-	-	-	-
54.00	55.00	-	-	-	-	-	-
55.00	56.00	-	-	-	-	-	-
56.00	57.00	-	-	-	-	-	-
57.00	58.00	-	-	-	-	-	-
58.00	59.00	-	-	-	-	-	-
59.00	60.00	-	-	-	-	-	-
60.00	61.00	-	-	-	-	-	-
61.00	62.00	-	-	-	-	-	-
62.00	63.00	-	-	-	-	-	-
63.00	64.00	-	-	-	-	-	-
64.00	65.00	-	-	-	-	-	-

(a)   Projected gross wages that Jane Doe would have earned, but for the injury, would have grown each year by the average rate of inflation.

(b)   Jane Doe's effective tax rate, which includes Federal, State, Social Security & Medicare taxes, would have reduced her gross wages had an injury not occurred.

(c)   Working condition fringe benefits that Company A would have provided to Jane Doe, but for the injury, would have been in addition to her gross wages.

(d)   The net economic benefit that Jane Doe would have earned, but for her injury, represents her gross wages adjusted for taxes and employer provided, working condition fringe benefits. The net economic benefit represents the income stream that would be subject to loss in the event of unemployment, had an injury not occurred, and had she remained employed with Company A.

(e)   The risk of unemployment for private industry workers in the same field as Jane Doe (Company A & Company B are in the same industry) have an unemployment rate that you derived from the US Department of Labor Statistics. The risk of unemployment reduces the net economic benefit.

(f)   The net economic benefit adjusted for the risk of unemployment represents the income that Jane Doe was projected to earn through worklife expectancy had she not suffered from a personal injury.

ENCLOSURE C - PROJECTED INCOME
POST INJURY EARNING CAPACITY BEFORE DISCOUNTING

Period by Age		(a) Projected Gross Wages	(b) Taxes	(c) Fringe Benefits	(d) Net Economic Benefit	(e) Risk of Unemployment	(f) Projected Income Age 44.50 - 65.00 *Before Discounting*
From	**To**						
44.50	45.00	$ -	$ -	$ -	$ -	$ -	$ -
45.00	46.00	-	-	-	-	-	-
46.00	46.50	-	-	-	-	-	-
46.50	47.00	-	-	-	-	-	-
47.00	48.00	-	-	-	-	-	-
48.00	49.00	-	-	-	-	-	-
49.00	50.00	-	-	-	-	-	-
50.00	51.00	-	-	-	-	-	-
51.00	52.00	-	-	-	-	-	-
52.00	53.00	-	-	-	-	-	-
53.00	54.00	-	-	-	-	-	-
54.00	55.00	-	-	-	-	-	-
55.00	56.00	-	-	-	-	-	-
56.00	57.00	-	-	-	-	-	-
57.00	58.00	-	-	-	-	-	-
58.00	59.00	-	-	-	-	-	-
59.00	60.00	-	-	-	-	-	-
60.00	61.00	-	-	-	-	-	-
61.00	62.00	-	-	-	-	-	-
62.00	63.00	-	-	-	-	-	-
63.00	64.00	-	-	-	-	-	-
64.00	65.00	-	-	-	-	-	-

(a)   Jane Doe secured alternate employment six months after her injury earning lesser wages. Those wages are projected to grow each year by the average rate of inflation through Jane Doe's worklife expectancy.

(b)   Jane Doe's effective tax rate, which includes Federal, State, Social Security & Medicare taxes, reduces her gross wages.

(c)   Working condition fringe benefits that Company B is projected to provide Jane Doe are in addition to her gross wages.

(d)   The net economic benefit that Jane Doe is projected to earn/receive with Company B represents her gross wages adjusted for taxes and employer provided, working condition fringe benefits. The net economic benefit represents the income stream that would be subject to loss in the event of unemployment.

(e)   The risk of unemployment for private industry workers in the same field as Jane Doe (Company A & Company B are in the same industry) have an unemployment rate that you derived from the US Department of Labor Statistics. The risk of unemployment reduces the net economic benefit.

(f)   The net economic benefit adjusted for the risk of unemployment represents the income that Jane Doe is projected to earn through her worklife with her alternate employment at Company B.

ENCLOSURE D - HOUSEHOLD REPLACEMENT COST
BEFORE DISCOUNTING

Period by Age		(a) Cost to Replace HouseHold Services
From	To	
44.50	45.00	$ -
45.00	46.00	-
46.00	46.50	-
46.50	47.00	-
47.00	48.00	-
48.00	49.00	-
49.00	50.00	-
50.00	51.00	-
51.00	52.00	-
52.00	53.00	-
53.00	54.00	-
54.00	55.00	-
55.00	56.00	-
56.00	57.00	-
57.00	58.00	-
58.00	59.00	-
59.00	60.00	-
60.00	61.00	-
61.00	62.00	-
62.00	63.00	-
63.00	64.00	-
64.00	65.00	-
65.00	66.00	-
66.00	67.00	-
67.00	68.00	-
68.00	69.00	-
69.00	70.00	-
70.00	71.00	-
71.00	72.00	-
72.00	73.00	-
73.00	74.00	-
74.00	75.00	-
75.00	76.00	-
76.00	77.00	-
77.00	78.00	-
78.00	79.00	-
79.00	80.00	-
80.00	81.00	-
81.00	82.00	-
82.00	83.00	-
83.00	84.00	-
84.00	85.00	-

(a)
On average, prior to her injury, Jane Doe performed approximately 10 hours per week on household tasks. After her injury, Jane Doe could no longer perform any of her household tasks. You researched the Occupational Employment Statistics Survey which publishes mean hourly wages for household workers in the same county that Jane Doe resides. Each year, the replacement cost is projected to grow by the average rate of inflation.

ENCLOSURE E - TOTAL ECONOMIC DAMAGES
PAST & FUTURE ECONOMIC DAMAGES (DISCOUNTED TO THE TRIAL DATE)

Period by Age		(a) Projected Income Pre Injury	(b) Projected Income Post Injury	(c) HH Replacement Value	(d) Net Economic Damages	Time from the Date of Trial	(e) Economic Damages Discounted to the
From	To						
44.50	45.00	$ -	$ -	$ -	$ -		$ -
45.00	46.00	-	-	-	-		-
46.00	46.50	-	-	-	-		-
					Total Past Economic Damages (I):		$ -
46.50	47.00	-	-	-	-	0.50	-
47.00	48.00	-	-	-	-	1.50	-
48.00	49.00	-	-	-	-	2.50	-
49.00	50.00	-	-	-	-	3.50	-
50.00	51.00	-	-	-	-	4.50	-
51.00	52.00	-	-	-	-	5.50	-
52.00	53.00	-	-	-	-	6.50	-
53.00	54.00	-	-	-	-	7.50	-
54.00	55.00	-	-	-	-	8.50	-
55.00	56.00	-	-	-	-	9.50	-
56.00	57.00	-	-	-	-	10.50	-
57.00	58.00	-	-	-	-	11.50	-
58.00	59.00	-	-	-	-	12.50	-
59.00	60.00	-	-	-	-	13.50	-
60.00	61.00	-	-	-	-	14.50	-
61.00	62.00	-	-	-	-	15.50	-
62.00	63.00	-	-	-	-	16.50	-
63.00	64.00	-	-	-	-	17.50	-
64.00	65.00	-	-	-	-	18.50	-
65.00	66.00	-	-	-	-	19.50	-
66.00	67.00	-	-	-	-	20.50	-
67.00	68.00	-	-	-	-	21.50	-
68.00	69.00	-	-	-	-	22.50	-
69.00	70.00	-	-	-	-	23.50	-
70.00	71.00	-	-	-	-	24.50	-
71.00	72.00	-	-	-	-	25.50	-
72.00	73.00	-	-	-	-	26.50	-
73.00	74.00	-	-	-	-	27.50	-
74.00	75.00	-	-	-	-	28.50	-
75.00	76.00	-	-	-	-	29.50	-
76.00	77.00	-	-	-	-	30.50	-
77.00	78.00	-	-	-	-	31.50	-
78.00	79.00	-	-	-	-	32.50	-
79.00	80.00	-	-	-	-	33.50	-
80.00	81.00	-	-	-	-	34.50	-
81.00	82.00	-	-	-	-	35.50	-
82.00	83.00	-	-	-	-	36.50	-
83.00	84.00	-	-	-	-	37.50	-
84.00	85.00	-	-	-	-	38.50	-
					Total Future Economic Damages (II):		$ -
					Total Economic Damages to Jane Doe (I + II):		$ -

Enclosure F - Summary of Economic Damages Due to Personal Injury on June 30, XXX3 Jane Doe		
		Reference
Total Past Economic Damages	$	*Enclosure E*
Total Future Economic Damages (at Present Value)		*Enclosure E*
Total Economic Damages	$	*Enclosure E*

* Adapted from Vol. 8, No. 2, Special Issue, 2016 of *Journal of Forensic & Investigative Accounting.*

CASE STUDY 31:

Adding Mathematical Statistics to the Auditor's Tool Box

Eddward Herron, Ph.D., CPA, CFE
University of Wisconsin – La Crosse

Jack Knorr, Ph.D.
Eli Lilly

Joseph T. Kastantin, MBA, CPA, CMA, ACCA
University of Wisconsin – La Crosse

LEARNING OBJECTIVES

After completing and discussing this case, you should be able to:

- Formulate analytical audit procedures based on professional skepticism and the element of surprise that, together with "standard" audit procedures, may expose anomalous evidence.
- Illustrate how the timing of "standard" audit procedures, including analytic procedures applied to judgment sampling, introduces an element of surprise to the audit client.
- Outline a possible brainstorming session prior to commencing the audit and how revisiting the brainstorming sessions throughout the audit are useful to helping the auditors understand the entity and its environment and assess the risk of material misstatement.
- Defend the notion that relevant audit experience directly affects how an auditor or bank examiner applies professional judgment in selecting or designing analytic procedures during an audit or investigation.
- Calculate the Poisson, binomial, and T-Distribution results based on data provided in the case study.
- Understand and appreciate the ethical dilemmas in crime and punishment.

THE ANTOGONISTS

Lemay ("Lee") Johnson sat in his spacious, well-appointed office at the Southern State Bank feeling restless and bored. Lee had been a perennial honor student at the prestigious Gravois Academy, in Gravois, Mississippi. He was always one of the top three students in a highly competitive prep-school class, and had gone on to graduate with high honors in mathematics from Princeton. Those were the days when anything seemed possible; when fame and fortune were so seemingly inevitable. Given his intellectual abilities, he did not give the future a second thought. He did well financially, especially compared to others in his graduating class. However, he had always expected to be involved in more *intellectually* superior and challenging business, and gain the recognition so deserving of a self-perceived "genius."

Lee had spent his first 12 years after graduating from college at one of the more prominent investment banks in New York, where education and earnings far exceeded his expectations. However, according to co-workers, he eventually left the firm after realizing that "90% of all business is sales," and large sums of money became less satisfying. Thinking that he could find satisfaction working for himself, he returned home to Gravois, Mississippi, a wealthy suburb of Jackson, with the goal of owning a commercial bank. His former high-school classmates and best friends, Tesson ("Tess") Ford and John St. Claire, were similarly successful. However, Tess also yearned to do something more challenging. St. Claire was not displeased with any part of his life, but he enjoyed the adrenal rush of being "hyper-challenged."

Similar to Lee, they had all attended highly competitive preparatory high schools and Ivy League schools. Tess had gone to Brown University and John to Harvard University. Similarly, they each found substantial business success after graduating, but intellectual recognition had eluded them. Tess was especially annoyed by the lack of recognition. She had gone to work for a pharmaceutical company after college graduation, but she found that research was painfully slow. Instead, she gravitated toward marketing, at first, and then finance. The "dot com" craze intrigued her most, and she soon left the more staid corporate finance firm for untold riches in that arena. Before the dot com bubble burst, she became bored and began searching for another pursuit. She was the only female in the trio of competitor friends, had the highest IQ, and was the first of the group to join MENSA. Over the years, she became the de-facto leader among this group of risk takers, thus feeling compelled to always be moving forward.

John St. Claire was overtly competitive. To him, life was to be enjoyed however one found it, but challenge and risk were his drugs of choice. He had become wealthy, but the wealth only afforded him greater toys and opportunities. Personally, he liked to say that he could have found fun and adventure in life even if he had worked at the local automobile assembly plant in Gravois, though not nearly through such elaborate activities as he had grown accustomed to enjoying. Whatever the game, though, he was usually interested. Therefore, John decided to follow the others back to Gravois in search of fun and adventure.

After carefully analyzing all of their opportunities, Lee, Tess, and John decided to purchase controlling interest in the Southern State Bank, although hometown banking was far from their plan. Because both Lee and John had been investment bankers, they planned to grow the bank's off-balance sheet (OBS) activities through loan origination, sales, and servicing rights. Naturally, they also wanted to dive into more exotic OBS activities, at least to the extent permitted by regulatory guidelines. Tess, a venture capital success story, planned on growing a subsidiary in technology-based start-up businesses, which would increase the bank's loan growth, as well as gambling on equity stakes in the start-ups.

Those equity stakes, in turn, would allow Tess access to investee-company accounting and operation records, a highly desirable advantage when business owners may not have sufficient expertise to manage their own businesses. She knew that the number one cause of business failure was poor management and, with her abilities, she could minimize the likelihood of that occurring.

As time progressed, the trio planned to acquire controlling interests in other small and regional banks and then manage those acquisitions along the same business plan. They were confident in their abilities to manage and grow the institution into "a major player," at least regionally.

The initial purchase of the bank was not as smooth as anticipated. However, by utilizing a few takeover tactics learned over several years in the big leagues, the purchase was at least completed, although at somewhat more than budgeted projections for time and money. Those takeover tactics were a bit too hostile for some in the area, though, and would return to haunt the trio as they pursued holding company formation (Southern Bancshares) and expansion, as well as subsequent acquisitions. Progress generally went forward as planned, but always took much longer than expected, whether due to regulatory road blocks or longer periods of decision-making (or deliberate foot-dragging) by almost everyone.

The holding company's headquarters remained in Gravois, but the majority of operations were moved to nearby Jackson, Mississippi for commercial reasons. Within 10 years the bank had grown from $300 million in total assets to Bank Holding Company (BHC) assets of more than $2 billion. Its OBS portfolio had similarly, but more impressively, grown from a relatively small $50 million to more than $1 billion at the holding company level. But that was during the heyday of the sub-prime market. Thereafter, mortgagees began to default when interest-only loans began to amortize, and worsened when the economy began to slow. Of course, most of the loans had been sold off to the secondary market, but many had already started to default during the waiting period required prior to sale of the loans. Therefore, they had to be retained by the bank.

Additionally, the organization invested substantially in securities derived from mortgage and other securitized assets. They classified those investments as "trading" assets, even though they more likely should have been available-for-sale (AFS). The trading classification meant continually rising holding gains could be taken directly to the income statement, versus through other comprehensive income (OCI) if they'd been treated as AFS. Earnings grew rapidly, of course, at least until the housing bubble burst at which time gains quickly became losses. Fair value accounting, indeed, is a two-edged sword, so then trading asset losses also were to be taken directly to the income statement. Regardless, losses mounted and capital dwindled, but not to the point of insolvency, but enough to make the owners' relatively "deep pockets" considerably shallower. Worse, the downward slide put the brakes on their strategic growth plans. To an outsider, they were still doing well, but not as well from an overachiever's perspective.

The demise of rapid growth necessarily meant an increase in the mundane business of conservative management that, in turn, seemed to bring on a certain malaise. That condition, in turn, became a slippery-slope into crimes and misdemeanors. Now, four years later, no one remembered precisely how their so-called "mundane" lives became so complicated and adrenal-powered, so quickly, but everyone seemed to feed on it. Slowly, and seemingly unintentionally, at least at first, the trio of comrades would later confess finding themselves slipping into discussions of deception. It probably started during an after-hours bull session, as John would later recall, when "what-if" scenarios flowed in tandem with libations: What if, we did X? Would anyone even notice? What would (or could) likely happen if someone did Y? Would the auditors (or bank examiners) find out? What would they look for? How could we conceal our little diversions from them? After several sessions, John titled the game "What Are the Odds?" and the three became increasingly enthusiastic players.

However, those questions eventually led to live testing through actual small, then increasingly large shell games with bank supervisors and auditors to see if the supervisors and auditors were paying attention, or if they were even "up to playing the game," as Tess liked to say. Small games grew larger and more complex over time, until the complexity gave way to an overall scheme of simplicity, and the trio found that simple schemes were most effective in both operation and evasion. Profits from the schemes were little more than a scorecard; however, the exhilaration of living on the edge was its own reward, and becoming "richer than the government" certainly had its own perks.

THE AUDITORS

Federal Reserve Bank examiner Eddie Coello arrived at the Southern State Bank (SSB) in Gravois, Mississippi with his team to conduct an examination of the bank. Mr. Coello, a senior examiner, was the most experienced member of the eight-person team, which included another senior examiner, two mid-level examiners, and four junior teammates who were still being trained in basic examination procedures. It seemed like a good opportunity for training, and wasn't expected to be a difficult exam. Earnings, liquidity, asset quality, and capital were seemingly moderate-high, and external audit reports consistently reported unmodified opinions, with only a few recommendations for managerial attention. Those findings were impressive, but were especially comforting given the bank and BHC's historical growth.

The examination merely reflected the bank's position in the examination cycle, and the examination was scheduled for four weeks of onsite work, which was not a great deal of time or resources for a large institution. But then, it was a targeted examination aimed at asset quality. As a favor to his field manager, Coello agreed to take on a training assignment for three rookie Bank Secrecy

Act examiners. Those specialists needed to check for compliance with federal laws regulating the inflows and outflows of large currency transactions among other things. That favor, like many chance-opportunities or encounters, proved to be serendipitous.

SSB had been growing rapidly over the previous decade, mostly through acquisitions of smaller institutions, but also through higher than average commercial loan and off-balance sheet growth. Most of the growth had been funded through deposit growth, plus a couple of small equity offerings. The BHC had even outgrown its information technology (IT) system about three years before, so the old system was replaced and its parallel run was completed about two years before the current inspection. Coello and his team would probably focus on some basic safety-and-soundness procedures, especially in the high growth areas of lending, financing and OBS activities, as well as provide some much needed training on anti-money laundering/counter terrorist financing (AML/CFT).

Pre-examination analysis is routinely conducted to allow bank examiners (such as auditors) to acquire a better understanding of the bank and search for anomalies or inconsistencies in the financial data. A full week of number crunching disclosed little about SSB or Southern Bancshares, which, along with positive external audit reports, was giving Eddie a comfortable feeling about the institution. Additionally, several other examiners and auditors he knew relayed multiple positive descriptions about the owners, such as "brilliant," "financial geniuses," and "he explained the mathematics of those derivatives so simply."

High praise, indeed, but Coello had learned long ago to keep initially positive (or negative) feelings in check. As he perused the file for the bank examination he and his team were about to commence, he had to remind himself that, in spite of the impeccable records of Southern Bancshares, he could not allow cognitive biases, negative *or* positive, to lull his team away from their obligations to maintain professional skepticism throughout the examination. Indeed, Southern Bancshares seemed to have an extended history of strong performance. Furthermore, the three principals of the bank were reputed to be "geniuses," who maintained a high level of control over all aspects of the institution's operations. The information file in front of him presented a picture of banking perfection. "Perfection," he whispered to himself. "Perfection is a very difficult standard to maintain."

THE AUDIT

Initial meetings with the owners were amicable, and Coello's impressions merely confirmed the praises of colleagues in describing the three owners. John seemed to be truly a great person with whom to socialize, inviting the entire team onto his yacht down in the Gulf when the assignment ended. Coello politely declined for the team, but suggested a less extravagant golf outing, where the losers had only to pay for lunch. John St. Claire immediately accepted, but laughingly agreed only if Coello's team would play a "best ball" game. They shook hands on the agreement, and Coello noticed that the banker had a warm and overtly friendly manner. His handshake was less than aggressive, but sufficiently firm to convey sincerity. Additionally, his eye contact was constant but in a manner that suggested true interest in the other party.

Tesson Ford was as brilliant as described, but also friendly, though she was not as open as John. She was a bit more fidgety and apparently anxious to return to work, but was willing to have the examination proceed. Still, she invited all who were interested to follow her through a "routine" investment analysis about whether to fund a fledgling chemical company from Alabama. "It might be fun and educational to see how those decisions are made," she coyly said, "and, besides, I'd like to see if you have any talent for the analysis. You can't logically examine my work if you don't, after all." It was probably a combination of her superior reputation, coupled with a bit of teasing in her voice that allowed her to avoid creating ill-feelings. Besides, her demeanor was so unpretentious that no one seemed offended.

"I'll take you up on that after I get settled in," said senior examiner Lynne Kupcinet. "I've always wondered what it would be like to play God with small companies to determine who might survive or fail," also in an obviously kidding manner.

"But surely you do that with banks all the time?" replied Tess, in kind.

"Not exactly," responded Lynne, "I only analyze the information and let others decide. Besides, there's no danger of closing a bank unless it's on the brink of failing or engaged in criminal activities." The two were smiling at each other as if they were old, slightly competitive, sorority sisters.

"So, we are safe at SSB?" asked Tess.

"That's what we are here to determine," said Lynne.

"OK," said John, getting up from his own chair and raising the arms of both ladies as if at a boxing match, "I declare this a draw, at least for the time being." His joviality brought the meeting back from the edge of an awkward moment.

"Well," said Tess, "let's go have a cold drink and plan our work. I think I'm going to actually enjoy this examination."

"I hope so," replied Lynne, and the two left the meeting together.

"That was a near miss"! St. Claire said. Even Lee Johnson laughed. He didn't seem nearly as cordial or social as John, or even Tess. Eddie thought Lee was much more serious. "Quintessential nerd," he thought, as Lee addressed all the standard issues of initial meetings, such as questions about strategy, growth, the bank's (or BHC's) market share, risks, and stability.

Coello thought he seemed to approach those and other issues like a mathematician would—precisely, dourly, and in stark contrast to John St. Claire, unemotionally. Toward the end of their meeting, Coello challenged Lee on the veracity of his risk modeling. "You seem so confident," said Eddie, "What if you're wrong? What's the potential down-side?"

"Ah, yes" said Lee, 'What if?' You know, that is one of the three greatest questions! The others are 'Why?' and 'So what?' But to me 'what if' is the beginning of inquiry, or creativity itself."

Eddie was surprised to hear Lee open up, if even only briefly. He'd been so reticent until now, obliging answers to all questions but always in a curt, precise, analytic manner. Now, it seemed, he was on the verge of . . . *philosophy*?

Lee continued, "Do you play chess?"

"A bit," replied Coello. "WHAT IF, I move a particular piece to a particular place? What chain of events will *probably* ensue? WHY did I move that piece? In other words, what was my strategy, and how did that particular move fit with that plan? SO WHAT? In other words, what is the likely or probable outcome of my strategic maneuverings? You see? It's all chess and chess is strategy, and strategy is based on probability!" Now he was, indeed, enthusiastic.

"Now you've done it," said a laughing John St. Claire. "He won't get any serious work done for the rest of the day, and neither will you if you stay on the subject of probability. The participants all laughed along with St. Claire, and even Lee Johnson was a little bemused by his own enthusiasm.

"I suppose John's right," he admitted. "But life is a series of probability estimates, nothing more or less, and those best able to model life should be the most successful and revered," Lee added.

Examiner Coello enjoyed the repartee, but added "You all seem to be the best of friends and to a degree I haven't seen much in life. How does that affect your business decisions? Is there a natural or decided leader?"

"We take turns at times," answered Lee, "and we divide up the rest. You're right in noticing that we're very close, very tight."

"Like the skin on a drum," added St. Claire. "We can kid around, we can be serious, we can talk to each other about *literally* anything, and everything we say to each other is seriously considered by the others. We're always in each other's corner, though, no matter what!"

"But," continued Coello, "how do you handle disagreements?"

The two looked at each other for a moment, and then St. Claire shrugged and said "We don't. If it's meaningful to any one of us, it's meaningful to all of us, no exceptions."

Coello challenged them, "Even if the decision is obviously bad in some way?"

"Without exception," replied St. Claire. "The biggest 'deal' to being rich, if I can use that term, is that we can afford to make mistakes and we can also afford our friends' mistakes."

"Agreed," said Lee Johnson. "Wealth provides us with the capital to take risks and possibly make mistakes. After all, that's what capital is, risk-funding. Otherwise, it serves no special purpose."

The meeting concluded shortly thereafter, and the team left to meet with functional managers for the respective areas of their work. Eddie Coello had found the meeting very cordial and informative. He had learned a good deal about the bank's standard examination issues (e.g., risk management, strategy), but also about the three majority owners.

FUNDS AND FUNDING ANOMALIES

Eddie Coello had a simple formula for examining banks. His four-point program was to check the veracity (i.e., reality) of:

1. Balances (including tie-ins and calculations);
2. Transactions (including tie-ins and calculations);
3. Presentations (including notes); and
4. Controls (overall and at various levels within the same area).

Even though Coello was a bank examiner, he was also a certified public accountant (CPA), so his four-point program paralleled the independent auditor's guidance in AU-C Section 315, primarily because of the large overlap of work performed by external, internal, and regulatory auditors. Most importantly, the purpose and use of data gathered are the primary separators of various types of audits and auditors, not necessarily the employer. Additionally, Coello, who had various types of auditor experience, would regularly remind his subordinates that regulatory auditors could always learn from their internal or external audit colleagues.

Regardless of the area, though, he stressed "detection of anomalies" so that limited sampling resources could be better used within limited boundaries surrounding those anomalies. AU-C Section 520, "Analytical Procedures," and AU-C Section 530, "Audit Sampling," address the independent auditor's responsibilities to plan, design, and carry out procedures, including the use of sampling techniques, throughout the audit.

AU-C Section 520 defines analytical procedures as: "Evaluations of financial information through analysis of plausible relationships among both financial and nonfinancial data. Analytical procedures also encompass such investigation, as is necessary, of identified fluctuations or relationships that are inconsistent with other relevant information or that differ from expected values by a significant amount." So, an exception (or, anomalous data) could be included in sampling parameters rather than spreading the sampling resources over a wide-range of data (which often was not anomalous in any respect). This sort of data profiling was essentially stratification on the basis of discovered anomalies, which usually meant more strata than is usually considered (or even envisioned) in regulatory or financial auditing.

AU-C Section 530 defines stratification as: "The process of dividing a population into subpopulations, each of which is a group of sampling units that have similar characteristics."

Aside from standard training procedures, Coello also had a standard technique that seemed to help young AML/CTF compliance auditors pare down the voluminous data through which they would ordinarily sift (looking for patterns or exceptions in the inflows and outflows of funds above and below $10,000). The three trainees were Mary Barnes, Joel Franklin, and Becca Malone. They met Coello in a corner of the main bank branch lobby, which housed 10 teller windows. The main branch was an original bank building from the 1930s, complete with marble, tile, high ceilings, ornamentation, and a giant bank vault door housed behind the teller windows of that era.

After reviewing the standard procedures for their work, Coello instructed the trainees simply to "observe teller operations at different times over the next two or three days in a pattern of similar time windows. For example, make your observations in one- or two-hour increments at the same time periods during the day. Choose among yourselves who will observe which tellers, but periodically switch with others so that by the time you are finished observing, everyone has observed each teller roughly an equal number of times, at different times during the day."

"But why?" asked Joel. "What's the point?"

"The usual procedure is to scan teller logs for dollar amounts, and that's what everyone expects you to do," replied Coello. "You should learn to periodically change the nature of your procedures, either by doing something different or at least changing the way you'd typically do the same work, to retain some amount of an element of surprise." This is similar to what independent auditors are supposed to do in response to risk assessment procedures, in accordance with AU-C Section 240, "Performing Audit Procedures in Response to Assessed Risks," and AU-C Section 330, "Evaluating the Audit Evidence Obtained."

"What is surprising about observing tellers?" asked Becca.

"Would you expect it?" Coello asked, rhetorically. "Afterwards, we'll compare what we observe to what the teller logs tell us. For now, we are only interested in how many transactions each teller processes, plus how much time is used to process each transaction and, literally, anything else that catches your eye as unusual (under the circumstances) or is seemingly out of place."

"But won't teller times differ with the types of transactions?" asked Mary.

"Sure," said their trainer, "but generally not by much. Besides, they'll process so many transactions that a good deal of the differential will be smoothed out." The three went off to discuss their schedule of teller observations, plus the usual work of pulling teller logs and scanning for numeric anomalies.

On the third day, Coello called the three trainees to discuss their observations and other work tasks. As there were 10 teller windows operating most of the day, except for lunch and break periods, he explained to the trainees that customers using the lobby tellers (overall) would likely choose a teller on a random basis. Consequently, he expected the average and median number of transactions to be roughly equal.

"And that's pretty much what we found," said Becca. "The average number of currency transactions processed over a two-hour time block sample was about 30."

"Were there any significant deviations from that average?" Coello inquired.

"Only one," Joel quickly chimed in, "but I vote that she gets a pass!"

"Why is that, Joel?" his trainer asked.

Mary said, "He thinks that one teller should be exempt from scrutiny because she looks like a model."

Joel jumped in, "She's so incredibly beautiful! Honestly, she could be a model of some sort, and here she is working in the bank and as a teller!"

Coello considered the situation for a moment, and then asked "Well, Joel, what would you expect to observe in her work habits given her obvious appearance?"

"Easy. Truly beautiful people have an easier life than the rest of us. So, I wouldn't expect such a beautiful woman to work as a bank teller. Next, I certainly wouldn't expect her to be so productive."

"Productive?" Coello asked.

"Yeah, she was about *twice* as productive as any other teller."

"And why is that an anomaly?" Coello asked.

"Because the truly beautiful people of the world don't have to work as hard as the rest of us, not usually anyway," Joel stated in a matter-of-fact manner.

"Well," Coello said, "You may or may not be correct in your analysis of 'the beautiful people' of the world, about where they are likely to work or how productive they may be. I don't have the data to say for certain one way or the other, but you *are* correct in recognizing that it seems anomalous. That's an important part of being an auditor of any type," he continued, "to identify anomalies. More importantly, it is *very* interesting that this particular teller, or anyone for that matter, completed double the average number of transactions during your sample window. That is something for which we can assign a number. You did verify your observations with data from the teller logs?"

"Absolutely," Joel replied, "twice in fact, since I couldn't believe it the first time."

PROBABILITY MODELS AND AUDITING

At that time, Coello went on to explain that there are probability models auditors may use to determine whether something (an activity, an amount of time, or some similar data) is likely to be true when compared to the average. Coello added, "Let me show you some simple models where you can plug in a few numbers and let the model work for you."

The trainer went on to explain the concepts of elementary probability, probability models, and probability distributions. "Probability is the chance that something will happen or, the likelihood that some event will happen. Sometimes you can measure **probability** with a number, such as referring to "a 10% chance" of rain. Other times you can use words such as impossible, unlikely, possible, even chance, likely, more likely than not, and virtually certain.

In *probability and statistics*, a **probability distribution** assigns a *probability* to each of the possible outcomes of a random *experiment*, such as randomly choosing one of 10 marbles from a box. In that case, the probability distribution would assign a 10% probability that any one marble would be selected. A **probability model** allows us to use the information in a probability distribution, as long as the requirements, or assumptions, are met. For example, if the **event** (i.e., possible outcome) is random or not, whether each of the data points is independent of the others, etc."

Coello explained that one particular probability distribution, known as the Poisson distribution, may be especially useful in the present set of circumstances. More specifically, it is a way to model the number of events over a given period of time (e.g., the number of cars that pass by on the freeway in an hour, or the number of teller transactions processed in a given period of time). He illustrated the math on a legal pad.

General form of Poisson distribution:

$$P(X) = \frac{e^{-\lambda} \lambda^x}{X!} \qquad \text{Where:} \quad X \text{ - \# of interest, and} \quad \lambda = \text{the average occurrence.}$$

Coello added, "Let me show you how an auditor can use this particular distribution. We want to know if one teller truly completed twice the number of transactions as the average. For example, the average is 30 transactions per observation period, but the anomalous teller completed 60 transactions. So the question becomes, in a world where 30 is the average, what are the odds that one member of the group completed 60 transactions. The probability that a teller processes *at least* 60 transactions in a given sample time period is given by:

$$P(X \geq 60) = P(X = 60) + P(X = 61) + P(X = 62) + \ldots$$

$$= \frac{e^{-30}30^{60}}{60!} + \frac{e^{-30}30^{61}}{61!} + \frac{e^{-30}30^{62}}{62!} + \ldots$$

Because the probability of each transaction value from 60 through infinity is conceptually difficult to calculate, the same value can be derived by calculating $1 - P(X < 60)$, which is finite and relatively easy to calculate.

$$1 - P(X \leq 60) = P(X = 60) + P(X = 59) + P(X = 58) + \ldots + P(X = 1)$$

$$= \frac{e^{-30}30^{60}}{60!} + \frac{e^{-30}30^{59}}{59!} + \frac{e^{-30}30^{58}}{58!} + \ldots + \frac{e^{-30}30^{1}}{1!}$$

Regardless, those calculations may be worked out using a simple business calculator or, better yet, some computer software.

Using one of their laptops, Coello quickly accessed Microsoft Excel, and found the statistical functions. "When we do that," he continued, "our answer is . . . surprising! Our answer is 0.000000953446!"

Coello continued, "To paraphrase the most famous fictional investigator of all time, Sherlock Holmes, 'When you have excluded the impossible, whatever remains, however improbable, must be the truth.'"

"*What* is the truth? Do we get truth from statistics?" asked Mary.

"No matter how tempting," Coello replied, "we wouldn't want to expect so much from statistics at this point. What this calculation can tells us, though, is that it is highly unlikely, if not impossible, that our anomalous teller truly performs twice as much work as the other tellers despite what the teller logs indicate. That, in and of itself, provides us with sufficient cause to investigate further."

Mary became very interested in this audit application of statistics. "Coello, is this the only model we can use for deriving anomalies in this situation?"

"No," her manager replied, "There are others that could be used if certain basic assumptions are met, such as the exponential distribution, or model. That distribution has more strenuous assumptions, so it would be more difficult to implement.

"I don't want to memorize a list of esoteric assumptions to do my job," Mary complained. "Isn't there something else I could use instead?"

"I agree," chimed in Becca, "We need a model with enough flexibility that we can easily use it on the job," she continued.

Coello explained, "In reality we do not need a fancy model for the overall data if we have a relatively large amount of data with which to work, as long as we remember the Central Limit Theorem, which states that, as long as the sample of data is large enough, the data tends to follow a normal distribution (which is represented by the popular symmetric bell shaped curve). Computing probabilities from a normal distribution requires using the so-called 'true' standard deviation of all sample items, but if we use the observed standard deviation from our sample as a substitute, we can compute probabilities using what we call the Student's T-Distribution."

"Hey," interrupted Joel, "even I remember studying that." "Anyone who has had a basic business stats course probably has, too, Joel. Let's create an example."

"Suppose we had chosen to gather data on tellers' transaction times. As you could guess, some customers' transactions may be more difficult or complicated than others, and so some transactions may take longer to process. One teller may also take more or less time per average transaction if they are new on the job or are engaged in some sort of manipulation. Suppose, then, that one teller at this bank had processing times far longer than the other tellers' transactions. For example, we may have calculated the average processing time for all of the tellers as 120 seconds per transaction, based on 60 observations. Suppose further that an anomalous teller had an average processing time of about twice that amount, or 240 seconds. If the discrepancy can be attributed to just chance, what is the probability that the processing time would take so long or even longer?"

"We can use the following general formula . . .

$$t = \frac{\bar{X} - \mu}{\frac{s}{\sqrt{n}}}$$

... where $\bar{X}$ is the average processing time from our anomalous teller, s is standard deviation from the sample of transactions processed by that teller, n is the number of transactions by that teller, and the mean processing time for tellers in general is given by the symbol μ. Finally, we have to know the degrees of freedom for our calculation, which is ..."

"I know," interjected Becca, "$n - 1$. That's an easy one."

"Right," answered Coello. "Now, let's use our excel program to make the actual calculation." "For our example," he continued, "the teller's average of two-minutes per transaction for our sample of 60 transactions produces a t score (with $60 - 1$, or 59 degrees of freedom) of:

$$\frac{240 - 120}{120\sqrt{60}} = 7.745$$

To approximate the probability of observing at least an average processing time of 4 minutes (or 240 seconds), we need to find the probability of observing a t score greater than 7.745. This answer ends up being incredibly small, 7.36×10^{-11} – or about 0.0000000000736. Hence, for this simple example, we have found another distinctly unlikely probability. Anyway, that's another potential procedure to add to your auditor toolbox."

Coello then asked Becca and Mary to find out all they could about the anomalous teller and report back to him later that day. He instructed Joel to pull the security videos of the teller area for several days and examine whether the anomalous teller was recorded as being equally busy across a broader time horizon.

REPORTING RISK

Later in the day Mary and Becca reported that the anomalous teller was none other than the "trophy wife" of John St. Claire. Reportedly, she'd wanted to have some part in her husband's business, but her limited formal education beyond high school landed her in the teller pool.

"What do you two think of that as an explanation?" Coello asked his trainees.

They both agreed that she could probably find other meaningful ways to participate in her husband's work and still feel satisfied. Joel also reported back, telling his trainer that the bank had installed a new video security system about two years ago when the new management information system had been fully implemented. The videos are routinely purged every three months, however, and technical difficulties in recording since the last purge date resulted in very few security videos of the anomalous teller area remaining useful. Joel reported that the security department apologized profusely for the error, but could not provide the recordings. To compensate for the lack of control, they had used extra security personnel while the system was experiencing difficulties. Regardless, the anomalies began to pile up around the hyper-busy teller.

ANOMALIES IN THE USE OF FUNDS

Eddie Coello had been pondering over the anomalous data, and actively considering whether and how fraud could have been conducted (per guidance given to auditors in AU-C Section 240). It crossed his mind that, *if* there was something illegitimate on the funding side of the balance sheet, perhaps he would find similar suspicious items on the asset side of the balance sheet. He concocted an experiment and then tested his theory with regard to loans.

Suppose that, on a monthly average, the sampled location (i.e., branch) receives 12,000 payments on outstanding loans. If we assume 24 average working days per month, that equates to a daily average of 500 payments. An examination of the bank's records was performed to look for significant deviations from that average. On one day, for example, the bank received 800 loan payments. If we assume loan payments are independent in a non-suspicious setting, then what is the probability that the bank could receive 800 or more *legitimate* loan payments in one day?

Coello had Joel do the mathematical calculations, again using excel, to show him that any comparison of actual to average (given that assumptions had been met) could be performed using the same Poisson distribution model. This time the question was how likely it may be that at least 800 commercial loan payments were received on a particular day when the average payments received was usually 500 per day? That probability during a sample time period is given by:

$$P(X \geq 800) = P(X = 800) + P(X = 801) + P(X = 802) + \ldots$$

$$= \frac{e^{-500}500^{800}}{800!} + \frac{e^{-500}501^{801}}{801!} + \frac{e^{-500}500^{802}}{802!} + \ldots$$

Again, using an excel spreadsheet Coello had provided the team, the result was surprising.

"Wow," said Joel. "It's only 0.00000000000000000000000000000000221717!"

"Clearly," said his trainer, "it is sufficiently anomalous to warrant further inquiry."

"How's that?" asked Joel.

"Unknown at this point," said Coello, but the calculation result provides a basis for further investigation simply because it is a significant anomaly."

"But," asked Mary, "since there is more than one model for finding anomalies with deposits, is there another model we could use to corroborate what we've just discovered in lending?"

"Sure," her trainer continued, "We can model the number of companies making payments on their loans using a binomial distribution." He began making notes on a legal pad. "If X is the observed number of payments, n is the total number of companies with outstanding loans, and p is the probability of a company making a payment on that specific day, then we can perform the calculation with this general formula:

$$P(X) = \binom{n}{x} p^x(1-p)^{n-x}$$

This model is dependent on the assumptions that each day the bank is open, it is equally likely to receive a loan payment and that each loan is paid independently of the others. If we assume 24 working days a month, that means an individual loan has a 1/24 chance (i.e., 4.1667%) of having a payment made on a specific day in that month. Furthermore, assume the bank has 15,000 outstanding loans. If these assumptions are met, the probability of observing *exactly* 800 loan payments on a given day can be computed by:

$$P(X = 800) = \binom{15{,}000}{800} (1/24)^{800} + (23/24)^{15{,}000-800}$$

Then, this calculation is carried out incrementally to estimate the probability that at least 800 companies who made payments on any given day is easily computed:

$$P(X \geq 800) \quad = \quad P(X = 800) \quad + \quad P(X = 801) \quad + \quad P(X = 802) \quad + \quad \ldots \quad P(X = 15000)$$

This calculation also results in a very small probability: 8.51673×10^{-13} – or about 0.000000000000851673. So, it seems unlikely then that these companies are *independently* making payments."

"But, isn't it also unlikely that payments will be made close to the average, for a lot of different reasons, to be able to use any of this," Becca asked.

"Good question, Becca," said Coello. "Keep in mind we're only looking for anomalies on which to base further investigation, just like we're directed to do in any analytical procedures (e.g., AU-C Section 520 for auditors), not unlike horizontal, vertical, or ratio analysis of financial data. **Finding anomalies of any sort simply helps us to better use our limited sampling and investigative resources.**"

Using the information from the probability model, Examiner Coello sampled all the loan payments on the anomalous day from the observations, and on others that were similarly anomalous throughout the year. His regulatory auditors discovered recurring individual and company names making the loan payments. When his team traced loan proceeds from those accounts he discovered that, in several instances, the borrowers seemed to be passing around loan proceeds in some sort of round-robin fashion. Firm A would borrow, for example, and then divide the funds between its own current account and two or three others. Those other firms would then either use the funds to repay their own commercial loans or transfer the funds to still other firms, who would behave in a similar fashion.

Quickly making a list of all those borrowers, he divided his entire staff into two-person teams and sent them out to physically inspect each suspicious business location. Performing this task in a small town, he had learned from previous experience, was a relatively simple task. Doing this verification in a big city would take longer but, again from personal experience, is still highly feasible. Findings substantially pointed out that many of the businesses did not exist. Others that did exist, were often too small to require so much borrowing, suggesting that they were acting as surrogate borrowers for others.

For example, one visit to a mom-and-pop neighborhood market seemed to have an inventory that could have been purchased for less than $10,000 and yet the bank had loaned the store $250,000 for working capital. Still other businesses legally existed, but were apparently defunct, although the financial statements supporting their borrowings showed viable (even strong) borrowers. In the days to come, Examiner Coello discovered that many of the financial documents were meticulously prepared for each company by the same local CPA, and that all legal documents could be traced to the same local law firm. Further, confirmations sent to any of the firms by external and, incredibly, internal auditors had been routed to a common address, apparently intercepted by bank insiders, and appropriately returned to all auditors disclosing no material deficiencies (in the case of positive confirmations) or not even returned at all (in the case of negative confirmations). AU-C Section 505, "External Confirmations," explains the requirements for use of all external confirmations, including inventory, bank accounts and status and trade accounts receivable.

Insiders had clearly perpetuated a massive loan fraud, but Examiner Coello could not pinpoint exactly how so many auditors and examiners had not recognized the crimes in progress previously. The data showed virtually nothing unusual, and itemizing every instance of fraud and would have been too voluminous to even rationally consider. He consulted with his chief assistant Lynne Kupcinet.

"Well," she said after talking at length about how the crimes could have been committed, "it's like you always say, 'when you have excluded the impossible, whatever remains, however improbable, must be the truth.'"

"So, it's *not impossible* to process so much data without leaving a trace?" he asked.

"You tell me," Lynne replied. "Could it have something to do with their new IT system?"

Immediately Coello recognized his error. Of course it had something to do with the new IT system! He and Lynne fairly ran to the office of Liam Banyans, vice president in charge of IT.

"Problems Lynne?" he asked when they burst into his office. They had met several times before on other exam-related matters, but this meeting was clearly more urgent.

"Maybe," she said, "you tell us." She handed him two pages of probability calculations underneath the headings "Probability of Anomalous Deposits," and "Probability of Anomalous Loan Payments." The very small probabilities were highlighted in bold print at the bottom of each respective page.

"I'm sure I don't know what you're talking about," he replied after taking a moment to scan the pages. "Can't get the data you want? That's all I do, you know, provide data," he continued jokingly.

"And," interjected Coello, "provide assurance about internal controls over the management information system."

"Well, yes," he conceded, regaining his usual efficient manner "and do you have a problem with some particular control?"

Lynne explained what they had found and what they now suspected, that the bank was either running a dual-management information systems (MIS) or that a single MIS had been compromised. "You must have stumbled onto the idea when the old system was replaced," she began. "Usually, when a new MIS is introduced a dual system is run for a few months until it is clear that the new system is satisfactorily capturing and processing information. The external and internal auditors check it out, then sign off when things appear satisfactory. So, here's what we think. The new system checks out, the old system is switched off, so auditors are satisfied and leave. They leave, and someone here with a good grasp of IT systems and processes, switches the old system back on. Am I on the right track?"

Liam was visibly shaken. "That's a pretty far-fetched story," he said, holding the arms of his chair to steady himself.

"Far-fetched but plausible," said Coello, "and so very, very easy to do."

"Who would think to check?" added Lynne. "The external auditors will not do anything they are not paid to do. The audit committee also approves the internal audit plan each year, so their work could be easily directed into any number of other areas. Besides, even if they did test the new MIS, how often would they even consider checking for a dual MIS or that the old system had been turned on again? I'm guessing almost never! Now, what we need to know is *who* gave the order to switch the old system back on?"

Liam was at least calm enough to indicate that his lawyer should be present for any further interrogation. At that point, the regulatory auditors turned the matter over to their own investigative unit and enforcement division. Both Eddie and Lynne stayed on and worked closely with the special units, however, until the case was prepared for trial.

EPILOGUE

The three principals of the bank had, indeed, engaged in loan fraud. The anomalous teller was not, in reality, processing an average of sixty transactions but, rather, one or two very large transactions. She was accepting a deposit of $300,000, for example, and breaking it up into unsuspicious, smaller deposits to a predetermined list of deposit accounts. She would process the "real" deposit entry on the old MIS, and the small deposits on the new MIS. Similarly, insiders used the old MIS to track "real" borrowing in the commercial loan portfolio, but distributed the insider loans to various fictitious, nominee, straw, or even legitimate borrowers on the new MIS.

The fraudulent loans had been siphoned off to fund a series of other investment projects, primarily decided by the three principal owners of the financial institution. Apparently, too, none of the three had actually embezzled or diverted the additional profits from the various other investments. It was just a game of growth outside the regulatory guidelines and apparently born out of a type of boredom probably known only to those with a certain type of "genius."

This was the second time the lead author had uncovered a fraud that was based on dual-MIS. He also had heard about other instances of fraud perpetuated by a dual MIS or other manipulation of the MIS. For example, the SEC discovered that Livent's accounting staff had developed computer software to track the company's "real" and bogus financial data and to conceal the fraud from their auditors. In later years, he also would read about Bernie Madoff's fraudulent investment schemes and Peregrine Financial Group/Russell Wassendorf, both of which frauds were MIS-related.

Generally speaking, though, economic loss is a primary determinant in litigating fraud. Out of court settlements between fraudsters, regulatory officials, and law enforcement agencies are similarly based, and this form of enforcement is even incentivized due to the backlog of cases destined for trial. A lack of measurable loss to the bank or holding company was likely what saved the three conspirators from significant jail time. Because the charges were settled out of court, less is known about the details of charges than would otherwise be the case. All three conspirators (and family members) had to divest themselves of ownership interests in Southern Bancshares and all subsidiaries. They were also similarly banned from banking for life. The three were penalized for a multiple of any gains derived from the frauds – despite the absence of economic loss sustained by loan frauds. They were also guilty of "lying to regulators," which ordinarily carries both civil and criminal penalties. Again, given the absence of economic loss to the institution criminal penalties resulted in extended probationary terms and civil penalties based on economic gains.

Afterwards, John and his anomalous teller-wife withdrew from business life and spent more than a year sailing around the coastal United States on their yacht. He and Tess eventually formed a small investment fund that they currently operate off-shore.

Lee embarked on a "self-awareness" odyssey for the next three years, and eventually found satisfaction working as a retired executive offering pro bono advisory services to fledgling businesses in developing countries. Southern Bancshares holdings sold at a premium to eager buyers, which helped the three fund their "rebooted lifestyles," as John described them, even after their extensive monetary penalties.

Liam Banyans received a similarly hefty civil money penalty and extended probation, and was also banned from banking for life. In all likelihood, his substantial monetary penalties were paid by the three primary conspirators. Notably, too, his part in the scheme effectively ended his rather lucrative career in MIS. Instead, he turned to teaching at a private, church-affiliated university, linking his path to tenure to his probationary term and performance, in addition to standard academic performance measures.

QUESTIONS

1. Explain the advantages of "knowing" client background.

2. Justify an auditor's decision to delve into the more personal aspects or histories of a business and/or its principals (at least conceptually).

3. Illustrate a situation in which the auditor might display cognitive biases, which could present threats to the auditors' objectivity during the audit.

4. Identify one or more safeguards that may mitigate the auditors' downside-risk from cognitive biases.

5. Identify two or more statements by management that might require further brainstorming by the audit team.

6. Speculate on the extent to which the personnel of an entity being audited may know in advance what auditors will audit, which procedures are likely to be used, and when those procedures are likely to be applied. How could they know these things?

7. Illustrate how the reliability of the audit might be adversely affected by personnel of the entity being audited having foreknowledge of the auditors' procedures and practices.

8. List some of the more useful points in the case section, "The Examination," that Eddie Coello may have gleaned from the exchanges with his forensic accounting team and key members of management.

9. Were there alternative hypotheses about possible causes of the apparently anomalous findings (i.e., teller productivity)? What could they have been?

10. Explain how use of the Poisson (or other) probability models could be used to improve the use of sampling methods.

11. Speculate on any other uses of the Poisson distribution as a non-financial method to test transactions and balances.

12. Discuss the penalties assessed on the primary culprits. Were they fair, too lenient, too strict, or simply indicative of the rights of rich people and not the average criminal under similar circumstances?

This case is adapted from Vol. 8, No. 3, July- December 2016, *Journal of Forensic & Investigative Accounting* article.

CASE STUDY 32:

Green Tech Manufacturing Company: Fraud and the Independent Auditor*

Diane Matson, Ph.D., CFE, CPA (inactive)

Lawrence Chui, Ph.D., CPA

University of St. Thomas

LEARNING OBJECTIVES

After completing and discussing this case, you should be able to

- Appreciate the value of an internal control questionnaire.
- Identify and define parts of the fraud triangle.
- Examine various accounting and bank records.
- Analyze suspicious activities.
- Understand separation of duties.

JUST THE FACTS

Background

Assume that you are an audit senior for Andrew and Andrew, CPAs, LLP. Your client is Green Tech Manufacturing Company, a privately held company involved in the production and sale of solar panels. Its primary customers are builders and home supply stores. You are reviewing the client's income statement accounts, and observe that your audit staff person, Jessica Kirner, has done some preliminary audit work in this area, as indicated by her comments and tick marks. Jessica has been called to another client, so you are taking over this audit area. You have workpapers relevant for the audit of income statement accounts: **W/Ps I-1 through I-4** that are provided below. *Note:* Identifying information has been altered and removed; any resemblance to actual companies or individuals is coincidental.

QUESTIONS

The questions are organized in five parts (**Parts I. – V.**). These are presented next.

Part I: Initial Analysis

Please refer to the Planning Comments and Internal Control Questionnaire (**W/P I-1**) and the Income Statement with Common-Size information (**W/P I-2**) to answer these questions in **Part I.**

Consider the income statement and the related common-size accounts.

A.   What trends and patterns do you see?

B.   What account(s), in particular, should be investigated more? Please be specific, and discuss your concerns.

Part II: Additional Information

Consider your findings in **Part I.**

A.   What additional information would you like to obtain? Where could you get this information?

B.   What are the costs of obtaining this information? What are the benefits of obtaining this information?

Part III: Analysis of Information

You have the Selling, General and Administrative (S, G and A) Expense Detail (**W/P I-3**) and Sample of Cancelled Checks (**W/P I-4**). Please consider your findings in **Part I.** and **Part II.,** and also use **W/P I-3** and **W/P I-4** to answer the questions in **Part III.**

A.   The client has a problem. What is the problem?

B.   Who could have done this? Why do you think this?

C.   Consider the fraud triangle. Identify and define each part of the fraud triangle. Apply the fraud triangle to this situation. Try to speculate on motive, opportunity and rationalization.

Part IV: Recommendations

A. Consider what recommendations would help the client prevent future frauds. Try to think of at least three recommendations.

B   Discuss how your recommendations would affect the parties involved.

Part V: Select One Recommendation

A. Assume you have to select one recommendation. What would it be?

B. Explain the advantages and disadvantages of this recommendation.

Green Tech Manufacturing Company
Workpaper I-1

12/31/2015
Initials J. A. K.

Planning Comments
Date: 1-15-16

Memo from Jessica Kirner   January 15, 2016

There has not been turnover in the top four client people: Marvin Green, Owner; Jacob Merriweather, Treasurer; Maeve Rehnhart, accountant; and Lucinda Washburn, factory manager. While talking at various times with these client people, I learned that a small piece of land was purchased from a nearby landowner, and the factory was expanded. In addition, some new equipment was purchased. This expansion is to allow a new product, Solar Panel Plus (Model X-4), to be produced. Builders are requesting this new solar panel, as it is easier to install than the other models.

Marvin thinks the new products will be a great seller. He has a new office, which is the corner office. Jacob recently returned from three-month paternity leave to take care of his new baby. He was able to work from home, so he said he is mostly current with his work. Maeve is getting a divorce and has missed some work to attend attorney meetings and court dates. Lucinda recently completed the second level factory manager-computer certification, so that she can run the new software related to the expansion.

In addition to reading Jessica's memo, you can talk briefly with four individuals. Here are a few of their comments.

KEY COMMENTS FROM PRIMARY INDIVIDUALS

Owner, Marvin Green: I'm not really into all the accounting, but we seem to have less cash than I would expect. Sales are up, but I'm not sure why we are not generating more cash."

Treasurer, Jacob Merriweather: "We took a loan of about $600,000 from the bank in the beginning of 2015. This notes payable is for the factory expansion."

Accountant, Maeve Rehnhart: "Where did the cash go? Well, we bought new equipment, added to our factory, and bought some land. These acquisitions reduced our cash. I can show you the contracts for the PPE."

Factory Manager, Lucinda Washburn: We have added to our building and productive capacity. I can give you a tour and show you the new area and items."

Green Tech Manufacturing Company Workpaper I-1
_____
12/31/2015
Initials J. A. K.
Internal Control Questionnaire
Date: 1-10-16

Internal Control Activity	Response	Comments
1. Does client have an internal control manual?	Yes.	Manual updated in May 2015.
2. Does client have independent checks on performance?	No.	Because of Jacob Merriweather's paternity leave, as well as the factory addition and the new product line, everyone has been too busy to check the work of others.
3. Does client have adequate documents and records?	Yes.	The accounting system is computerized. All paper and electronic documents are pre-numbered.
4. Does client have physical control over assets and records?	Yes.	File cabinets, storage rooms, and vault are locked. Passwords are required to access all critical computer programs and applications.
5. Does client have proper authorization of transactions and activities?	No.	An individual tends to authorize transactions in his or her area. Lucinda Washburn authorizes all factory activities. Maeve Rehnhart authorizes cash disbursements. Jacob Merriweather authorizes banking relationships and investment strategies.
6. Does client have adequate separation of duties?	No.	Accountant Maeve Rehnhart authorizes cash disbursements and prepares checks. Treasurer Jacob Merriweather handles deposits and authorizes banking activities.

Green Tech Manufacturing Company
12/31/2015
Income Statement with Common-Size Information

Workpaper 1-2
Initials *J. A. K.*
Date 1-15-16

Income Statement	Unaudited For Year Ending 12/31/2015	Common-Size 12/31/2015	Audited For Year Ending 12/31/2014	Common-Size 12/31/2014
Sales Revenue	$ 11,000,000	100%	$ 8,000,000	100%
Cost of Goods Sold Expense	$ 8,250,000	75%	$ 5,920,000	74%
Gross Profit	$ 2,750,000	25%	$ 2080,000	26%
S, G and A Expenses	$ 2,420,000	22%	$ 1,520,000	19%
Operating Income	$ 330,000	3%	$ 560,000	7%
Interest Expense	$ 121,000	1%	$ 80,000	1%
Income Before Taxes	$ 209,000	2%	$ 480,000	6%
Income Tax Expense	$ 62,700	1%	$ 144,000	2%
Net Income	$ 146,300	1%	$ 336,000	4%

Green Tech Manufacturing Company
12/31/2015
S G & A Expense Detail

Workpaper 1-3
Initials *J. A. K.*
Date 1-16-2016

Selling, General and Administrative Detail

Account Descriptions	Detail Amounts 12/31/2015 Unaudited	Subtotal 12/31/2015 Unaudited	Subtotal 12/31/2016 Audited
Corporate Headquarters			
Depreciation			
Office Building	$ 100,000.00	$ 100,000.00	$ 100,000.00
Utilities			
Heating and Cooling	$ 121,000.00		
Electricity	$ 47,000.00		
Water	$ 15,000.00	$ 183,000.00	$ 125,000.00
Repairs and Maintenance			
Ace Supplies *	$ 16,000.00		
XYZ Furnace and Air	$ 50,000.00		
Fred's Painting	$ 35,000.00		
Norstein Electrical	$ 32,000.00	$ 133,000.00	$ 45,000.00
Administrative			
Salaries and Benefits			
Executive	$ 550,000.00		
Managers	$ 282,000.00		
Customer Reps	# 300,000.00		
Support	$ 90,000.00	$1,222,000.00	$ 928,000.00
Training			
Enhanced Communications	$ 40,000.00		
M and R Motivation *	$ 50,000.00		
Computer Strategies	$ 30,000.00		
Diversity Plus *	$ 18,000.00	$ 138,000.00	$ 47,000.00
Travel			
Executive	$ 60,000.00		
Customer Reps	$ 75,000.00	$ 135,000.00	$ 102,000.00
Entertainment			
Customer Meetings	$ 37,000.00		
Holiday Party	$ 9,000.00	$ 46,000.00	$ 36,000.00
Professional Services			
Auditing			
Andrews and Andrews	$ 42,000.00	$ 42,000.00	$ 37,000.00
Tax			
Andrews and Andrews	$ 16,000.00	$ 16,000.00	$ 14,000.00
Legal			
Norris and Morris *	$ 33,000.00		
Claremont and Cirrus	$ 2,000.00	$ 35,000.00	$ 17,000.00
Consulting			
Acme Consulting *	$ 38,000.00		
Environo Consultants	$ 65,000.00		
ProProfits Business Power	$ 4,000.00		
MAR Software Consulting *	$ 50,000.00	$ 157,000.00	$ 37,000.00
Engineering			
Factory Synergy	$ 68,000.00		
Chemstart Performance *	$ 45,000.00		
High Power Engineering *	$ 47,000.00		
Mechanix Water Tech	$ 53,000.00	$ 213,000.00	$ 32,000.00
Totals		$ 2,420,000.00	$1,520,000.00

Tichmark Legend * Selected expenses as sample items to test. Traced vendor name and check amount to scanned copy of check paid by and received from the bank. (see workpaper series 1-4)

Green Tech Manufacturing Company	Workpaper 1-3
Sample of Cancelled Checks	Initials *J. A. K.*
For Year Ending 12/31/2015	Date 1-15-2016

(1) Front and Back of Check #2001

Green Tech Manufacturing Company	2-402/710	#2001
1117 Industrial Road		Date: February 2, 2015
Bloomington, MN 55422		
Payee ACE Supplies, Inc.		$ 16,000.00
Sixteen thousand and no/100s		¥
Water pipe repair		Signed Maeve Rehnhart
Second state bank		
31-0041 1967 5607198002 2001		

Pay to Order of Prime Bank
Farmington, MN
For Deposit Only
#100-376-0871
Ace Supplies, Inc.
2-6-15

(2) Front of Check and Back of Check #2007

Green Tech Manufacturing Company	2-402/710	#2007
1117 Industrial Road		Date: March 19, 2015
Bloomington, MN 55422		
Payee Acme Consulting		$ 38,000.00
Thirty eight thousand and no/100s		¥
Installation Assistance for New Computers		Signed Maeve Rehnhart
Second state bank		
31-0041 1967 5607198002 2007		

Deposit Only 3/24/15
Capitol View Bank
St. Paul, MN
#179-675
Acme Consulting

(3) Front and Back of Check #2017

Green Tech Manufacturing Company	2-402/710	#2017
1117 Industrial Road		Date: April 22, 2015
Bloomington, MN 55422		
Payee Chemstart Performance		$ 45,000.00
Forty five thousand and no/100s		¥
Engineering Support for New Product Line		Signed Maeve Rehnhart
Second state bank		
31-0041 1967 5607198002 2017		

Chemstart Performance
Northfield Division
#147-0099
Deposit Only 04-25-2015
Farmer's State Bank
Northfield, MN

(4) Front and Back of Check #2025

Green Tech Manufacturing Company	2-402/710	#2025
1117 Industrial Road		Date: June 29, 2015
Bloomington, MN 55422		
Payee MAR Software Consulting		$ 50,000.00
Fifty thousand and no/100s		¥
Consulting for New Factory Design		Signed Maeve Rehnhart
Second state bank		
31-0041 1967 5607198002 2025		

MAR Software Consulting
Capitol View Bank
St. Paul, MN
#179-675
July 5, 2015
Deposit Only

(5) Front and Back of Check #2035

Green Tech Manufacturing Company	2-402/710	#2035
1117 Industrial Road		Date: July 30, 2015
Bloomington, MN 55422		
Payee Norris and Morris Law Firm		$ 33,000.00
Thirty three thousand and no/100s		¥
Tax Advice for Potential Acquisition		Signed Maeve Rehnhart
Second state bank 31-0041 1967 5607198002 2035		

Pay to Order of
Big First Bank
Minneapolis, MN
Norris and Morris
Deposit Only
#417-22-0954
August 5, 2015

(6) Front and Back of Check #2045

Green Tech Manufacturing Company	2-402/710	#2045
1117 Industrial Road		Date: September 22, 2015
Bloomington, MN 55422		
Payee M and R Motivation		$ 50,000.00
Fifty thousand and no/100s		¥
Training for Executives		Signed Maeve Rehnhart
Second state bank 31-0041 1967 5607198002 2045		

Capitol View Bank
St. Paul, MN
#179-675
September 24, 2015
Deposit Only
Restricted Endorsement

(7) Front and Back of Check of #2051

Green Tech Manufacturing Company	2-402/710	#2051
1117 Industrial Road		Date: October 15, 2015
Bloomington, MN 55422		
Payee Diversity Plus		$ 18,000.00
Eighteen thousand and no/100s		¥
Training for Managers		Signed Maeve Rehnhart
Second state bank		
31-0041 1967 5607198002 2051		

Diversity Plus
10/18/2015
Central City Bank
St. Paul, MN
ACCT# 88-19071
Deposit Only

(8) Front and Back of Check of #2058

Green Tech Manufacturing Company	2-402/710	#2058
1117 Industrial Road		Date: November 5, 2015
Bloomington, MN 55422		
Payee High Power Engineering		$ 47,000.00
Forty seven thousand and no/100s		¥
Engineering Outsourcing		Signed Maeve Rehnhart
Second state bank		
31-0041 1967 5607198002 2058		

High Power Engineering
Deposit Only
November 7, 2015
Capital View Bank
St. Paul, MN
Deposit Only
ACCT# 179-675

¥ Traced vendor name and check amount to S G & A Expense Detail (See **W/P I-3**).

*Adapted from Vol. 8, No. 2, Special Issue, 2016, *Journal of Forensic & Investigative Accounting*.

CASE STUDY 33:

The Fraud at High Flying Corporation: Developing Audit Interview Skills*

Diane M. Matson, Ph.D., CFE, CPA (inactive)

Kristine M. Sharockman, MBA, CPA

Janice M. Raffield, CPA, MPA

University of St. Thomas

LEARNING OBJECTIVES

After completing and discussing this case, you should be able to

- Learn effective interviewing skills.
- Understand inquiry skills.
- Identify and understand communication evidence.
- Participate in a role-playing situation.
- Recognize and investigate a fraud.

INTRODUCTION

This case study simulates an audit client interview. Based on an actual audit fraud, the case includes several "red flags" for students to identify and investigate. Analytical procedures involving both financial and non-financial data are useful in helping students identify key issues in the case. Students need to ask questions effectively in order to make professional judgments about the reasonableness of the financial statements and the information provided by the client; simultaneously, students experience real time pressure and client behaviors intended to evoke negative emotional reactions and undermine their confidence.

Each student interviews a client portrayed by a practicing accountant from the business community. The accountants portraying the client are asked to display behaviors that clients seeking to conceal information might actually exhibit. The participation of practicing accountants helps to simulate a realistic audit environment where young auditors are expected to perform under pressure.

Each student's interview is videotaped. The instructors review each interview and select one or more excerpts to include in a DVD that will be used to demonstrate both effective and ineffective inquiry techniques during a follow-up session. Selected excerpts are intended to capture the complex dynamics that may occur between the client and the auditor during an interview, particularly when the client is attempting to conceal a fraud. Excerpts usually demonstrate: (1) the client evading questions by discussing unrelated issues; (2) the client providing information that is inconsistent with data in the work papers; (3) the client making statements that conflict with prior statements; (4) the students leading the client, answering their own questions or failing to properly ask follow-up questions; (5) the students appropriately redirecting the dialogue; (6) the students asking strong follow-up questions; and (7) the students maintaining a calm professional demeanor. The DVD with excerpts is shown in a follow-up session that provides students with constructive feedback on their performance and helps them reflect on their experience.

This case introduces effective client inquiry skills and the concept of emotional intelligence through a role playing exercise. Students practice and analyze effective interviewing techniques and, as importantly, identify and analyze ineffective techniques. The case can also be used as a written assignment, instead of or in conjunction with an interview simulation.

The article is organized into two major sections. The first section provides an overview of the case and the case materials. These materials include client information, financial statements, and various details relevant to the audit. (*Note:* The data files, which are Word and Excel files, are available upon request from the corresponding author). The second section presents the teaching notes, which include the learning objectives, instructional approach, and implementation ideas. The teaching notes also provide case instructions, suggested assignments and solutions, and excerpts from representative interviews. (*Note:* The teaching notes are available upon request from the corresponding author).

CASE MATERIALS

Purpose of Case

The purpose of this case is for you to assume the role of an audit senior. As such, you will focus on cash; accounts receivable; sales revenue; and property, plant and equipment for a client with a fiscal year-end of June 30, 2014. You will be given background information, financial statements, various schedules, a bank statement and cash confirmation, and a charter agreement.

List of Case Materials

The list of case materials is as follows:
1. Exhibit A: Memorandum for Planning Meeting
2. Exhibit B: Draft of President's Letter
3. Exhibit C: Audit Program—Cash
4. Exhibit D: Audit Program—Sales Revenue and Accounts Receivable
5. Exhibit E: Statements of Income
6. Exhibit F: Balance Sheets

7. Exhibit G: Schedule of Trade Accounts Receivable
8. Exhibit H: Schedule of Monthly Sales Revenue for Year ending June 30, 2014
9. Exhibit I: Schedule of Sales Revenue for the Month ending July 31, 2013
10. Exhibit J: Schedule of Sales Revenue for the Month ending June 30, 2014
11. Exhibit K: Schedule of Aircraft
12. Exhibit L: Bank Statement and Standard Bank Confirmation
13. Exhibit M: Terms and Conditions for all Charter Agreements
14. Exhibit N: First Assignment for Case
15. Exhibit O: Second Assignment for Case
16. Exhibit P: Third Assignment for Case

Overview of Client

The client, High Flying Charter Company (HF), is a privately-held aviation company based at Holman Field, an airport near downtown St. Paul, Minnesota. Its main line of business is providing air charters for executives and groups, primarily to four large customers. HF has 19 employees. The major shareholders are also employed as top executives. The primary contacts at the client are Mr. Calvin Kemper, chief executive officer (CEO) and Ms. Valerie Walsh, chief financial officer (CFO). More information on the client is found in Exhibits A and B.

The CPA Firm

Smith Franklin CPAs LLP, a regional CPA firm, specializes in small manufacturers and distributors. This is the first year that the firm has conducted HF's audit. Larry Lemay is the audit partner. More information on the CPA firm is found in Exhibit A.

Purpose of Audit

The client needs an audit as a condition of its debt agreement and in anticipation of seeking new private investors. More information on the audit is found in Exhibit A.

Industry Information

The charter flight industry is greatly affected by economic conditions and travel-related trends. The industry has started to recover after some tough years, and industry revenues are expected to grow during the fiscal year ending June 30, 2014. The audit team will need to assess how the market pressures faced by the industry will impact HF's ability to achieve its projected aggressive revenue growth. In addition, the industry faces significant regulation by government agencies. More information about the industry is found in Exhibit A.

ASSIGNMENTS

Interview Format. Your professor may require you to prepare for and conduct an interview of the client contact. If so, there are two related assignments. The first assignment, Exhibit N, is an individual assignment. It involves preparing for an interview with someone portraying either Mr. Kemper or Ms. Walsh and conducting this interview. To prepare for this interview, you should carefully review and analyze the Exhibits, looking for unusual amounts, patterns and activities, while considering the client and the industry. Compile a list of questions to ask the client person. When you conduct the interview, take notes. Be sure to follow up on answers that are confusing, incomplete, or inconsistent.

The second assignment, Exhibit O, is a group assignment that involves reflecting on the information received in the interview and identifying additional questions and concerns.

Written Format. Your professor may require some written evaluation and analysis of the case materials, in addition to, or in place of, preparing for and conducting an interview of the client contact. If so, there is one related assignment, Exhibit P. In this individual assignment, you are asked to identify and analyze unusual amounts, patterns and activities, and to present your findings in a written paper.

CASE MATERIALS

Exhibit A

Smith Franklin CPAs LLP
High Flying Charter Company
Memorandum for Planning Meeting
FYE June 30, 2014

General
You have been assigned as the audit senior on High Flying Charter Company (HF). It is July 10, 2014, and you are starting your audit fieldwork.

Audit Firm Information
Smith Franklin CPAs LLP is a regional CPA firm with three offices in the Midwest. The firm has 100 professional staff in assurance, taxation, and litigation support. The firm specializes in small manufacturers and distributors. This is the first year that the firm has conducted HF's audit. Previously, the audit was conducted by a very small local public accounting firm.

The client needs an audit for its bank, as a condition of its debt agreement. It also wants an audit because it will be seeking private investors. The usual engagement letter, outlining the responsibilities of the client and the auditors, has been obtained. An important point in the engagement letter is that the audit should be completed by August 1, 2014, as required by the bank.

The audit partner, Larry Lemay, is known for great client service. He is all about client service. Client service is his top one priority. Even though he is a favorite with clients, he also expects quality audit work.

Client Information

HF is an aviation company based at Holman Field, just south of downtown St. Paul, Minnesota. Its main line of business is providing air charters for executives and groups, primarily in Minnesota, Wisconsin and Illinois. The company has been experiencing good growth despite fluctuating fuel oil prices and a tough economy.

Mr. Calvin Kemper, CEO, has explained that HF primarily works with several large corporate clients. These clients do not want the expense and hassle of maintaining their own airplanes, so they rely on HF to fly their executives to various cities in the midwest. The executives typically fly to branch offices or factories, and then fly back to corporate headquarters. Four major customers are: Big Builders Buying (BBB); Commercial Money and Finance (CFM); National Air Service (NAS); and PIP (Progressive Industrial Products).

The client has eight employees in the office, five licensed pilots, five attendants, and one baggage handler. Repairs and maintenance services are contracted out to an unrelated company, Airplane UpKeep, Inc.

HF is a privately-held corporation. The major shareholders are also top executives.

Mr. Kemper displays his pilot licenses in his office, which indicate that he is licensed to fly 20 types of large airplanes. His employees have mentioned that, after returning from the Air Force, he started several successful businesses before launching HF in 2004. Recently, in *The Aviation Reporter*, he stated, "I earned my first pilot license when I was only 16. Anything related to aviation, that's where I want to be." When he engaged the auditing firm he explained that he earned his aviation management degree from the University of North Dakota and a MBA from Northwestern University.

Valerie Walsh is the CFO. She has been with HF since 2004, first as a secretary and office manager, then as the accountant, then as CFO. She loves to fly, although she is not a licensed pilot. In a feature article in *Take Off*, she explained the company's business model: "Well, we aim for the stars, so to speak. We look towards consistent, yet aggressive growth over the next five years. We see an untapped market in small to medium sized businesses, who need to get their executives here and there, but who do not want the hassle of maintaining their own fleets of aircraft." Mr. Kemper provided a little information about Ms. Walsh's background. She holds an economics degree from Richmond College and an MBA from the University of Minnesota—Duluth.

Industry Information

The Charter Flights Industry, which provides non-scheduled air transport services for passengers and cargo, has started to recover after a 12.6% decline in revenues in 2009. The 2009 decline was primarily attributable to an overall decrease in travel spending, particularly among corporate clients. Economic conditions and travel-related trends are the key factors driving the Charter Flight Industry.

In the fiscal year ending June 30, 2014, industry revenues are expected to grow 4.8% due to the recovery of corporate profits and per capita disposable income. However, during the prior five-year period the number of companies operating in the Charter Flight Industry declined by 1.7% annually. The industry is highly sensitive to changing conditions in the corporate sector. A large portion of revenues come from business trips carrying executives to outlying locations. Since 2009 corporate clients have taken a razor to their budgets resulting in drastic cuts to funds for chartered and private flights. In 2011, indications of an improving economy eased fears surrounding the state of the economy resulting in a small increase in the number of business people and consumers traveling. This trend has continued into 2012 and 2013. Despite these trends, industry profitability and demand is threatened by rising fuel prices and the corresponding increase in charter flight costs.

The audit team will need to consider the possible impact market pressure has on the industry and on HF's ability to achieve their aggressive revenue growth and maintain their premium charter pricing. The reasonableness of industry-specific non-financial data such as aircraft capacity and range should also be considered.

HF operates under Federal Aviation Regulations, Part 135. Part 135 is applicable to HF, because, as a smaller charter airline, it provides transportation to persons for compensation. HF has a Part 135 commercial operating certificate. Mr. Kemper indicates that the company is currently in the process of applying for a 121 Certificate, which is required for higher capacity aircraft.

Board of Directors
Calvin C. Kemper, Chairman of the Board, CEO and President
Michael L. Medford, Vice Chairman and Executive Vice President
Valerie Hansen Walsh, CFO
Kirkland Jones, COO
Margaret Wilmington
Yvette Kemper Dupree

Exhibit B
Draft of President's Letter

PRESIDENT'S LETTER (Draft for Auditors)

To Our Shareholders:

We are pleased to report that our projections and previous predictions of greater revenues and profits for the fiscal year 2014 have not only been realized for High Flying Charter Company, but have exceeded our expectations significantly. Several plans and projects presently in progress at HFCC lead us to believe that 2015 should not only be a record year in revenues and profits but also greatly enhance HFCC's position in the marketplace of general aviation.

We are presently involved in the following projects:

Application for our own 121 certificate to allow us to be a commercial non-scheduled air carrier. This would allow us to conduct large group charters in the Dassault Falcon 2000 XL, carrying over 150 passengers. These aircraft will be operated at full capacity on longer flights from all parts of the midwest United States into Europe, Japan, the Cayman Islands, and Mexico.

Continuation of computer system upgrade to make it possible to implement growth plans. We have added hardware and software capacity to help track our growth in the future. We feel that accurate cost accounting is the key to our success in the charter business. Most charter operators think of accounting as a necessary evil, but we consider it a sound business practice necessary for an efficient operation. Our accounting system also allows us to maintain strict control over maintenance parts inventory, aviation fuel, and pilot supplies.

Planning to seek approval to be a FAA Certified Helicopter Repair Station. We expect to expand and improve our maintenance facilities to accommodate this approval, when received.

These are a few projects in progress. We are anticipating a very healthy new fiscal year. You may be assured that we will proceed with caution as our growth has been rapid. Our dedication to you, our employees and our customers, is of utmost importance here at HFCC.

We sincerely thank you for your past support and your belief in us.

Calvin Kemper

Exhibit C

Smith Franklin CPAs LLP
High Flying Charter Company
Audit Program—Cash
June 30, 2014

Audit Steps

Smith Franklin, CPAs, LLP	Initial and Date
Cash Audit Program	
Client: High Flying Charter Company Year-End: 06/30/2014	

(1) Check the mathematical accuracy of all schedules.   ❏

(2) Trace deposits in transit on the bank reconciliation to the cash receipts journal and the cutoff bank statement. Note any discrepancies.   ❏

(3) Trace outstanding checks on the bank reconciliation to the cash disbursements journal and the cutoff bank statement. Review copies of the cancelled checks, if necessary. Note any discrepancies.   ❏

(4) Review the standard bank confirmation for any other activity that needs to be reflected in the financial statements.   ❏

(5) Review the activity reflected in the bank reconciliation for reasonableness.   ❏

(6) Identify and explain any problems you find with the bank reconciliation and supporting detail.   ❏

(7) Discuss problems you have identified with the client. Consider what questions you should ask. Consider your satisfaction with the answers.   ❏

(8) State your conclusion about this account. If any adjustments are needed, document the reasons and amounts involved.   ❏

Exhibit D

Smith Franklin CPAs LLP
High Flying Charter Company
Audit Program—Sales Revenue and Accounts Receivable
June 30, 2014

Smith Franklin, CPAs, LLP	Initial and Date
Cash Audit Program	
Client: High Flying Charter Company Year-End: 06/30/2014	

(1) Check the mathematical accuracy of all schedules.	❏
(2) Trace a sample of sales revenue amounts to underlying documentation. This documentation includes the sales contracts (charter agreements).	❏
(3) Trace collections on accounts receivable made around the end of June 2014 to deposits in transit on the bank statement.	❏
(4) If cash sales are made around the end of June 2014, trace the cash receipts to deposits in transit on the bank statement.	❏
(5) Review the activity reflected in sales revenue and accounts receivable for reasonableness.	❏
(6) Identify and explain any problems you find with the sales revenue, accounts receivable, and supporting detail.	❏
(7) Discuss the problems you have identified with the client. Consider what questions you should ask. Consider your satisfaction with the answers.	❏
(8) State your conclusion about these accounts. If any adjustments are needed, document the reasons and amounts involved.	❏

Exhibit E

High Flying Charter Company
Statements of Income
For the Years ended June 30

| | (unaudited) | |
	2014	2013
Net Sales Revenue	$80,387,340	$31,585,050
Expenses		
Cost of Sales	67,650,300	26,082,650
Selling, general administrative	6,646,330	4,142,950
Interest - net	415,180	177,890
Total Expenses	74,711,810	30,403,490
Income before income taxes	5,675,530	1,181,560
Income taxes	2,490,000	130,000
Net Income	$3,185,530	$1,051,560
EPS	$0.27	$0.14

Exhibit F
High Flying Charter Company
Balance Sheets
June 30

ASSETS	(unaudited)	
	2014	2013
Current assets:		
Cash (including cash in escrow of $500,000)	$7,113,890	$168,050
Trade accounts receivable	3,148,920	2,951,440
Insurance claim receivable	—	1,512,740
Inventories	1,523,030	4,142,870
Prepaid expenses	2,079,890	854,930
Total Current Assets	$13,865,730	$ 9,630,030
Property, plant & equipment, at cost		
Buildings and improvements	$4,545,810	$4,477,930
Aircraft	14,896,260	136,900
Furniture & equipment	2,478,610	289,230
Vehicles	1,110,570	575,890
Aircraft purchase deposits	3,200,000	—
	26,231,250	5,479,950
Less depreciation and amortization	1,509,490	653,470
Total PPE, net	24,721,760	4,826,480
Other Assets	956,300	—
Total Assets	$39,543,790	$14,456,510

LIABILITIES AND STOCKHOLDERS' EQUITY

	(unaudited)	
	2014	2013
Current liabilities:		
Bank overdraft	—	$430,770
Notes payable	$4,477,430	2,441,410
Current portion of long-term debt	241,310	2,439,340
Accounts payable	870,500	1,323,090
Accrued expenses	445,660	287,970
Income taxes	2,259,720	—
Total Current Liabilities	8,294,620	6,922,580
Deferred income taxes	190,000	—
Long-term debt	7,668,870	2,307,220
Commitments and contingencies	—	—
Total Noncurrent Liabilities	7,858,870	2,307,220
Stockholders' equity:		
Common stock, $.01 par value; authorized - 30,000,000 shares;		
issued and outstanding - 14,653,800 shares in 2014 and 9,000,000		
shares in 2013	146,540	90,000
Paid in capital	20,528,230	5,606,710
Retained Earnings (deficit)	2,715,530	(470,000)
Total Stockholders' Equity	23,390,300	5,226,710
Total Liabilities and Stockholders' Equity	$39,543,790	$14,456,510

Exhibit G

High Flying Charter Company
Schedule of Trade Accounts Receivable
June 30

| | (unaudited) | |
	2014	2013
National Air Service	3,148,920	2,951,440
Total Trade Accounts Receivable	$3,148,920	$ 2,951,440

Exhibit H

High Flying Charter Corporation
Schedule of Monthly Sales Revenue
For the Year ending June 30, 2014

Month	Revenue
July, 2013	$ 5,960,300
August, 2013	5,625,270
September, 2013	5,992,160
October, 2013	5,886,300
November, 2013	5,841,920
December, 2013	6,583,000
January, 2014	6,623,100
February, 2014	6,933,900
March, 2014	6,965,590
April, 2014	7,622,850
May, 2014	7,988,100
June, 2014	8,364,850
Total	$ 80,387,340

Exhibit I

High Flying Charter Corporation
Schedule of Sales Revenue
For the Month ending July 31, 2013

Date	Customer/Contact	Description	Amount	FAA Flight Plan
1-Jul	NAS/Y. Dupree	Round Trip St. P/GraCay	$200,700	√
1-Jul	NAS/Y. Dupree	Round Trip GraCay/St. P	234,200	√
2-Jul	BBB/B. Wilson	Round Trip St. P/Chicago	189,500	√
2-Jul	CFM/T. Smither	One Way St. P/Milwau	94,700	√
3-Jul	PIP/C. Nottingham	One Way St. P/Peoria	87,300	√
3-Jul	NAS/Y. Dupree	Round Trip GraCay/Chic	200,300	√
3-Jul	NAS/Y. Dupree	Round Trip Chic/GraCay	230,200	√
5-Jul	BBB/B. Wilson	One Way St. P/Chic	98,500	√
9-Jul	CFM/T. Smither	One Way St. P/GreBay	77,500	√
9-Jul	CFM/T. Smither	Round Trip St. P/GreBay	159,000	√
10-Jul	CFM/T. Smither	One Way GreBay/Chic	145,200	√
11-Jul	CFM/T. Smither	One Way Gre Bay/Fargo	142,000	√
11-Jul	NAS/Y. Dupree	Round Trip Chic/GraCay	318,800	√
12-Jul	PIP/C. Nottingham	Round Trip St. P/Peoria	204,400	√
13-Jul	BBB/B. Wilson	Round Trip St. P/Chicago	197,100	√
13- Jul	PIP/C. Nottingham	One Way St. P/Duluth	100,400	√
16-Jul	PIP/C. Nottingham	One Way St. P/Duluth	100,400	√
17-Jul	PIP/C. Nottingham	One Way St. P/Peoria	302,900	√
18-Jul	BBB/B. Wilson	Round Trip GraCay/Fargo	580,300	√
Round Trip St.				
18-Jul	BBB/B. Wilson	Round Trip St. P/Chicago	269,400	√
19-Jul	PIP/C. Nottingham	Round Trip Fargo/Duluth	144,400	√
20-Jul	NAS/Y. Dupree	One Way St. P/GraCay	400,700	√
23-Jul	BBB/B. Wilson	Round Trip Chic/GreBay	163,200	√
24-Jul	PIP/C. Nottingham	Round Trip St. P/Duluth	122,700	√
24-Jul	PIP/C. Nottingham	One Way St. P/Madiso	86,500	√
25-Jul	PIP/C. Nottingham	Round Trip Milwau/Madiso	125,000	√
27-Jul	CFM/T. Smither	One Way St. P/Milwau	187,100	√
27-Jul	BBB/B. Wilson	Round Trip St. P/Fargo	294,100	√
30-Jul	PIP/C. Nottingham	Round Trip St. P/Peoria	198,600	√
31-Jul	NAS/Y. Dupree	Round Trip Chicago/GraCay	305,200	√
		Total	$5,960,300	

Exhibit J
High Flying Charter Corporation
Schedule of Sales Revenue

Date	Customer/Contact	Description	Amoun	FAA Flight Plan
3-Jun	BBB/B. Wilson	Round Trip Chic/Fargo	$210,500	√
3-Jun	PIP/C. Nottingham	One Way Duluth/Chicago	130,900	√
4-Jun	CFM/T. Smither	One Way St. P/Milwau	156,100	√
5-Jun	BBB/B. Wilson	Round Trip St. P/Fargo	150,100	√
6-Jun	PIP/C. Nottingham	Round Trip St. P/Peoria	150,400	√
7-Jun	CFM/T. Smither	One Way St. P/GreBay	220,500	√
7-Jun	CFM/T. Smither	Round Trip St. P/GreBay	240,000	√
10-Jun	CFM/T. Smither	One Way GreBay/Chic	120,200	√
10-Jun	CFM/T. Smither	One Way Gre Bay/Fargo	150,000	√
11-Jun	NAS/Y. Dupree	Round Trip Chic/GraCay	300,600	√
12-Jun	BBB/B. Wilson	Round Trip St. P/Chicago	371,400	√
13-Jun	PIP/C. Nottingham	One Way St. P/Duluth	150,300	√
13-Jun	PIP/C. Nottingham	One Way St. P/Duluth	150,800	√
14-Jun	PIP/C. Nottingham	One Way St. P/Peoria	190,300	√
17-Jun	CFM/T. Smither	Round Trip GreBay/Fargo	280,500	√
17-Jun	CFM/T. Smither	Round Trip GreBay/Fargo	272,900	√
18-Jun	BBB/B. Wilson	Round Trip Chic/Fargo	200,700	√
19-Jun	PIP/C. Nottingham	Round Trip St. P/Duluth	260,900	√
19-Jun	CFM/T. Smither	One Way GreBay/Fargo	191,500	√
19-Jun	PIP/C. Nottingham	One Way Duluth/Milwau	199,300	√
20-Jun	PIP/C. Nottingham	Round Trip Duluth/Chic	300,200	√
20-Jun	PIP/C. Nottingham	Round Trip Duluth/Chic	300,200	√
21-Jun	PIP/C. Nottingham	Round Trip GreBay/Madiso	300,540	√
24-Jun	NAS/Y. Dupree	One Way St. P/GraCay	300,700	√
24-Jun	NAS/Y. Dupree	One Way GraCay/St. P	320,900	√
24-Jun	NAS/Y. Dupree	One Way St. P/GraCay	330,700	√
25-Jun	BBB/B. Wilson	One Way St. P/Chicago	190,500	√
25-Jun	NAS/Y. Dupree	One Way GraCay/St. P	350,300	√
26-Jun	NAS/Y. Dupree	One Way St. P/GraCay	350,400	√
26-Jun	NAS/Y. Dupree	One Way GraCay/Chicago	370,700	√
27-Jun	BBB/B. Wilson	Round Trip St. P/Chicago	250,100	√
27-Jun	BBB/B. Wilson	Round Trip St P/Chicago	180,500	√
28-Jun	NAS/Y. Dupree	One Way Chicago/GraCay	200,400	√
28-Jun	BBB/B. Wilson	Round Trip St. P/Fargo	200,110	√
30-Jun	NAS/Y. Dupree	One Way GraCay/Chicago	320,700	√
		Total	$8,364,850	

Exhibit K

High Flying Charter Corporation
Schedule of Aircraft
June 30, 2014

Aircraft Internal ID	Plane	Cost	Acquisition Date
Hwk	Hawker 4000	$5,105,480	June 15,2014
DF	Dassault Falcon 2000 LX	$5,050,000	May 22, 2014
GS-150	Gulf Stream 20	$1,000,200	March 18, 2014
CE-II	Citation Eagle II	$1,180,000	February 10, 2013
GG	Gulfstream G-IIB	$1,100,000	November 14, 2012
BK	Beech King Air	$1,460,580	September 30, 2012

Exhibit L

Bank Statement and Standard Bank Confirmation

Crowne Royal Chartered Bank
P. O. Box 717
97 Fort Street
Grand Cayman, Cayman Islands KY1-1222
(345) 949-0202
Discretion. Security. Safety.

Bank Statement for General Account #T 1411
High Flying Charter Company

Beginning Balance 06/01/2014	$17,759,900
Add: Deposits	2,845,400
Less: Checks Paid, Withdrawals	13,491,410
Ending Balance 06/30/2014	**$7,113,890**

Detail of Deposits:			Detail of Checks Paid:
6/11/2014	*wire transfer*	$300,600	No Activity
6/24/2014	*wire transfer*	300,700	
6/24/2014	*wire transfer*	320,900	
6/24/2014	*wire transfer*	330,700	Details of Withdrawals
6/25/2014	*wire transfer*	350,300	
6/26/2014	*wire transfer*	350,400	$13,491,410
6/26/2014	*wire transfer*	370,700	
6/28/2014	*wire transfer*	200,400	
6/30/2014	*wire transfer*	320,700	
Total Deposits		**$2,845,400**	

STANDARD FORM TO CONFIRM ACCOUNT

BALANCE INFORMATION WITH FINANCIAL INSTITUTIONS

High Flying Charter Company
Checking Account Balance as of 06/30/2014

non-interest bearing

#T 1411   no compensating balance

$7,113,890

Signature   Philipě Van Andressen

Date   5.Jul.2014

Philipě Van Andressen
Assistant Vice-President, International Banking

Crowne Royal Chartered Bank
P. O. Box 717
97 Fort Street
Grand Cayman, Cayman Islands KY1-1222
(345) 949-0202
Discretion. Security. Safety.

Please return to:
Smith Franklin CPAs LLP
1470 West 32nd Street
Minneapolis, MN USA 55405

Exhibit M

High Flying Charter Company
Terms and Conditions for all Charter Agreements
Effective July 1, 2013

Name of Charterer _____

Street Address _____

_____

City   State   Zip Code

_____

Date Charter Commences   Date Charter Concludes

Flight Schedule:

Outbound City	Return City
Departure Time	Departure Time
Arrival Time	Arrival time

One-way or Round-trip   Number of Passengers _____

	Date and Initial
Flight Price _____	Payment Received in full
_____	Charter Aircraft Assigned
Catering	Flight Crew Scheduled
	Cabin Crew Scheduled
_____	Catering Confirmed
_____	
Other Services	Additional Services Confirmed

Fuel Surcharge _____

Misc. Charges _____

Total Charter Price _____

The parties hereto have caused this agreement to be executed in their names and on behalf of their respective officers thereunto duly authorized, as of this date and year.

Agreed:

_____

High Flying Charter Company   Charterer

_____

Name   Name

_____

Date   Title   Date   Title

The following terms and conditions apply to all air charters conducted by *High Flying Charter Company*, a Minnesota corporation with offices at Holman Field, St. Paul, MN 55107, and every charter *Customer* who executes an agreement with High Flying Charter Company, except to the extent that the agreement contains special terms and conditions that specifically replace those set forth below.

A. *Basic Agreement*: Customer and High Flying Charter Company agree that the following terms and conditions shall apply to all charters from the point at which High Flying Charter Company has received Customer's passengers until the aircraft arrives at the final destination, except as otherwise modified on page one of the agreement.

B. *Charter Price, Other Charges and Related Conditions.*
    1. *Booking*: For each charter, Customer will sign and date the Agreement where indicated. Full payment of the contract price must be received by High Flying Charter Company prior to dispatching the aircraft.
    2. *Price*: Customer shall pay High Flying Charter Company the total charter price plus any additional billing per this Agreement, which shall be deemed irrevocably earned unless transportation hereunder is canceled. The price is based on the planned itinerary and anticipated charges. Additional flight time charges may be incurred in the event of weather avoidance, holding and ATC routing changes. The contract price does not include after-hours airport operation fees, parking fees, aircraft de-icing, or hanger-related expenses due to ice or inclement weather, catering, or itinerary changes. Should any part of the itinerary change, the trip may be re-quoted.
    3. *Flight Crew Duty Time*: In order to comply with Federal Aviation Regulations, the parties shall provide for no more than ten (10) flight hours and fourteen (14) duty hours within any twenty-four (24) hour period. There shall be ten (10) hours of uninterrupted rest within each twenty-four (24) hour period. Duty time shall normally begin two (2) hours before each daily flight sequence and end a half (1/2) hour after each daily flight sequence, unless provisions such as a hotel room for each crewmember is provided for a rest period in between flights; otherwise, the duty time continues.
    4. *Rest Period*: An uninterrupted rest period of ten (10) consecutive hours shall begin a half (1/2) hour after a flight sequence if that rest period includes the use of a hotel room or other suitable area for crew rest. The rest period normally ends two (2) hours prior to the scheduled departure.
    5. *Responsible Party Additional Charges*: All fuel, crew salary, and aircraft maintenance shall be paid by High Flying Charter Company. Fuel surcharges, if any, shall be paid by Customer. Customer shall pay all other charges, including but not limited to, transportation taxes,

foreign taxes, catering, ground transportation, de-icing, hangar fees for inclement weather, landing fees, airway fees, security fees, after-hours airport

6. *Airborne Phone and Airborne Internet*: If an airborne telephone and/ or airborne Internet service is available and used during the charter, Customer will be charged for the service.

C. *Prohibited Activities; High Flying Charter Company's Right of Refusal to Conduct Flight*: All aircraft travelers are restricted from the following activities:
1. Smoking tobacco or other products of any type.
2. Transportation of pets or animals of any type.

Client agrees and acknowledges that High Flying Charter Company reserves the right to refuse to commence a charter trip, or to terminate a charter trip as soon as is reasonably practicable, in the event Client attempts to bring any type of pet, or to smoke on board the aircraft.

D. *Payment*: High Flying Charter Company must receive payment in full for all anticipated charges prior to origination of the charter. High Flying Charter Company will accept the following methods of payment: (i) Wells Bank customers via online transfer; or (ii) wire transfer; or (iii) credit card charge that shall include a four (4) percent processing fee. All Funds must be payable in U.S. dollars and must clear High Flying Charter Company's bank account prior to dispatching the aircraft. In addition, a credit card shall be provided, or other arrangements made, by Customer for any additional charges incurred beyond those paid for in accordance with the payment procedures herein.

E. *Price and Payment*: The contract price has been set based on current local taxes and other public fees and fuel prices and fuel surcharges as of the date of the agreement. High Flying Charter Company reserves the right to adjust prices in the event price increases are imposed by Governmental Authorities.

F. *High Flying Charter's Rights and Responsibilities*:
1. High Flying Charter Company is responsible to exercise due diligence in the delivery of charter services but does not guarantee route, speed or specific departure or arrival dates or times.
2. High Flying Charter Company will attempt to accommodate Customer requests for specific aircraft and crew but does not guarantee the availability of any requested aircraft or crew.
3. During Charter Services, High Flying Charter Company shall, at all times, have exclusive control over the aircraft, the aircraft crew, passengers and all cargo onboard.

4. High Flying Charter Company maintains the exclusive right to refuse to transport any cargo or luggage that the company determines to be hazardous or unsafe for any reason at its sole discretion.

5. High Flying Charter Company may terminate a charter without prior notice, in its sole discretion, if the company makes a determination that transportation would be hazardous or ,

G. *Customer Rights and Responsibilities*:
    1. Prior to boarding for flight departure, Customer is responsible to provide a passenger manifest, including each passenger's full name and weight to High Flying Charter Company. The manifest for international flights must include date of birth, passport country of issue, and passport number for each passenger.
    2. Customer is responsible to ensure that each passenger has a proper photo ID, including passports for international flights. Passengers without proper identification will not be permitted to board the aircraft.
    3. Each passenger is allowed one 30- pound bag plus one carryon item.
    4. Passengers may not pack any hazardous cargo or weapons in their luggage. Any weapons brought aboard the aircraft must be declared five days in advance of departure and a proper permit to carry documentation must be provided to High Flying Charter Company at the time of declaration.
    5. Customer is responsible for any damage or loss of property aboard the aircraft attributable to the Customers cargo or passengers.
    6. High Flying Charter Company will arrange catering for your trip. Our team will strive to accommodate your specific catering request; however, at times some items may be unavailable.
    7. In the event we are unable to provide a requested item, we will provide a substitution of comparable quality.

H. *Assigning or Subletting Aircraft Utilization*: Customer is not entitled to assign or sublet any portion of his rights under this Charter Contract without the express written permission of High Flying Charter Company.

I   *Cancellation Due to Conditions Beyond the Control of High Flying Charter Company*: The company may cancel or delay flight departure without liability if said cancellation or delay is the result of conditions or circumstances beyond the control of High Flying Charter Company including but not limited to strikes, civil unrest, riots, embargo, fire, flood, storms, or epidemics.

J.   *Law and Jurisdiction*: This charter shall be governed by the laws of the State of Minnesota and any dispute arising in connection with this charter or the transportation of the passengers or cargo hereunder shall be brought in state or federal court located in Minnesota with the prevailing party to recover its legal fees and costs.

Integration: This document, the air waybill, and any agreed attachment constitute the entire contract between the parties with respect to the charter described herein and supersede all prior or contemporaneous written or oral agreements. This agreement may only be modified or amended by the express written consent of all parties.

Customer Initials _____ Date _____

Client Initials _____Date_____

Exhibit N

First Assignment for Case

Please prepare for and conduct an interview with the client contact.

Background. This is an individual assignment. You, as the audit senior on the HF audit, will interview a person portraying one of the client contacts, Mr. Kemper or Ms. Walsh. To prepare for this interview, you should carefully review and analyze the Exhibits. For example, you could look for unusual amounts, patterns and activities, while considering the client and industry.

Required. Compile a list of questions to ask the client. When you conduct the interview, ask these questions. Take notes. Be sure to follow up on answers that are confusing, incomplete, or inconsistent. In the follow-up class session, you will be asked to report on what you did and did not learn from the client. You will be asked to reflect on how you could have acquired more and better information from the client.

Exhibit O

Second Assignment for Case

Please reflect on your interview experience.

Background. This project is a team assignment. Your professor will assign you to a team. Please prepare the responses with word processing.

Required. Prepare responses to the questions below. Submit your paper in the office before you leave for the day. We will discuss the responses in our follow-up session.
1. How did you feel when you were interviewing your client?
2. Did you get the information you needed? Please explain.
3. What questions/follow-ups do you have for your audit senior, manager, or partner?
4. What are your concerns, especially, in relation to this specific audit?

Exhibit P

Third Assignment for Case

Please evaluate and analyze possible issues and problems at the client.

Background. This is an individual assignment. Please identify, analyze, and discuss unusual amounts, patterns, and activities at the client. Prepare the responses with word processing and spreadsheets.

Required. Please answer the following questions. Provide details and analysis as appropriate.
1. Analyze profitability. Do you see any unusual activity related to profitability? If so, what?
2. Consider the prices charged for flights. Do these seem reasonable? Why or why not?
3. Evaluate the bank statement and bank confirmation. Do the amounts seem reasonable? Why or why not? Does ending cash tie to the balance sheet? What concerns might you have about cash?
4. Consider the relationship between cash and sales revenue. What concerns might you have about this relationship?
5. Are there any related party transactions? If so, who or what is involved with this transaction? Why is this a concern?
6. How would you characterize the environment at the client? Does this characterization lead to any concerns?

7.   Do you have specific concerns about the top executives at this client?
8.   Consider various analytical procedures that could be helpful in this situation. Identify these analytical procedures and prepare them. Comment on what you see.
9.   Consider property, plant and equipment (PPE). Do the items of PPE look reasonable? If not, discuss what looks unusual.

*Adapted from Vol. 7, No. 2, July-December, 2015, *Journal of Forensic & Investigative Accounting.*

CASE STUDY 34:

Uncovering Majority Shareholder Fraud in a Closely-Held Corporation: A Case Study to Develop Forensic/Tax Investigation Skills*

Cynthia E. Bolt, CPA, MTax
The Citadel

Richard W. Powell, Ph.D., JD, CPA
Pepperdine University

LEARNING OBJECTIVES

After completing and discussing this case, you should be able to

- Recognize and identify tax, forensic, and legal issues.
- Understand and recognize assumptions and inferences, as opposed to concrete facts.
- Improve research and investigative skills.
- Think analytically and critically.
- Understand and assess interpersonal relationships between majority and minority shareholders.
- Develop written communication skills.
- Enhance professional judgment.
- Communicate ideas and opinions.
- Make and defend decisions.

INTRODUCTION

Financial "irregularities" often arise in closely-held businesses. When the majority shareholder controls the accounting records, employs family members, and conducts all legal and accounting transactions, opportunities are abundant for self-dealing and breach of fiduciary duty.

Students are placed in the role of a forensic accountant working with a small, closely-held business in tax and financial statement preparation. A client, a minority shareholder in a construction company, engages the accountant after the majority shareholder states that cash flow is weak, salaries must be reduced, and shareholders must make cash contributions to maintain liquidity. The client expresses concerns with the cash flow situation due to his knowledge and experience with recent collections of large accounts receivable, which is contrary to the majority shareholders' claims.

The case addresses issues regarding the widespread problem of shareholder fraud within a closely- held business. The student is required to determine an appropriate course of action, including the acquisition of corporate records withheld from the minority shareholder, analysis of records, potential coordination with forensic accountants, legal issues related to the discovery of personal expenses paid by the company, and failure to properly comply with associated laws. The client to date has only seen his personal K-1. Financial statements, Form 1120S tax returns, and other financial information have not been shared. The minority shareholder expresses concerns with what appears to be corporate self-dealing, including company vehicles for office personnel, excess rent paid for property owned by the majority shareholder, family member employment, and several expenses that appear personal in nature.

ACME CONSTRUCTION COMPANY FACTS

The client, Bob Mitchell, is a minority shareholder in a closely-held construction company, Acme Construction. Annually you prepare Bob's individual return, which includes a K-1 from his company's Form 1120S. You have no responsibilities related to Acme Construction, and you have never seen any records other than the annual K-1 and the W-2 Bob receives as an Acme employee. Aside from the preparation of his individual return, you have not been involved in Bob's financial affairs.

Bob sets up an appointment with you to discuss a recent situation with his company. Bob tells you that all shareholders in the company are related parties except for himself, and he was asked to join as an investor due to his extensive experience and sales base. When you talk to him before the appointment, he says that the majority shareholder called a meeting recently, requested a $10,000 contribution from each shareholder, and indicated extensive cash flow problems leading to an inability to meet payroll requirements. Bob expresses extreme doubt, as he knows sales are strong and, to his knowledge, there are no large receivables outstanding.

Bob is responsible for company sales and operations. Family members, both shareholders and non-shareholders, conduct administrative and business matters including accounting and legal dealings. Bob has limited experience with the administrative side of the business, and after 10 years he has stayed out of any management issues. According to Bob, any requests for financial information were discouraged by the majority shareholder/president of the company. You ask him to provide you with prior years' financial information, including tax returns and financial statements.

When Bob arrives for his appointment, he does not have any of the information requested. His request to the majority shareholders was denied, and he was told that his job was to "manage the construction sites, not the company business." Given the harsh tone of this statement, you ask further questions about suspicious activity. Bob tells you that the majority shareholders consist of four family members owning 85%. Bob's share is 15%. The majority shareholder who serves as president of Acme is employed full time elsewhere, but his immediate family members run office operations. His wife, one of the shareholders, is "CFO."

Specific details from Bob include the following:

- Most of the office employees are family members:
    - The majority shareholders' parents are employed, as well as the majority shareholders' college-aged children (during their holiday breaks and summer).
    - Family members work inconsistently throughout the week, and Bob has observed that personal chores are frequently performed at the office during business hours.
    - The majority shareholder, employed fulltime at another company, draws a rather large salary. He has explained to Bob that he works in Acme management as needed during the day, during the evenings, and on weekends.
- Family member employees each appear to have received a cell phone and automobile paid for by the company.
- Operations are run from a business location that provides storage for equipment and construction inventory. Company trucks are parked there and employees meet daily before going to job sites. Construction project managers are provided office space, and there are several empty offices. A small break room is available. The land and building used for operations is owned by the majority shareholder.
- The office/administrative operations are located at a separate site in a family member's spare bedroom (presumably for convenience).

Bob asks you to assist with investigating the cash flow issue, but he's concerned that he does not have any rights to access the accounting records. At your request, Bob calls the tax preparer directly and copies of the prior three years' returns are emailed. As Bob leaves, you provide him with a copy of the state's laws related to minority shareholder rights, including an explanation of the laws against minority shareholder oppression. Bob plans to contact the majority shareholder to request accounting records given this new information.

When Bob leaves, you examine the S corporation tax return. Immediately several areas of concern appear:

- Travel expenses for the local company are extensive.
- The company has reported a net loss for several years.
- Consulting fees, found in "other expenses" on the tax return, are in excess of $150,000.
- Cell phone charges confirm the minority shareholder's suspicion, as it appears there are numerous, large cell phone bills being included in "other expenses" on the tax return.

- Office rent is extremely large, in contrast to Bob's statement that the location of business operations are on property owned by the majority shareholder. An online search of ownership records for the county confirms this fact.
- Meals and entertainment expenses for the company are large, as are donations to charities.

You call the signing tax preparer, who states that he does not review records. He only uses the Acme trial balance (prepared by the majority shareholder), updates depreciation, and has a staff member prepare the return based on the client's information. His nominal involvement is done to ensure the client fees are kept to a minimum.

Bob returns the following week with electronic copies of the general ledger and financial statements. Bob and you pull up the information and project it on a screen to provide details of transactions in questionable accounts. Suspicions of self-dealing are confirmed, including several unexpected costs for personal expenses buried in the construction supplies expense account. It appears there are extensive issues with the due to/due from shareholder account, including mislabeled deposits and withdrawals, revealing considerable uncertainty as to the transactions recorded. Additionally, payroll tax withholding, including insurance and taxes, appears to be unreconciled and incorrect.

REQUIRED:

Identify the tax, legal, and potential fraud issues associated with Acme Construction. How should these issues be investigated? What assistance will you need? How do you proceed?

Provide details on your approach towards assisting Bob, the minority shareholder, with the challenge he is facing in a company where he is affiliated as not just an owner but also as an employee.

Write a report for your accounting firm's files and also write a letter to Bob. Thoroughly explain the approach you have chosen and the challenges faced in this situation. Consider IRC Section 162, Circular 230, and Statements on Standards for Tax Services.

Issues for Discussion
- What questions should be asked of the majority shareholders working in management?
- What questions should be asked of the current tax advisor/CPA? Has he violated any professional standards?
- How should the reasonableness of compensation, rent, and other expenses paid to family members be determined?
- How should the compliance or lack of compliance with government regulations (such as the filing of a W-2 or Form 1099 for the company president) be addressed?

- What if management doesn't comply?
- Should legal counsel be hired? Is a forensic accountant required?
- What tax laws have been violated by the majority shareholders?
- Has the CPA who prepares the Form 1120S violated any laws or standards?
- What other issues should be addressed?
- Do these irregularities require an amended return? If so, what if management or the company's CPA fail to amend the return?

*Adapted from Vol. 8, No. 2, July-December, 2016, Journal of Forensic & Investigative Accounting.

CASE STUDY 35:

DIAMOND FOODS' PAYMENTS TO NUT GROWERS

Priscilla Burnaby, Ph.D., CPA
Bentley University

Susan Hass, MBA, CPA, CGMA
Simmons College

Donna McConville, CPA, JD
Bentley University

LEARNING OBJECTIVES

After completing and discussing this case, you should be able to

- Recognize a food company recording costs in the wrong period.
- Understand how company culture and senior management can influence behavior and lead to the wrong decisions.
- Recognize how financial statements and reporting are impacted by fraudulent activities.
- Identify how fraud can be prevented and appreciate how other stakeholders respond to fraud allegations.

The leadership of Diamond Foods (DF), the global California-based premium snack food company, was excited. In the fall of 2011, the company was close to finalizing an agreement with Proctor & Gamble to acquire the Pringles brand in exchange for DF stock.[1] This acquisition would help the company achieve the number two position in the U.S. snack foods industry behind PepsiCo. DF product lines currently included potato chips (Kettle), popcorn (Pop-Secret), and nuts (snack nuts, in-shell nuts and culinary nuts) (Emerald and Diamond of California). DF started in 1912 as a grower-owned cooperative called Diamond of California. The company originally focused on walnuts, but more recently they transformed into a diverse snack food company. The business changed from a co-operative business status and went public in 2005 with the NASDAQ ticker DMND. The stock price increased, and in September 2011, the price was at an all-time high of $92 per share.[2]

The person who orchestrated the company's expansion and growth was CEO and President Michael Mendes, who was hired in 1997. He had previously

---

[1] Alpert, Bill (2011, November 7). Getting to the Nut of the Problem. *Barron's*. http://online.barrons.com/article/SB50 00142405274870427020457701393387895O486.html

[2] Diamond Foods, Inc. website, (accessed 2013, November 30). Hardesty, Shermain D. (2009). The conversion of Diamond Walnut Growers. *Journal of Cooperatives*. Vol.23. oo. 44-45.

worked at Hormel Foods Corporation and Dole Food Company. Mendes was very competitive and implemented the companywide philosophy of 'bigger is better.' This viewpoint was the corporate culture, and it had a significant impact on employees of DF. This aggressive company culture resulted in an emphasis on financial performance and some bold and very expensive acquisitions (e.g., Kettle and Pop-Secret). The most expensive acquisition was to be Pringles. DF was making this acquisition so it could be a significant player in the very competitive snack foods space where it felt pressure for financial success and greater market share amid increasing industry competition.[3]

In fall 2011, Mark Roberts, founder of the Off Wall Street Consulting Group, received an anonymous call.[4] For the fiscal year ending in July 2011, the caller indicated that DF was making 'momentum payments' to growers for walnuts delivered in September 2011. It appears that the approximately $60 million payments could be impacting the wrong fiscal year financial statements. Roberts accused DF of incorrectly reporting its payments to suppliers on the company financial statements. DF denied any illegal actions, and they replied that the payments were an advance on the fiscal 2012 crop and had nothing to do with fiscal 2011. Unfortunately, the nut growers disagreed. They were told by the company to keep the money even if they were not going to provide crops for 2012. Supposedly, they were told that the payments were for the prior year.[5]

Investigation into the situation ascertained that an additional approximately $20 million of 'continuity payments' were made by DF to growers in fall 2010. Again, the question arose as to what fiscal year did these payments relate. Were the payments recorded in the proper year? Were the books cooked? Would the Pringles acquisition occur?

[3]   Alpert, Bill (2011, November 7). Getting to the Nut of the Problem. *Barron's*. *http://online.barrons.com/article/SB5 00014240527487042702045770139338789 50486.html*. Herel, Suzanne. (2010, July 11). Meet the Boss: Diamond Foods CEO Michael Mendes. SFGate. Jannarone, John (2011, September 27). Hidden Flaw in P&G's Diamond Deal. *http://online.wsj.com/news/articles/SB10001424052970204831304576595000985103090*. Michael Mendes. (2013, April 13). Forbes. *http://www.forbes.com/profile/michael-mendes/*

[4]   Roberts, Mark (2012, August 15). Interview with Suraj Srinivasan and Tim Gray. Cambridge, MA. Summarized in HBS Diamond Foods, Inc. case 9-113-055.

[5]   Off Wall Street Consulting Group (2011, September 25). Diamond Foods. *http://www.offwallstreet.com/reports/ NEW_DMND_9-25-11.pdf*.

QUESTIONS

1. Review Research Diamond Foods' website. Find and read articles written about the problems they had with payments to the nut growers in 2010 and 2011. Did Diamond record payments to the nut growers in the wrong period? Did the company commit fraudulent acts?

2. What financial accounting rules are applicable in this instance?

    a. In what fiscal periods should fall 2010 and fall 2011 payments have been recorded in the DF income statements?

    b. Is this a different period than when the cash was paid to the growers?

    c. What was the impact on the company's financial statements in those years?

3. What other factors were occurring at the company that may have contributed to this situation? Consider hints in the case and the articles you reviewed in question (1) above as you answer this question.

4. Who found the fraud? How could it have been prevented? What actions did the company take as a result of these events?

5. Did Diamond Foods acquire the Pringles line from Proctor & Gamble?

CASE STUDY 36:

The Dixon City Embezzlement: A Rita Crundwell Story

Priscilla Burnaby, Ph.D., CPA
Bentley University

Susan Hass, MBA, CPA, CGMA
Simmons College

Donna McConville, CPA, JD
Bentley University

LEARNING OBJECTIVES

After completing and discussing this case, you should be able to

- Learn how fraudsters conceal fraud and the disadvantages of two sets of auditors.
- Identify false invoices, bank accounts, and other red flags.
- Develop ways to prevent fraud.
- Appreciate the aftermath of a significant fraud.

Rita Crundwell was convicted of embezzling approximately $54 million from the city of Dixon, Illinois over a period of 22 years. Rita's crimes makes her the biggest municipal embezzler in U.S. history. She ranks fifth among embezzlers of *any* kind.[1] The amount that the FBI alleges that Rita Crundwell stole from September 2011 to February 2012 is more than Dixon budgeted on police, fire, and other essentials combined. Rita spent her embezzled funds on expensive jewelry, fancy clothes, a custom motor coach, boats, property in Florida, luxury cars, and the finest horses the city's money could buy. The question that should have been asked: how could a small-town, high school bookkeeper afford to dazzle her friends and coworkers with her horse ranch and trophy room?[2]

From 1983 to April 2012, Rita Crundwell was the comptroller and treasurer of Dixon, Illinois right up until the time she was arrested. Rita embezzled the funds to support her multimillion dollar American Quarter Horse breeding operation. She was considered one of the best-known quarter horse breeders in the country. Her breeding program produced 52 world champions. (Keyser, 2012) For eight consecutive years prior to her arrest, Rita was named the leading owner by the American Quarter Horse Association. Crundwell was 59 years old when

[1] Smith, B. (2012, November 14). Rita Crundwell and the Dixon embezzlement. *Chicago Magazine*. http://www. chicagomag.com/Chicago-Magazine/December-2012/Rita-Crundwell-and-the-Dixon-Embezzlement/
[2] Keyser, J. (2012, April 27). Rita Crundwell: Dixon, Illinois comptroller allegedly spent embezzled millions on horses. *The Huffington Post.http://www.huffingtonpost.com/2012/04/27/rita-crundwell-dixon-illi_n_1460180.html*

she was arrested and sentenced to almost 20 years in prison for her crimes. Who was she and how did she committed the fraud?

Rita came from humble beginnings. She grew up on the family farm near Dixon, where the population of only 16,000 consisted of low to middle class individuals.[3] In school, Rita was on the National Honor Society. While in high school at the age of 17 through her school's work-study program, Rita began working at the Dixon City Hall. Rita worked her way up from secretary to treasurer. She worked for the city of Dixon for nearly three decades. Crundwell was a trusted employee who was a participant in budget meetings with city council members.[4] Her coworkers said she was wonderful to work with. The mayor of Dixon, who knew Rita Crundwell since she was a teenager, said that Rita was very smart and almost brilliant.[5] This view may explain how she could pull off something of this magnitude.

QUESTIONS

1. Describe the fraud scheme committed by Rita Crundwell, including how she concealed the fraud.

2. How could this fraud have been prevented? In your discussion, be sure to explain the controls that were missing at City Hall.

3. Explain how the auditors for the City of Dixon did not detect the fraud.

    a. How was this fraud continued for so many years?

    b. What red flags did the auditors miss?

4. How was the fraud finally detected? Explain the legal side of the case?

[3]   Keyser, J. (2012, April 27). Feds: Ill. suspect spent stolen millions on horses. *Associated Press. http://www.boston. com/news/nation/articles/2012/04/27/feds_ill_suspect_spent_stolen_millionson_horses/?page=full.*

[4]   Pavlo, W. (2013, February 14). Fmr Dixon, IL comptroller, Rita Crundwell, sentenced to 19 ½ years in prison. *Forbes. http://www.forbes.com/sites/walterpavlo/2013/02/14/fmr-dixon-il-comptroller-rita-crundwell-sentenced-to-19-12-years-in-prison/.*

[5]   Keyser, J. (2012, April 27). Feds: Ill. suspect spent stolen millions on horses. *Associated Press. http://www.boston. com/news/nation/articles/2012/04/27/feds_ill_suspect_spent_stolen_millionson_horses/?page=full.*

CASE STUDY 37:

MANI/PEDI? CREDIT CARDS NOT ACCEPTED

Cynthia E. Bolt, CPA, MTax
The Citadel

LEARNING OBJECTIVES

After completing and discussing this case, you should be able to

- Describe the situation at a business that would lead an IRS examiner to suspect underreported income.
- Develop a suitable approach to address the suspicion of underreported income.
- Recognize the types of nonfinancial data available to estimate the amount of unreported income.
- Understand the importance of an accurate accounting system for reporting.

SALON NAILS FACTS

Salon Nails, a fictitious nail salon located in the suburbs of a large northeastern city, provides manicures and pedicures for its customers. The business operates as an S-corporation with 100% of shares owned by Gina Lee. Opened seven days a week from 9:00 am until 7:00 pm, the salon currently employs ten nail technicians. Gina has six pedicure chairs and eight stations for manicures and other nail services and has owned the business for three years.

Alex Ray is a revenue agent with the Internal Revenue Service (IRS), assigned to examine Salon Nails. The company reported a net loss since its opening. The IRS has selected the business for audit. Alex receives the following information from the prior three years regarding tax filings for Salon Nails:

- Salon Nails employs 8-10 employees annually, with wages ranging from $2,000 to $35,000 per year.
- The employer files payroll tax returns and W-2 information in a timely fashion, paying withholdings as required.
- Salon Nails files form 1120S and the owner has properly reported income from the K-1 and her own W-2 on her individual tax return.
- Salon Nails uses the cash method of accounting.
- Net losses for the prior three years were ($220,000), ($150,000) and ($75,000) respectively.
- Salons in the area with a similar-size business, employees, and payroll report net income on their tax returns in excess of $100,000, as the nail salon business is quite lucrative in this affluent suburb.

Alex sets up an appointment with Ms. Lee to examine the business accounting records. He requests a meeting at the business location during office hours. Alex will determine the scope of the audit work, as no specific area of concern has been identified.

When Alex meets with Ms. Lee, she is noticeably nervous, which is not unusual in an IRS audit situation. The appointment time, 2:00 pm on a Thursday afternoon, was intentionally set to provide a sense of the average business flow for Salon Nails. The salon is busy, with three customers in the waiting area, three pedicure stations operating, and four customers receiving nail services. There are seven employees in the salon.

Immediately, Alex notes that the business is properly licensed with the state board of cosmetology. Technicians are wearing gloves and masks, the disinfecting equipment is operating, and the salon is well-kept. Customers and technicians are chatting and music is playing lightly. Women receiving pedicures are enjoying sodas while they read magazines and relax in massage chairs. The clientele appears to be high-income, based on expensive cars in the parking lot, as well as personal appearance.

A sign displays the cost for services: manicures cost $17 and pedicures are $38 with a package deal of $50. At the front of the salon is a display case where customers can buy nail polish, nail dryers, electric manicure kits and special lotions and spa items. Prices are handwritten on a sticker on the side of each product.

There is no cash register, and Alex sees one technician receive cash from a customer, and another using a card to pay for her pedicure. One of the customers receives a receipt for the transaction, and the other does not. There is a visible sign at each station stating "no credit cards accepted." Another sign states "debit cards or cash only." A folded card is on the appointment desk up front in calligraphy: "All tips in cash please."

Alex notices that the customer received a handwritten receipt from a receipt pad similar to those found at the office supply store. Alex notes these invoice forms do not have the business logo or the services provided. As Alex observes, the nail technicians ask customers if they would like a receipt. It appears receipts are optional.

Ms. Lee takes Alex to her office in the back of the building. Alex notices a new MacBook Air and several file cabinets in the room, along with a sofa, widescreen television, refrigerator, table and chairs as well as a private restroom. Several accordion files are on the table with post-it notes separating stacks of receipts that appear to be bundled by date. The room is well decorated and organized, as it appears Ms. Lee has pulled out files for the meeting.

Alex tells Ms. Lee that this is just an initial meeting to see what type of records are kept at Salon Nails. As she turns the television off, Ms. Lee explains that she does not really have a formal computerized accounting system, but she says "my system works and I know where every penny goes." Each day the technicians bring her their receipts and the cash plus debit card slips, from their individual stations. She adds up the receipts and records them in her columned ledger. After counting the cash and ensuring it matches the receipts, she deposits it in the bank or leaves it in the vault in the office until the next day's bank trip. Technicians keep their own cash tips.

Ms. Lee shows Alex a ledger and tells him that this is her record from the prior year. In the book are neatly written penciled entries, separating the day's receipts into three columns: (1) manicures, (2) pedicures, and (3) product sales. As if reading Alex's mind, she opens a file cabinet where he notices stacks of receipts bound by rubber bands. "This is last week's receipts" she tells him, "and I can show you how I add up all these receipts and they total the amount in my accounting records and my cash deposits at the bank."

Alex notices an adding machine tape on top of each stack of receipts. She pulls one specific date out and shows how the receipt matches her entry in the ledger. Alex asks if he can see her appointment book, but since the business is open, Ms. Lee says he should look at the one from last year, as the current book is needed for today's customers. "Do all customers make appointments?" he asks? Ms. Lee explains that it's about 50/50, but that most customers sign in when they first walk in the door so that she knows the type of service they need. "Do you have a receipt book for product sales?" he asks. She shows him a similar invoice book, with no logo, from the prior year and says all sales and sale tax are recorded accurately in the book.

Moving on to deductions from the 1120S, Alex questions her regarding the expenses, and shows her the prior year's tax return. Payroll and payroll taxes, property taxes, sales tax and interest expense were all confirmed through the IRS electronic systems prior to the audit. Other expenses are listed in very broad categories: Cost of Goods Sold, Office Supplies, Rent, Insurance, and "other." Ms. Lee shows him her payroll files, all kept in pencil in the same ledger as receipts. She explains that her nail technicians are straight salary, with no commission, ranging from $8 to $10 per hour, with a bonus paid each month based on production. "I give them cash bonuses, like the salon I used to work for did" she explains. Ms. Lee pulls out her checkbook, business style, with three checks on a page. "It's all in here, and I add up my check stubs at the end of the year and use this to prepare my tax return. I bought the tax preparation software online and it works well. I run the business and manage the technicians so I can ensure our business is operated properly," she says.

"May I see your receipts for other expenses?" Alex asks. Gina shows him her ledger entry which details each check in numerical order. "These checks match my receipts, which are in a box, by month, separated by type. I only write checks, as I know the IRS needs records" she replies. Again she opens a drawer that holds a similar accordion file, this one with a variety of receipts and computer printouts. "I can show you how these receipts match the checks I write," she explains.

Alex nods and tells Ms. Lee that he appreciates her information and that he'll be back next week with more specific questions. This is just a fact finding meeting, and since all files are manual, Alex has nothing to take with him. He thanks Ms. Lee for her time and says he will be in touch.

She walks him to the door. He's parked beside a rather expensive sports car, and a teenage girl gets out and goes to Ms. Lee. "Thanks for letting me borrow your car Mom," she says.

QUESTIONS AND REQUIREMENTS

1. What specific conditions indicate unreported income at Salon Nails?

2. Given the accounting system and Alex's observations, what approach should he take when he returns for a more in-depth examination?

3. What documents and files should Alex request to help him verify the suspicion of underreported income?

4. Has Salon Nails fulfilled obligations with the IRS related to recordkeeping? Support your answer.

CASE STUDY 38:

EXCLUSIVE RESTAURANT OR A FRONT FOR ILLEGAL GAMBLING?

Cynthia E. Bolt, CPA, MTax
The Citadel

LEARNING OBJECTIVES

After completing and discussing this case, you should be able to

- Analyze a scenario where a taxpayer over-reports gross revenue, with rumors pointing to potential money laundering.
- Examine data from five consecutive years to determine possible irregularities in financial information.
- Understand a tax preparer's responsibilities, under Circular 230 and the AICPA's standards, to report suspicious illegal activities occurring in a client's business.

THE EXTRAORDINARY CHEF FACTS

The Extraordinary Chef is an exclusive restaurant in the city. Reservations are difficult to obtain and the menu is pricey. The owner, Andrew, is rumored to be running an illegal gambling operation on the side, with revenue flowing through the restaurant to ensure there will be appropriate reporting of revenue and thus no consequences for tax fraud.

Elaine prepares the corporate tax return for The Extraordinary Chef, based on amounts from Andrew's computerized general ledger, which he shares with her at year-end. After 10 years of working with Andrew in the preparation of his corporate tax return, she feels she understands the business fairly well.

Elaine, a licensed CPA in the state and member of the AICPA, heard stories of the gambling operation, but having worked with Andrew for so long, dismisses the accusations as rumors. This year, however, the business showed a sharp increase in net income as well as revenue, including a large tax liability. Andrew did not complain about the taxes due, as he typically did when he first started.

Information for the prior five years is shown below:					
Year	2011	2012	2013	2014	2014
Revenue	$750,000	$875,000	$1,200,000	$1,700,000	$2,000,000
Cost of Goods Sold	240,000	262,500	324,000	442,000	400,000
Operating Expenses	375,000	410,500	506,250	690,500	625,000
Net Income before Taxes	$135,000	$202,000	$369,750	$567,500	$975,000
Income Tax (34% tax rate)	$45,900	$68,680	$125,715	$192,950	$331,500

QUESTIONS AND REQUIREMENTS

1. What caused Elaine to question her client's tax return?

2. Using data provided, does Elaine have any support for her concerns?

3. What is Elaine's responsibility, under Circular 230 and other tax preparer ethics guidelines, regarding her suspicions?

CASE STUDY 39:

Madon Oilfield Services, Inc.*

Christopher E. Peters, MBA, CFE, CIDA, MAFF
GPS Consultants, LLC

LEARNING OBJECTIVES

After completing and discussing this case, you should be able to

- Use data analysis tools such as CaseWare IDEA® - Data Analysis Software.
- Detect ghost employees.
- Find fraudulent payroll and bonus transactions.
- Discover account mirroring schemes.
- Compare information across data sets.
- Detect anomalies.
- Discover vendor collusion schemes.

This interactive data analysis case study is designed for participants to uncover and investigate realistic fraud schemes using forensic data mining techniques. This case includes an overview of the company, case study engagement, several figures, and other company data that present the red flags and risk areas that participants will further investigate by data mining Madon Oilfield Services, Inc.'s company databases. The data files are now accessible at the URL *http://ideasupport.caseware.com/public/downloads/Madon Database Files.zip*. Download instructions are provided in the "Part I Exercise Hints" that follow.

Case Study Learning Objectives: After effectively completing this case, participants should be capable of using data analysis tools, such as IDEA® - Data Analysis Software, to detect ghost employees, fraudulent payroll and bonus transactions, account mirroring schemes, cash disbursement schemes, and vendor collusion false billing schemes. The emphasis of this exercise is to arm anti-fraud professionals with innovative techniques for mining organizational data to investigate allegations and suspicions of fraud, waste, or abuse. Participants should be able to leverage data analysis to identify transactions that deviate from the business rules, compare information across data sets, and detect anomalies that go unnoticed due to the complexity and/or volume of transactions in an organization's database.

About Madon Oilfield Services, Inc.: Madon Oilfield Services, Inc. ("the Company" or "Madon") was founded by Bernie Madon in August 1995, and is

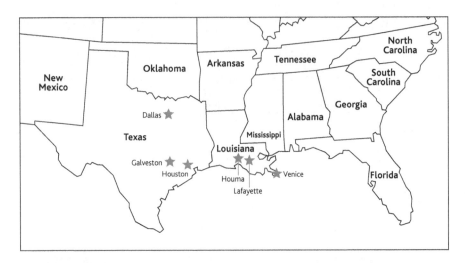

headquartered in Lafayette, Louisiana. Prior to founding the Company, Bernie Madon had a decorated career in the oilfield industry, having managed and founded several successful oilfield service companies.

The Company has a total of six branches. There are three branches in Louisiana: Lafayette, Houma, and Venice and three branches in Texas: Dallas, Galveston, and Houston. The Company has experienced rapid growth as annual revenue increased from $40 million to $300 million over the past 10 years. Knowing that the company had outgrown its administrative policies and procedures, Bernie Madon decided to hire a Controller, Ona Scott, to enhance the business processes, implement an internal control environment, improve financial reporting, and standardize business processes to streamline anticipated expansion.

The Company is one of the largest regional distributors of pipe, valve, and fitting products, and they service the oilfield and industries primarily in the gulf south. Customers include oil refineries, oil transporters, freight exporters, and offshore and inshore drilling companies. The Company offers customers products such as pipes, valves, fittings and flanges, drilling equipment, and other specialty products.

Organizational Structure. Each branch has a branch manager, a small sales team, a warehouse manager, warehouse/yard crew, receptionists/administrative assistants, and delivery truck drivers. The CEO, the controller, and the accounting staff are based out of Lafayette, and all accounts payable and payroll processes are centralized and processed out of this branch. This central location is the Company's original branch and is still one of the top revenue-producing branches. The past 12 months have been record-breaking months, as new shale discoveries have customers investing heavily in new and existing projects in the area.

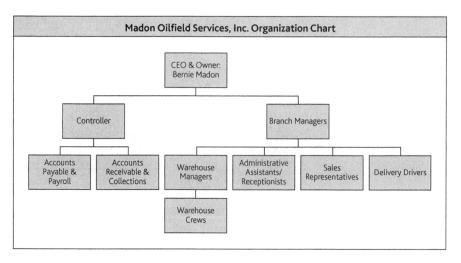

Bernie Madon OWNER & CHIEF EXECUTIVE OFFICER (CEO): Bernie demands excellence and is feared by many employees. He manages through intimidation and focuses on identifying "what is wrong." But he never discusses "what is right" with his staff's performance. His staff does not want to get caught doing something other than the way "Bernie would want it," because they fear being made an example in front of everyone. Most of the staff admires him, but they know that his iron fist management style can be frightening when mistakes are made. So most of the employees would rather conceal problems and issues to avoid potential ridicule from Bernie. Bernie has always compensated his management team very well, which he uses as leverage to demand longer hours and more commitment.

Ona Scott, CONTROLLER: Ona was recently hired to improve the accounting and administrative functions of the company. She brings a strong analytical skill set that has been lacking since the company was founded in 1995. The company has never been audited (internally or externally), and Ona has her hands full with everything she has identified since joining the company in October 2012.

Tim Spies, LAFAYETTE BRANCH MANAGER: Tim has been with the company since 1996, and he is one of Bernie's most trusted managers. He is extremely knowledgeable about the products and has always been excellent at resolving customer complaints and management challenges. He has been very involved with establishing and modifying branch processes. Tim played a major role in the start-up of the other five branches and played a key role in the hiring and training of the other branch managers. He has had a close relationship with Bernie Madon for years, in and out of the office, and they share many of the same hobbies and interests.

Ross Tanory, HOUMA BRANCH MANAGER: Ross has been with the company since 1999. He has a strong management background, but he is not a strong sales representative (which continues to cause disagreements with Tim Spies in sales meetings).

Andy Strong, Venice Branch Manager: Andy has been with the company since 2004. He has been a good manager and operates one of the company's smaller branches.

Boyce Chaz, Houston Branch Manager: Boyce has been with the company since 2005. He was hired from a competitor due to his contacts in the Houston area. He has built strong relationships and likes to entertain his customers.

Brent Saia, Galveston Branch Manager: Brent has been with the company since 2007. He is Bernie Madon's nephew, and was hired shortly after his graduation from college. He has limited experience in the industry.

Stuart Rigby, Dallas Branch Manager: Stuart has been with the company since 2008. He operates the fastest growing branch, and is quickly becoming a leader in the company.

Case Study Engagement. During her first six months with the company, Ona Scott observes the company's rapid growth; however, its control environment has not evolved and there is a lack of segregation of duties and oversight in several areas. For example, Sherika Spies, Tim Spies' wife, has been the accounts payable and payroll clerk since 1997 and processes all accounts payable and payroll. She has been entrusted with handling these processes for over a decade, and Bernie Madon has always been confident in her ability to get the job done with minimal oversight.

Due to her observations and concerns, Ona hired a firm to perform a risk assessment of the company's control structure, and they uncovered and confirmed several control weaknesses as Ona had suspected.

In addition to the risk assessment report, Bernie received customer complaints regarding some recent invoices. One of the most troubling tips came from a Lafayette branch customer who complained of unexplainable pricing differences for the same or similar products. Upon further review, management determined that

GPS CONSULTANTS

Madon Oilfield Services, Inc.
Risk Assessment
As of May 30, 2012

Department	Risk Area	Function	Probability	Impact	Risk Score
Accounting	Accounts Payable	Vendor Setup & Maintenance	Likely	Medium	3
Accounting	Accounts Payable	Vendor Contract Monitoring	Likely	High	4
Accounting	Accounts Payable	Bank Reconciliations	Very Likely	Very High	5
Accounting	Accounts Payable	Payment Authorization	Very Likely	High	4
Accounting	Payroll	Employee Setup & Maintenance	Likely	Medium	3
Accounting	Payroll	Management Monitoring	Unlikely	Low	2
Accounting	Payroll	Non-standard Runs	Very Likely	Medium	2
Accounting	Payroll	Payroll Taxes	Very Unlikely	Medium	1
Accounting	Accounts Receivable	Deposit Reconciliations	Likely	High	4
Accounting	Accounts Receivable	Customer Billing & Statement Generation	Very Unlikely	High	2
Accounting	Accounts Receivable	Account Write-offs	Unlikely	High	2
Accounting	Accounts Receivable	Collections	Unlikely	Medium	1
Management	Information Technology	Security	Unlikely	High	2
Management	Information Technology	Database Maintenance	Likely	High	4
Management	Information Technology	Exception Monitoring	Very Likely	High	4
Management	Information Technology	Backup Maintenance	Unlikely	High	2
Management	Information Technology	Disaster Planning	Very Unlikely	High	2

the sales representative who sold and authorized this particular Outside Purchase transaction (see Part III: Sales) was the most senior and trusted branch manager.

Ona has hired your firm to conduct a forensic investigation based on her observations, risk assessment, and customer complaints. The key areas of your investigation should include a detailed analysis of sales transactions, payroll transactions, and accounts payable transactions. Management has gathered the following information in preparation of your detailed investigation.

PART I: PAYROLL

Overview of the payroll process. All employees (hourly, salary, and commissioned) are paid on a weekly basis. Payroll is processed every Friday by Sherika Spies. As a control measure, Bernie Madon signs the payroll checks each week when he is in town. Bernie travels often, so Sherika uses a signature stamp when Bernie is out of town or when he is too busy. In 2006, Sherika pushed to move all salaried employees to direct deposit to reduce the number of paper checks and postage. Bernie agreed with the initiative, and he also encouraged hourly employees to move to direct deposit; however, several have been resistant to change and most still receive a paper check each week. Ona finds Bernie's concept of personally signing payroll checks as a control measure to be ineffective because the majority of payroll funds are disbursed through direct deposit. Ona also noticed that Bernie does not review the payroll registers monthly, and he can only recall reviewing them at the end of each year.

Bernie Madon is generous and rewards his staff for their hard work. Annual discretionary bonuses have become routine for the company. Bernie has always paid his salaried employees a bonus at the beginning of December, but when business is thriving, Madon has been known to issue an additional bonus to incentivize quality results. The bonus process is very informal. Bernie simply provides Sherika a handwritten listing of the employee names and their applicable bonus amounts. Sherika then processes the bonus transactions, but she does not retain the handwritten document provided by Bernie on file.

Ona was not comfortable with the current process and began asking Bernie some questions after discovering a few red flags. The first red flag Ona noticed was that Sherika was extremely protective of the current payroll process, which she stated "had been fined tuned over the years and did not need any further tweaking." A second red flag was the lack of supervision and monitoring over the payroll process. No one ever followed behind Sherika to verify the transactions she had processed. The third red flag Ona noticed was that Sherika processed her own payroll, and she also processed her husband's payroll, Tim Spies. Tim was one of the highest compensated branch managers in the company. These red flags did not indicate that fraudulent activity had occurred, but they indicated that opportunity to commit fraud existed and that the process needed improvements (such as segregation of duties and additional monitoring to limit the company's exposure).

After Ona's discussions with Bernie and Sherika, Ona obtains a payroll data set for your analysis in which she isolates only salary transactions for 2011 and 2012. Ona wants to audit the hourly wage and commission transactions separately from the salary transactions due to the nature of the analysis. She asks for your assistance in data mining the salary transactions. Her main concerns are related to the transactions for Sherika and Tim Spies, who were both salary employees.

PART I QUESTIONS:

1. Who has the ability to commit payroll fraud at Madon Oilfield Services, Inc.?
2. How could payroll fraud be committed? Brainstorm and list the potential payroll schemes that could have occurred at Madon and how you might detect them. important to ensure that the date format in the Madon Database
3. What is a ghost employee?
4. Describe ways to detect ghost employees.
5. What might motivate internal personnel at Madon to perpetrate payroll fraud?
6. In some payroll frauds, how might the victim organization's total loss differ from the actual economic gain received by the perpetrator?
7. Would you be able to quantify the financial gains to the internal perpetrator through analyzing the victim organization's data? If not, explain why.
8. What internal control recommendations can you provide to Madon's management team?

PART I EXERCISE HINTS:

OBTAINING THE DATA

The following data files have been made available for the audit of Madon's accounts payable, payroll, and valve sales. The file is saved in Excel and is titled *Madon Database Files v1.xlsx* and contains the following work sheets:

- Madon Payroll Data
- Madon Employee Data
- Madon AP Data
- Madon Valve Trans-24mn
- Madon Valve Trans-6mn
- Madon Vendor Database
- Madon Branch Data

Data files (above) for the Madon Oilfield Services, Inc. Problem are available as a zip file at: *http://ideasupport.caseware.com/public/downloads/Madon Database Files.zip.*

A demo version of IDEA can be downloaded for free at: *http://www.caseware. com/IDEACDBook1.* To learn how to use IDEA and get started on the IDEA Project, the tutorial is available to be downloaded at the install screen.

If you have problems downloading the software or accessing the data files, you may contact *Ideasupport@caseware.com.*

AUDIT SET-UP

In order to begin the audit of Madon Oilfield Services, Inc. it will be necessary to set up a Managed Project to facilitate file management. Use the steps found on page 17 of the IDEA Version Nine Tutorial , which is available to be down-loaded at the install screen at *www.caseware.com/IDEACDBook1*, as a reference for creating a Managed Project using the following information:

- Project Name: Madon Audit

    STEP 1: Click the Select icon on the Home tab of the ribbon tool bar (see below)

STEP 2: Click the "Create…" icon and enter "Madon Audit" into the Project Name box listed under the Managed Project selection, then click "OK" on both open windows (see below)

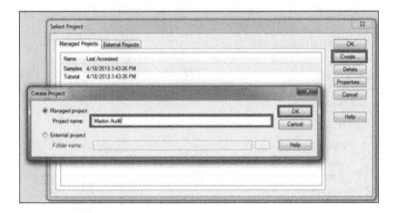

IMPORTING THE FILES

Prior to importing the necessary files, it is important to ensure that the date format in the Madon Database Files file has been input properly. In the Microsoft Excel document ensure that dates are formatted correctly (see screen shot below).

STEP 1: Format all dates using "MM/DD/YY" mask in Excel

STEP 2: Click the icon listed under the "Home" tab

 in IDEA

STEP 3: Select "Microsoft Excel" and click the "…" icon to left of "File name" in the Import Assistant Window (see below)

STEP 4: Browse to the location where the "Madon Data Files v1.xlsx" file is saved on your computer or desktop and double click the file name

STEP 5: Check each box next to the sheet names in the "Select sheets to import:" section. Check the box next to "First row is field names." Name the Output file and select "OK" (see below)

The files should appear in IDEA as shown below:

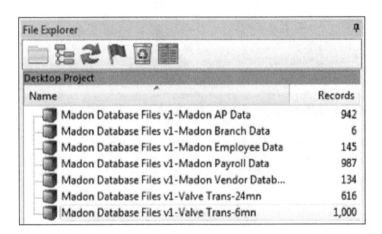

(Instructions for IDEA)

1. Import the *Part I – payroll data*, *Part I – employee data*, and *Part I – branch data* into your data analysis tool.
2. Analyze the *Part I – payroll data* for ghost employee and other suspicious payroll activity.

3. Leverage the Join function to analyze the *Part I – payroll data* and *Part I – employee data* to identify anomalies.
4. Leverage the Summarization function to analyze the *Part I – payroll data* to identify anomalies.
5. Leverage the Project Overview and History sections in IDEA® - Data Analysis Software to document the specific procedures performed to uncover each group of specific suspicious transactions your firm detects.

PART II: ACCOUNTS PAYABLE

Overview of the Accounts Payable Process. The accounts payable process is handled in the central office by Sherika Spies. Invoices received through the various branches are forwarded to the Lafayette branch for payment. Invoices are input when received and checks are typically cut on Tuesdays; however, checks are occasionally printed throughout the week as needed. The only authorized signor on the account is Bernie Madon. As evidence of authorization for expenditures, Bernie signs the checks each week when he is in town. Sherika uses a signature stamp when Bernie is out of town or when he is too busy. Mary Gonzalez in the Accounts Receivable department reconciles the bank statement on a monthly basis. She heavily relies on Sherika for explanation and documentation of any discrepancies noted through her reconciliation process. Bernie has not reviewed any bank reconciliations in years due to his lack of interest in this function of the business.

All branch managers and Bernie have a company American Express credit card. They are required to provide supporting documentation for the transactions on the credit card. Bernie also has a personal American Express and a personal Chase credit card that he has Sherika pay out of the business.

While Bernie was on a two-week vacation, Ona asked Sherika to provide her with the check register, checks, and supporting invoices prior to mailing. During her review, Ona noticed a check on the check register that was classified to specific vendor; however, when she inspected the check, the payee on the check was not the same vendor. Ona was also unaware of any recent activity with this vendor. When Ona asked Sherika about the discrepancy, Sherika was unable to provide an answer. Ona has requested that your firm perform an accounts payable audit to investigate this issue and look for other potential suspicious activity.

PART II QUESTIONS:

1. How could accounts payable fraud be committed? Brainstorm and list the potential schemes that could have occurred at Madon and how you might detect them.
2. What types of expenses are susceptible to *account mirroring schemes* at Madon Oilfield Services, Inc.?
3. What might motivate internal personnel at Madon to perpetrate an accounts payable fraud scheme and how could they benefit from perpetrating fraud?

4.   Who could perpetrate an accounts payable fraud scheme at Madon Oilfield Services, Inc.?
5.   Would you be able to quantify the financial gains to the internal perpetrator through analyzing the victim organization's data? If not, explain why.
6.   What internal control recommendations can you provide to Madon's management team?

PART II EXERCISE HINTS:

1.   Import the *Part II – accounts payable data* and *Part II – check register* into your data analysis tool.
2.   Leverage the Pivot Table function to analyze the *Part II – accounts payable data* by month to identify anomalies.
3.   Leverage the Summarization function to analyze the *Part II – accounts payable data* by vendor to identify anomalies.
4.   Leverage the Project Overview and History sections in IDEA® - Data Analysis Software to document the specific procedures performed to uncover each group of specific suspicious transactions your firm detects.

PART III: SALES

Overview of the Sales Process. Bernie Madon believes that the sales function is the backbone to the company's existence, and he focuses the bulk of his energy motivating sale representatives to always outperform their previous results. Bernie traveled a lot, but he always participated in the weekly sales meeting which is a conference call with all of the branch managers to discuss all of the latest effective approaches that had helped increase sales. Bernie is aggressive and is known for blasting poor performing managers on these conference calls week after weekly.

The company has five main product lines: (1) valves, (2) fittings and flanges, (3) pipes, (4) drilling equipment, and (5) specialty products. The company has experienced rapid growth in valve revenue, and Bernie attributes the growth to the new oil shale discoveries in Louisiana and Texas. Drilling activity has increased dramatically, and customers are focusing on completing drilling projects quickly to get the oil pumping and revenues generating to appease investors. Below is an illustration of the shifts in the company's product mix over the past three years.

	2012		2011		2010	
Product	Revenue ($M)	%	Revenue ($M)	%	Revenue ($M)	%
Valves	109.8	37%	82.3	32%	64.9	29%
Fittings and Flanges	71.1	24%	69.9	27%	63.4	29%
Pipes	57.9	19%	53.4	20%	40.2	18%
Drilling Equipment	46.5	15%	41.1	16%	39.1	18%
Specialty Products	15.0	5%	13.9	5%	14.0	6%
	300.4	100%	260.8	100%	221.7	100%

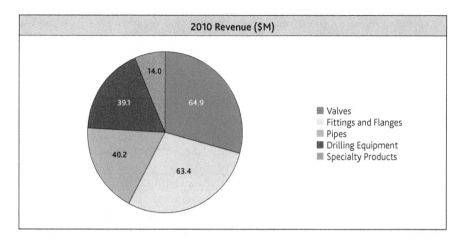

2010 Revenue ($M)

- Valves
- Fittings and Flanges
- Pipes
- Drilling Equipment
- Specialty Products

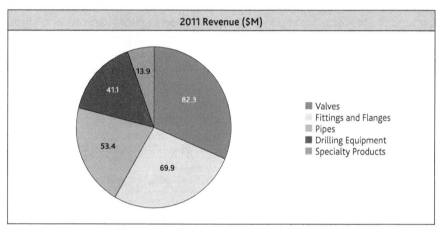

2011 Revenue ($M)

- Valves
- Fittings and Flanges
- Pipes
- Drilling Equipment
- Specialty Products

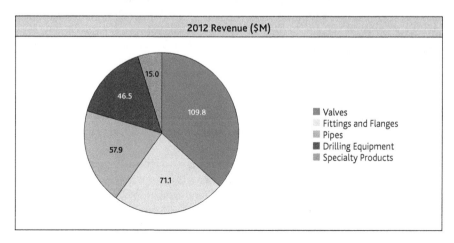

2012 Revenue ($M)

- Valves
- Fittings and Flanges
- Pipes
- Drilling Equipment
- Specialty Products

Timely Delivery. Quality and timeliness are key customer priorities and the focus of management. Due to the nature of the customers' projects, timely delivery of specific products can be priced at a premium. For example, the customers can justify paying $300 for a pair of rubber boots to avoid any delays in production. The same pair of boots may only cost $20 at Wal-Mart; however, the customer values timely delivery over short-term costs. This same concept applies, for example, when customers need a critical valve or fitting. This factor creates an environment in which excessive markups on missing critical products can go undetected. The company keeps a large inventory at each branch, but they also use outside vendors to purchase these time- sensitive products upon customer request. Purchases from outside vendors require branch manager authorization and are referred to as "Outside Purchases" or "OSP." All products, whether in inventory or purchased from an outside vendor are sold to the customer with an 18% markup to maintain the company's required profit margins. However, the customer pays a premium for an OSP because the products are typically purchased at retail with a delivery premium, and the total cost is marked up by Madon versus an inventory item bought at wholesale with no delivery premium.

Recently, a long standing customer and friend of Bernie's contacted him regarding unexplainable pricing differences for the same or similar products. The customer told Bernie that he had made the same complaints to Tim Spies, but no resolution efforts had occurred. The customer described two invoices he had received. The first invoice, dated April 8, 2013, charged him approximately $3,500 for a 12" valve. The second invoice, dated May 27, 2013, charged him approximately $72,000 for the same 12" valve.

In order to investigate the customer concerns, Ona performed data analysis on the last 24 months of valve transaction data (January 2011 – December 2012). She has requested your firm's assistance with analyzing the raw data from the transaction database for the first six months of 2013. Ona is hoping that this comparison helps shed light on the issues. Ona's historical analysis and the raw data for January – June 2013 have been provided to your firm for further analysis and comparison.

PART III QUESTIONS:

1. What is a vendor collusion false billing scheme?
2. What types of transactions are susceptible to vendor collusion false billing schemes at Madon Oilfield Services, Inc.?
3. What might motivate internal personnel at Madon to perpetrate a false billing scheme, and how could they benefit from participating?
4. Who could perpetrate a false billing scheme at Madon Oilfield Services, Inc.?
5. Would you be able to quantify the financial gains to the internal perpetrator through analyzing the victim organization's data? If not, explain why.

6. What outside economic trends and factors were present at Madon that might help conceal a false billing scheme?
7. What internal control recommendations can you provide to Madon's management team?

PART III EXERCISE HINTS:

1. Import the *Part III – 6mn valve transaction data* and the *Part III – 24mn summarized valve transaction data.*
2. Leverage the Join function and compare the *Part III – 6mn valve transaction data* and the *Part III – 24mn summarized valve transaction data* to identify anomalies and deviations from the overall transaction population's trends.
3. Leverage the Project Overview and History sections in IDEA® - Data Analysis Software to document the specific procedures performed to uncover each group of specific suspicious transactions your firm detects.

CASE STUDY EXERCISE:

The company would like a formal written report of your scope, procedures, findings, and recommendations. The findings should include:

▪ Quantification of any fraud, waste, or abuse uncovered by your firm.
▪ Perpetrator(s) of each fraud scheme your firm detected.
▪ Description of the fraud scheme(s) detected.
▪ Detailed listing of the specific suspicious transactions detected by your firm with references to the specific procedures performed.

Madon Oilfield Services, Inc. Statements of Operations By Branch 3 Year Comparison						
All Branches	2012		2011		2010	
	Amount ($)	%	Amount ($)	%	Amount ($)	%
Sales						
Valves	109,820,148	37%	82,314,725	32%	64,935,784	29%
Fittings and flanges	71,149,688	24%	69,974,124	27%	63,434,789	29%
Pipes	57,958,147	19%	53,422,456	20%	40,221,466	18%
Drilling Equipment	46,526,732	15%	41,145,244	16%	39,143,215	18%
Specialty Products	14,989,755	5%	13,956,868	5%	14,012,192	6%
	300,444,470	**100%**	**260,813,417**	**100%**	**221,747,446**	**100%**
Cost of Sales						
Valves	90,052,521	30%	67,498,075	26%	53,247,343	24%
Fittings and flanges	58,342,744	19%	57,378,782	22%	52,016,527	23%
Pipes	49,264,425	16%	44,874,863	17%	33,786,031	15%
Drilling Equipment	38,151,920	13%	33,739,100	13%	32,097,436	14%
Specialty Products	11,991,804	4%	11,025,926	4%	11,209,754	5%
	247,803,415	**82%**	**214,516,745**	**82%**	**182,357,091**	**82%**
Gross Profit						
Valves	19,767,627	7%	14,816,651	6%	11,688,441	5%
Fittings and flanges	12,806,944	4%	12,595,342	5%	11,418,262	5%
Pipes	8,693,722	3%	8,547,593	3%	6,435,435	3%
Drilling Equipment	8,374,812	3%	7,406,144	3%	7,045,779	3%
Specialty Products	2,997,951	1%	2,930,942	1%	2,802,438	1%
	52,641,055	**18%**	**46,296,672**	**18%**	**39,390,355**	**18%**
SG&A Expenses	**15,149,878**	**5%**	**14,325,587**	**5%**	**14,422,136**	**7%**
Operating Income (loss)	**37,491,177**	**12%**	**31,971,085**	**12%**	**24,968,219**	**11%**

Madon Oilfield Services, Inc. Statements of Operations By Branch 3 Year Comparison						
Lafayette Branch	2012		2011		2010	
	Amount ($)	%	Amount ($)	%	Amount ($)	%
Sales						
Valves	39,048,726	41%	23,048,123	32%	21,428,809	29%
Fittings and flanges	21,344,906	22%	19,592,755	27%	20,933,480	29%
Pipes	17,387,444	18%	14,958,288	20%	13,273,084	18%
Drilling Equipment	13,958,020	15%	11,520,668	16%	12,917,261	18%
Specialty Products	4,496,927	5%	3,907,923	5%	4,624,023	6%
	96,236,023	**100%**	**73,027,757**	**100%**	**73,176,657**	**100%**
Cost of Sales						
Valves	32,019,956	33%	18,899,461	26%	17,571,623	24%
Fittings and flanges	17,502,823	18%	16,066,059	22%	17,165,454	23%
Pipes	14,779,327	15%	12,564,962	17%	11,149,390	15%
Drilling Equipment	11,445,576	12%	9,446,948	13%	10,592,154	14%
Specialty Products	3,597,541	4%	3,087,259	4%	3,699,219	5%
	79,345,224	**82%**	**60,064,689**	**82%**	**60,177,840**	**82%**
Gross Profit						
Valves	7,028,771	7%	4,148,662	6%	3,857,186	5%
Fittings and flanges	3,842,083	4%	3,526,696	5%	3,768,026	5%
Pipes	2,608,117	3%	2,393,326	3%	2,123,693	3%
Drilling Equipment	2,512,444	3%	2,073,720	3%	2,325,107	3%
Specialty Products	899,385	1%	820,664	1%	924,805	1%
	16,890,799	**18%**	**12,963,068**	**18%**	**12,998,817**	**18%**
SG&A Expenses	**6,044,963**	**6%**	**5,511,164**	**8%**	**6,259,305**	**9%**
Operating Income (loss)	**10,845,836**	**11%**	**7,451,904**	**10%**	**6,739,512**	**9%**

Madon Oilfield Services, Inc. Statements of Operations By Branch 3 Year Comparison						
Houma Branch	**2012**		**2011**		**2010**	
	Amount ($)	%	Amount ($)	%	Amount ($)	%
Sales						
Valves	8,363,813	33%	9,877,767	32%	8,441,652	29%
Fittings and flanges	6,403,472	25%	8,396,895	27%	8,246,523	29%
Pipes	5,216,233	20%	6,410,695	20%	5,228,791	18%
Drilling Equipment	4,187,406	16%	4,937,429	16%	5,088,618	18%
Specialty Products	1,349,078	5%	1,674,824	5%	1,821,585	6%
	25,520,002	100%	31,297,610	100%	28,827,168	100%
Cost of Sales						
Valves	6,858,327	27%	8,099,769	26%	6,922,155	24%
Fittings and flanges	5,250,847	21%	6,885,454	22%	6,762,149	23%
Pipes	4,433,798	17%	5,384,984	17%	4,392,184	15%
Drilling Equipment	3,433,673	13%	4,048,692	13%	4,172,667	14%
Specialty Products	1,079,262	4%	1,323,111	4%	1,457,268	5%
	21,055,907	82%	25,742,009	82%	23,706,422	82%
Gross Profit						
Valves	1,505,486	6%	1,777,998	6%	1,519,497	5%
Fittings and flanges	1,152,625	5%	1,511,441	5%	1,484,374	5%
Pipes	782,435	3%	1,025,711	3%	836,606	3%
Drilling Equipment	753,733	3%	888,737	3%	915,951	3%
Specialty Products	269,816	1%	351,713	1%	364,317	1%
	4,464,095	18%	5,555,601	18%	5,120,746	18%
SG&A Expenses	863,489	3%	1,219,070	4%	1,374,878	5%
Operating Income (loss)	3,600,606	14%	4,336,530	14%	3,745,868	13%

Venice Branch	Madon Oilfield Services, Inc. Statements of Operations By Branch 3 Year Comparison					
	2012		2011		2010	
	Amount ($)	%	Amount ($)	%	Amount ($)	%
Sales						
Valves	9,362,015	33%	9,054,620	32%	12,987,157	29%
Fittings and flanges	7,114,969	25%	7,697,154	27%	12,686,958	29%
Pipes	5,795,815	20%	5,876,470	20%	8,044,293	18%
Drilling Equipment	4,652,673	16%	4,525,977	16%	7,828,643	18%
Specialty Products	1,498,976	5%	1,535,255	5%	2,802,438	6%
	28,424,447	**100%**	**28,689,476**	**100%**	**44,349,489**	**100%**
Cost of Sales						
Valves	7,676,852	27%	7,424,788	26%	10,649,469	24%
Fittings and flanges	5,834,274	21%	6,311,666	22%	10,403,305	23%
Pipes	4,926,442	17%	4,936,235	17%	6,757,206	15%
Drilling Equipment	3,815,192	13%	3,711,301	13%	6,419,487	14%
Specialty Products	1,199,180	4%	1,212,852	4%	2,241,951	5%
	23,451,941	**82%**	**23,596,842**	**82%**	**36,471,418**	**82%**
Gross Profit						
Valves	1,685,163	6%	1,629,832	6%	2,337,688	5%
Fittings and flanges	1,280,694	5%	1,385,488	5%	2,283,652	5%
Pipes	869,372	3%	940,235	3%	1,287,087	3%
Drilling Equipment	837,481	3%	814,676	3%	1,409,156	3%
Specialty Products	299,795	1%	322,404	1%	560,488	1%
	4,972,506	**18%**	**5,092,634**	**18%**	**7,878,071**	**18%**
SG&A Expenses	**1,014,988**	**4%**	**1,075,815**	**4%**	**2,384,427**	**5%**
Operating Income (loss)	**3,957,518**	**14%**	**4,016,819**	**14%**	**5,493,644**	**12%**

Madon Oilfield Services, Inc. Statements of Operations By Branch 3 Year Comparison						
Houston Branch	**2012**		**2011**		**2010**	
	Amount ($)	%	Amount ($)	%	Amount ($)	%
Sales						
Valves	21,840,231	35%	18,109,240	32%	11,688,441	29%
Fittings and flanges	14,941,434	24%	15,394,307	27%	11,418,262	29%
Pipes	12,171,211	20%	11,752,940	20%	7,239,864	18%
Drilling Equipment	9,770,614	16%	9,051,954	16%	7,045,779	18%
Specialty Products	3,147,849	5%	3,070,511	5%	2,522,195	6%
	61,871,339	100%	57,378,952	100%	39,914,540	100%
Cost of Sales						
Valves	17,908,989	29%	14,849,576	26%	9,584,522	24%
Fittings and flanges	12,251,976	20%	12,623,332	22%	9,362,975	23%
Pipes	10,345,529	17%	9,872,470	17%	6,081,486	15%
Drilling Equipment	8,011,903	13%	7,422,602	13%	5,777,539	14%
Specialty Products	2,518,279	4%	2,425,704	4%	2,017,756	5%
	51,036,677	82%	47,193,684	82%	32,824,276	82%
Gross Profit						
Valves	3,931,242	6%	3,259,663	6%	2,103,919	5%
Fittings and flanges	2,689,458	4%	2,770,975	5%	2,055,287	5%
Pipes	1,825,682	3%	1,880,470	3%	1,158,378	3%
Drilling Equipment	1,758,710	3%	1,629,352	3%	1,268,240	3%
Specialty Products	629,570	1%	644,807	1%	504,439	1%
	10,834,662	18%	10,185,268	18%	7,090,264	18%
SG&A Expenses	3,181,474	5%	3,151,629	5%	2,595,984	7%
Operating Income (loss)	7,653,187	12%	7,033,639	12%	4,494,279	11%

Madon Oilfield Services, Inc. Statements of Operations By Branch 3 Year Comparison						
Galveston Branch	**2012**		**2011**		**2010**	
	Amount ($)	%	Amount ($)	%	Amount ($)	%
Sales						
Valves	7,285,612	32%	6,585,178	32%	4,545,505	29%
Fittings and flanges	5,691,975	25%	5,597,930	27%	4,440,435	29%
Pipes	4,636,652	21%	4,273,796	20%	2,815,503	18%
Drilling Equipment	3,722,139	17%	3,291,620	16%	2,740,025	18%
Specialty Products	1,199,180	5%	1,116,549	5%	980,853	6%
	22,535,558	**100%**	**20,865,073**	**100%**	**15,522,321**	**100%**
Cost of Sales						
Valves	5,969,200	26%	5,399,846	26%	3,727,314	24%
Fittings and flanges	4,667,420	21%	4,590,303	22%	3,641,157	23%
Pipes	3,941,154	17%	3,589,989	17%	2,365,022	15%
Drilling Equipment	3,052,154	14%	2,699,128	13%	2,246,821	14%
Specialty Products	959,344	4%	882,074	4%	784,683	5%
	18,589,271	**82%**	**17,161,340**	**82%**	**12,764,996**	**82%**
Gross Profit						
Valves	1,316,412	6%	1,185,332	6%	818,191	5%
Fittings and flanges	1,024,556	5%	1,007,627	5%	799,278	5%
Pipes	695,498	3%	683,807	3%	450,480	3%
Drilling Equipment	669,985	3%	592,492	3%	493,205	3%
Specialty Products	239,836	1%	234,475	1%	196,171	1%
	3,946,286	**18%**	**3,703,734**	**18%**	**2,757,325**	**18%**
SG&A Expenses	**711,990**	**3%**	**646,047**	**3%**	**509,550**	**3%**
Operating Income (loss)	**3,234,296**	**14%**	**3,057,687**	**15%**	**2,247,775**	**14%**

Madon Oilfield Services, Inc. Statements of Operations By Branch 3 Year Comparison						
Dallas Branch	2012		2011		2010	
	Amount ($)	%	Amount ($)	%	Amount ($)	%
Sales						
Valves	23,919,751	36%	15,639,798	32%	5,844,221	29%
Fittings and flanges	15,652,931	24%	13,295,084	27%	5,709,131	29%
Pipes	12,750,792	19%	10,150,267	20%	3,619,932	18%
Drilling Equipment	10,235,881	16%	7,817,596	16%	3,522,889	18%
Specialty Products	3,297,746	5%	2,651,805	5%	1,261,097	6%
	65,857,101	**100%**	**49,554,549**	**100%**	**19,957,270**	**100%**
Cost of Sales						
Valves	19,619,197	30%	12,824,634	26%	4,792,261	24%
Fittings and flanges	12,835,404	19%	10,901,969	22%	4,681,487	23%
Pipes	10,838,173	16%	8,526,224	17%	3,040,743	15%
Drilling Equipment	8,393,422	13%	6,410,429	13%	2,888,769	14%
Specialty Products	2,638,197	4%	2,094,926	4%	1,008,878	5%
	54,324,394	**82%**	**40,758,182**	**82%**	**16,412,138**	**82%**
Gross Profit						
Valves	4,300,553	7%	2,815,164	6%	1,051,960	5%
Fittings and flanges	2,817,528	4%	2,393,115	5%	1,027,644	5%
Pipes	1,912,619	3%	1,624,043	3%	579,189	3%
Drilling Equipment	1,842,459	3%	1,407,167	3%	634,120	3%
Specialty Products	659,549	1%	556,879	1%	252,219	1%
	11,532,707	**18%**	**8,796,368**	**18%**	**3,545,132**	**18%**
SG&A Expenses	**3,332,973**	**5%**	**2,721,862**	**5%**	**1,297,992**	**7%**
Operating Income (loss)	**8,199,734**	**12%**	**6,074,506**	**12%**	**2,247,140**	**11%**

* The publisher acknowledges CaseWare IDEA® Inc.- Data Analysis Software for hosting the data sets for the Madon Oilfield Services case and for making available to us the demo version of IDEA for student use. We also acknowledge Audimation Services, Inc., U.S. Distributor of IDEA, for their help and coordination with this case.

CASE STUDY 40:

Southlake Hematology/Oncology Associates

Wilson A. LaGraize, Jr., CPA, CFF, Cr.FA
Kushner LaGraize LLC

LEARNING OBJECTIVES

After completing and discussing this case, you should be able to

- Understand the work of an accounting expert witness.
- Understand some basic steps required to calculate monetary damages in litigation.
- Review pleadings in a courtroom dispute.
- Prepare a discounted cash flow calculation with factual data.

The principal questions in this matter are whether the defendant's actions violated a contract that the plaintiff alleges it had with the defendant and, more particularly, whether such a contract existed; and whether defendant's actions are in violation of any other Louisiana law. If so, the Court must determine what damages the plaintiff suffered as a result of the defendant's actions.

The main factual issue in this dispute surrounds the negotiation of the contract between Southlake Hematology/Oncology Associates (A Professional Medical Corporation) [hereinafter referred to as "Southlake") and David M. French, M.D. with respect to his employment. Many of the facts surrounding the plaintiff's allegation that a contract existed are undisputed. The balance of the dispute surrounds whether a contract was entered into based upon certain communications between the parties in April through June of 2004 as well as the actions of the parties.

The events leading to this lawsuit occurred in early 2004 when two independent but related circumstances occurred: Louisiana University decided to close its oncology clinic in Hammond and Dr David French, an oncologist, decided to leave his position at Foundation Hopsital to enter private practice.

Dr. Hebert first met Dr. French in 2004. Dr. Hebert owned an oncology/hematology practice[1] based in Slidell, but also operated offices in Coving-

---

[1]   R. Dale Herbert, M.D., Inc., would later be renamed Southlake Hematology/Oncology Associates, A Professional Medical Corporation (hereinafter referred to as "Southlake"), effective June 1, 2004.

ton, LA and Picayune, MS. Dr. Allen Calamia was one of its employees. Dr. Hebert and Dr. French discussed the possibility of Dr. French joining the practice, which would eventually be named Southlake Hematology/Oncology. Southlake made an offer of employment to Dr. French, which included a non-competition agreement. Dr. French decided instead, to accept a position at Ochsner, another clinic.

Dr. French signed an employment contract with Ochsner that contained a non-competition provision. Dr. French testified that he negotiated his contract with Ochsner so that he would only be prohibited from competing in the parishes of Orleans and Jefferson, in which he would be working for Ochsner.

Eventually, Dr. French again communicated with Dr. Hebert regarding an association for practice. In late 2003 or early 2004, Dr. French called Dr. Hebert to find out how his practice was doing. Dr. French told Dr. Hebert that he wanted to leave Ochsner. Shortly thereafter, Dr. Calamia received word from his colleagues and prior mentors at LU that LU was closing its hematology and oncology practice in Hammond, Louisiana. Dr. Calamia had had prior relationships with some of the LU doctors working at that clinic. These colleagues indicated a desire to have Dr. Calamia and Southlake serve the patients and staff the Hammond clinic, which LU was closing.

Doctors Hebert and Calamia set up a meeting with the doctors of LU and invited Dr. French to the meeting. The LU doctors were concerned about their patients having continuing care once the practice closed and agreed to refer their patients to Dr. Hebert's group, if it would open an office in Hammond. The staff of the LU clinic was also discussed; Dr. Hebert agreed to hire them. After this meeting, Dr. Hebert discussed hiring Dr. French and gave him a copy of Dr. Calamia's employment agreement as a starting point of discussion. Dr. French had already declined overtures from the LU doctors to take over the clinic himself.[2]

Hiring of Dr. French was crucial to the opening of Southlake's Hammond Practice. Dr. Hebert decided that he had to move quickly or risk losing some of the LU patients. He had located a potential office but wanted to get a firm commitment from Dr. French before he started spending money on establishing the Hammond office.

In March and April of 2004, Dr. Hebert and Dr. Calamia met with Dr. French to hammer out details of his employment agreement. Dr. French would have to pay Ochsner $10,000 to terminate his contract and Dr. Hebert agreed to pay it. After the last meeting and after agreeing to most of Dr. French's requests for revisions to the agreement, Dr. Hebert felt that they had an agreement and, in reliance thereon, proceeded to take steps to open the Hammond office. Dr. French was to join the practice on June 1, 2004.

Dr. Hebert signed a lease for the Hammond office, renovated it, bought furniture and supplies, and installed equipment. He changed the name of his

---

[2]   Dr. French testified that the LU doctors had also contacted him about taking over the practice but he declined because he did not have sufficient knowledge of how to run a private oncology practice.

practice from R. Dale Hebert, MD, Inc. to Southlake Hematology/Oncology Associates, A Professional Medical Corporation. In addition, Southlake hired the secretary, nurse and other staff of the former LU Clinic. LU's volunteer came to work with Southlake as well. Southlake made a substantial financial investment in developing this practice ("Southlake's Hammond Practice").

Dr. French was hired by Southlake to staff Southlake's Hammond Practice. LU referred its patients to Dr. Calamia and directed its patients to Southlake. Eventually, Southlake picked up almost all of LU's patients and Dr. French started seeing patients as an employee in June of 2004.

Southlake, through its president Dr. Hebert, tendered a copy of the written employment agreement between Southlake and Dr. Calamia to Dr. French as a template for the terms and conditions of Dr. French's contract. Dr. French understood that this template was an offer for employment. In subsequent litigation, that contract was introduced into evidence.

Following tender of the agreement, Dr. French wrote to Southlake on March 29, 2010 and made a counter offer. The counter offer specifically states that Dr. French has "outlined below terms of a counter proposal for terms of my contract and employment." The counter offer further states that "1 would like to get a general agreement with you by the end of this week, so if possible, I'd appreciate it if you would accept, reject, or counter this proposal by Wednesday night." The counter offer indicates Dr. French's offer for terms and conditions of employment and the desire to have an agreement in place shortly. This indicated written desire is consistent with Dr. French's testimony that he was leaving Ochsner at the end of May and wanted to have an agreement with Southlake prior to his departure so as to solidify his future.

The counter proposal contains seven (7) enumerated items where Dr. French would either like changes to Dr. Calamia's contract or has questions. Dr. Hebert, Dr. Calamia and Dr. French all testified that a meeting convened in April of 2004 on a Saturday shortly after receipt of this memo. During that meeting there was consensus reached among the three physicians with respect to a productivity bonus, the outside professional activities, professional meetings, rules for equity partnership and the other items outlined in Dr. French's March 29, 2004 counter proposal. Dr. French testified that his impression of this meeting was that his concerns were worked out and that there was some level of understanding and a basic understanding of the terms and conditions of his employment.

All physicians testified that Dr. Hebert was to take the handwritten notes from this meeting to his attorney and have the contract for Dr. Calamia modified based upon the notes from this meeting. Dr. Hebert did take the contract to his attorney and had a draft created. In subsequent litigation, that draft was introduced into evidence.

On May 29, 2004, Dr. Hebert met with Dr. French to review the written version of what he thought was the final agreement. That agreement was deficient, however, in large part because it did not recognize that the practice had expanded from when Dr. Calamia was hired to points in Mississippi and certain modifications relevant to that were needed. After Dr. Hebert and Dr. French met and reviewed the contract, and agreed that the contract would be modified to make the changes associated with Mississippi, Dr. French accepted the signing bonus of $10,000[3] on May 29, 2004.

Importantly, the changes that Dr. French requested be made to the non-competition agreement contained in Dr. Calamia's contract [both in his written memo of March 29 and orally at the meeting in April] were all made and contained in the written contract reviewed on May 29, 2004. No changes were suggested by Dr. French to the non-competition provision other than Dr. French and Dr. Hebert agreeing that Mississippi would have to be inserted into the areas where competition would be prohibited.

Shortly thereafter, Dr. Calamia became eligible for partnership in the practice, and, apparently, Dr. Hebert and Dr. Calamia focused their attention on achieving that goal, rather than following up on having Dr. French actually sign the employment agreement under which all parties were operating.

Southlake's counsel modified the agreement and furnished same to Dr. Hebert on June 9, 2004. Dr. Hebert faxed the employment agreement to Dr. French on June 9, 2004. Dr. French made handwritten changes on pages 4, 5 and 16 that he testified were clarifications of provisions already contained in the contract. Because the first clarification [on pages 4 and 5] was actually dealt with in a later provision of the same contract [section E on page 5], and the clarification [on page 16] was unnecessary to the contract, those changes were not made. However, the testimony of Dr. Hebert and Dr. French was that Exhibit A to the contract, which listed the physician services upon which bonuses and equity buy-in would be calculated, needed to be revised according to Dr. French. Dr. French's notes related to Exhibit A from the June 9 contract were provided in subsequent litigation.

Both Dr. Hebert and Dr. French operated according to the terms of the June 9, 2004 agreement until July, 2005. One dispute arose as to the calculation of Dr. French's bonus after his first six months of employment.[4] Other than that, all other terms of the agreement were followed.

Dr. French's testimony that he reviewed the contract and made a couple of clarification notes but never intended to agree to its terms is simply not supported by his testimony or actions.

First, Dr. French understood clearly that a non-competition provision was going to be part of his relationship with Dr. Hebert. He received Dr. Calamia's contract and in his response made a minor change in the non-competition provision, which was accepted along with the other changes Dr. French requested in April of 2004. Those changes were incorporated into the May 28 draft of the

---

[3]   This amount funded his buy-out of his Ochsner contract.
[4]   It would not be until December 17, 2004, on the eve of calculating Dr. French's productivity bonus under the contract, that Dr. French would finally furnish the CPT codes. The testimony was that Dr. Herbert, on behalf of Southlake, agreed to use whatever CPT codes for professional services were utilized by and furnished by Dr. French.

contract. Dr. French made no further suggested changes. In addition, when he tendered the contract on June 9, 2004, Dr. French made no further changes to the non-competition provision.

Dr. French's testimony that he did not intend to be bound by the non-competition provision is not credible based on other extraneous written documentation. Most particularly, documentation was introduced into evidence namely a written memorandum from Dr. French dated July 23, 2004 to Southlake's office manager. That memorandum states, in pertinent part: "I would really like to see the billing of patients, units + billing + collections from "physician services" *as shown on Exhibit A of my contract* [emphasis added]. I wouldn't mind seeing overall billing + collections as well, but would like to track service bill/collection separately as that affects my personal bottom line!"

Dr. French's references to "my contract" and his "bottom line" [which he testified to be the bonus calculation under the contract's terms] indicate his intention to be bound by the agreement. If Dr. French did not believe he had an agreement, he would not have referred to the agreement as "my contract" or expected the bonus according to the terms set forth in the agreement.

Dr. French's testimony regarding his expectations presents additional reasons why he did not intend to be bound by the contract. These assertions cannot be accepted and fly in the face of the evidence presented in this case. Dr. French expected and accepted the following benefits under the contract: 1) a salary; 2) an increase in salary after one year of employment to the amount stated in the contract; 3) malpractice insurance; 4) all of the employee benefits called for in the contract; 5) a productivity bonus paid at six months and at twelve months under the contract; and 6) that he was accruing time towards an equity buy-in (i.e., partnership). The Court found particularly compelling Dr. French's expectation that he would receive a bonus as called for *under the formula in the contract,* and that he testified he was accruing time to become an equity partner *under the provisions of the contract.* It would be unjust enrichment for Dr. French to expect performance by Southlake under the contract and to receive all of the benefits provided to him under the contract, without him having an obligation to fulfill the terms of the contract, including the non-competition provision.

Dr. French's justification for why he believed there was no contract was that he intended to have a lawyer review the contract, and that he would sign it before he would become bound. As previously found by the Court, this type of contract does not need to be signed to be binding or even to be in writing to be binding. Further, Dr. French himself testified that he never had a lawyer review the contract at any time after it was given to him in June of 2004. In fact, when Southlake's attorney found out that the contract had not been signed, in connection with putting together an assemblage of documents for purposes of a CPA evaluation of the practice in the spring of 2005, Dr.

Hebert sent another copy of the contract to Dr. French for his signature [5] Dr. French did not even have this contract reviewed by a lawyer.

In July, 2005, Dr. Hebert and Dr. French met to review Dr. French's bonus for the year and review how the practice was progressing. Dr. Hebert also brought the written employment agreement for signature. Dr. French stated that he was leaving the practice and that he wanted to take over Southlake's offices in Hammond and Covington. Dr. Hebert was shocked and told Dr. French that he would think about it. Because of this development, Dr. Hebert never presented the employment agreement for signature.

Dr. French, after giving notice to Southlake of his intended departure, offered to keep the office staff, equipment, furniture, fixtures and the office of Southlake's Hammond Practice. Dr. French, Dr. Hebert and Dr. Calamia desired to continue the practice in Hammond.

Dr. French testified that he then started trying to locate an office in Hammond and was told by someone at LU hospital that the lease to the existing Hammond office was in his name and he could just "take it over".[6]

It is undisputed that Dr. French in July of 2005 gave notice, in accordance with the terms of the employment agreement, to Southlake that he would be leaving Southlake. The Court found the subsequent actions of Dr. French to be unconscionable. Dr. French, who testified that he was relying on the representation made by a person at LU Hospital, and without checking the accuracy of same, then proceeded to take possession of the office space, telephone number and telephone system, equipment, furniture and fixtures of Southlake's Hammond Practice, effectively taking them away from Southlake. He simply changed the name on the door to "Pontchartrain Oncology Associates" and embarked on his own practice, converting Southlake's Hammond Practice to his own on or around September 3, 2005. He hired all of Southlake's Hammond Practice employees, including the volunteer, and made arrangements to continue to possess the office space with LU Hospital.

To be enforceable in Louisiana, a non-competition provision must adhere to the requirements of LSA-RS 23:921. Subsection C of LSA-RS 23:921 provides that an employee may agree with his employer to refrain from carrying on a business similar to the business of the employer or from soliciting customers of the employer within a specified parish or parishes for a period not to exceed two years after termination of the employment. That provision does not require that

---

[5]   Dr. French argues that because there was a slight modification in this contract forwarded in April by Dr. Herbert that it demonstrates that there was no agreement to the terms and conditions of the contract. This argument is contrary to the actions and testimony and fails for two other reasons. First, the modification to the contract in April is a clarification on page 5 which does two things: 1) changes from 45 days to 60 days the amount of days for purposes of paying the bonus; and 2) clarifies how the productivity bonus is to be paid consistent with the parties' agreement. The first change was orally agreed to by Dr. Herbert and Dr. French in December of 2004. The second change was one suggested by the attorney based upon an unrelated relationship and is consistent with the agreement of the parties. In addition, the forwarding of this document in April in no way discounts the fact that the parties already had a contract based upon on a written document and the terms and conditions therein.

[6]   The lease is somewhat ambiguous in that the lessee is listed as "R. Dale Herbert, M.D., Inc., on behalf of recruit Dr. David French". No explanation was given at trial as to why the lease was worded as it is. Dr. Herbert negotiated the lease and obligated his personal medical corporate entity to pay the rent and fulfill all other lessee's obligations under the lease. His company paid the rent up until the time Dr. French commenced his conversion of the practice.

the contract be signed. The Court previously held that Dr. French's agreement not to compete or solicit pursuant to subsection C of LSA-RS 23:921 did not have to be signed. The written document contains the terms and conditions of Dr. French's non-competition agreement with Southlake and it satisfies all of the conditions of LSA-RS 23:921.

Dr. French suggests numerous legal assertions for why the Court should refuse to enforce the non-competition provision and the non-solicitation provision of the June 9, 2004 contract on the legal grounds that the Court previously denied in a summary judgment. However, Dr. French continued to assert several of those grounds at trial herein and, therefore, those arguments will be briefly addressed.

First, Dr. French argues under Louisiana Civil Code Article 1947 that where the parties contemplate that there will be no agreement unless it is written and signed, no contract can exist unless signed. In fact, Dr. Hebert does testify that he intended for this agreement to be in writing and signed by all parties. However, a contract in Louisiana is formed by the consent of the parties. In Louisiana, partial performance of a contract constitutes consent to the contract even though the parties contemplated that the contract would be reduced to writing and signed. *Southern Scrap Material Company v. Commercial Scrap Materials Corp.,* 129 So.2d 491 (La. 1960). In Louisiana, when the parties substantially comply with the agreement, neither party can back out on the grounds that they failed to execute a writing, even though they had agreed to reduce their agreement to written form. *Id.* In this case, not only was there an oral agreement but there is a written document containing the terms of such agreement, although not signed. Pothier stated the foregoing general rule of law that:

> " ... it must appear to be the intention of the parties to make the perfection of the agreement depend on the writing, for, if it was merely contemplated to secure a more authentic mode of proof, then neither party can pretend the contract was not complete ...."

Pothier, *Traite des Obligations,* No. II. See also, *Segura* v. *La. Architects Selection Bd.,* 349 So.2d 369, 371 (La.App. 1st Cir. 1976), *rehearing den., writ refosed* (1977) [citing, Litvinoff, *Offer and Acceptance in Louisiana Law: A Comparative Analysis,* 28 La.L. Rev. 1, 9 (1967); and *The Work of the Louisiana Supreme Court for the 1954-1955 Term,* Smith, Conventional Obligations, 16 La.L.Rev. 237, 238(1956)].

"A party need not accept a contract expressly by his signature. He does so by availing himself of its stipulation." *Willis* v. *Allied Insulation Co.,* Inc., 174 So.2d 858 (La.App. 1st Cir. *1965), rehearing denied* [quoting, *Shear* v. *Carne,* 150 So.2d 916 (La.App. 4th Cir. 1963)]; *Ashy* v. *Trotter,* 2010-612 (La.App. 3 Cir. 11110/10), 888 So.2d 344).

Secondly, Dr. French asserts that enforcement of the non-competition and non-solicitation provisions of the employment agreement would be against public policy and in violation of the AMA Principles of Medical Ethics. The court notes, preliminarily, that the AMA Principles (there was no testimony directly on what the AMA Principles were) do allow a physician to be free to choose with whom to serve, but where a physician specifically agrees not to compete, he therefore limits his own right and creates the problem if he goes out and violates that agreement. Secondarily, the Court has already held that there is no public policy in Louisiana prohibiting physicians from agreeing not to compete. The Court further finds that it is the legislature's province to set public policy. The Louisiana Supreme Court confirms that the power to set public policy is reserved to the legislature. *State of Louisiana v. Edwards*, 2000-1246 (La. 6/1/01), 787 So.2d 981,993.

LSA-RS 23:921 provides in subsection H as follows:

> Any agreement covered by Subsections B, C, E, F, or G of this Section shall be considered an obligation not to do, and failure to perform may entitle the oblige to recover damages for the loss sustained and the profit of which he has been deprived. In addition, upon proof of the obligor's failure to perform, and without the necessity of proving irreparable injury, a court of competent jurisdiction shall order injunctive relief enforcing the terms of the agreement.

The following information is included:

1. Additional information for an estimation of damages.
2. Original petition filed to the court.
3. The defendant's expert witness report.

The following represents additional factual information developed in arriving at an estimate of damages.

Exhibit 1 Southlake Hematology/Oncology Associates Estimated Receipts Less Expenses — Hammond For the 8 months ending 8/31/05	
Receipts	**As of 8/31/05**
David French	$ 1,983,896.00
Net Receipts:	1,983,896.00
Expenses:	
Salaries — French	164,531,00
Salaries — staff	62,682.00
Payroll taxes — French	8,211.00
Payroll taxes — staff	5,230.00
Continuing Education	1,005.14
Dues & Subscriptions	600.00
Rent Expense	32,297.80
'Telephone	1,939.00
Utilities	2,485.27
Total Expenses:	278,981.21
Excess Receipts Over Expenses Before Taxes	$ 1,704,914.79

Note: Based upon information supplied by Mr. James Lichardi CPA for Southlake Hematology/Oncology Associates.

Exhibit 2
Southlake Hematology/Oncology Associates
Patient Experience and Receipts

Month/ Year	Number of Patients			Hospital Charges	Office and Hospital			YTD Receipts
	Office	Chemo	Hospital		Charges	Receipts	Adjusts	
Jan-04								$0.00
Feb-04								$0.00
Mar-04								$0.00
Apr-04								$0.00
May-04								$0.00
Jun-04	190	23	8	$1,880.00	$160,306.00	$300.00	$0.00	$300.00
Jul-04	180	35	45	$6,560.00	$180,451.00	$34,342.33	$28,964.47	$34,642.33
Aug-04	238	47	150	$20,700.00	$344,174.00	$93,015.22	$50,808.08	$127,657.56
Sep-04	259	53	8	$835.00	$347,996.00	$94,887.40	$59,271.82	$222,544.95
Oct-04	285	48	175	$23,885.00	$353,844.00	$117,831.68	$69,241.26	$340,378.63
Nov-04	261	59	48	$7,385.00	$360,740.00	$200,842.75	$104,099.46	$541,219.38
Dec-04	296	70	305	$44,790.00	$456,965.00	$128,869.14	$84,788.19	$868,088.52
Total of 2004	1697	335	740	$105,915.00	$2,204,286.00	$688,088.52	$395,193.28	
					% of Charges	30.31%	17.93%	

Month/ Year	Number of Patients			Hospital Charges	Office and Hospital			YTD Receipts
	Office	Chemo	Hospital		Charges	Receipts	Adjusts	
Jan-05	264	62	156	$21,540.00	$360,604.00	$200,584.15	$126.968.58	$200,684.15
Feb-05	232	43	20	$2,205.00	$267,916.00	$218,864.69	$138,647.58	$419,428.84
Mar-05	292	55	−16	−$1,340.00	$351,307.00	$244,886.36	$158,288.10	$864,315.20
Apr-05	267	69	109	$12,190.00	$337,353.00	$249,228.19	$189,736.61	$913,543.39
May-05	313	91	272	$42,865.00	$537,801.00	$268,886.53	$161,369.25	$1,180,429.92
Jun-05	327	86	239	$34,180.00	$518,671.00	$283,643.83	$199,219.56	$1,464,273.75
Jul-05	274	78	18	$2,410.00	$471,099.00	$256,926.47	$172,084.42	$1,721,202.22
Aug-05	293	73	115	$15,930.00	$516,064.00	$262,693.79	$217,092.99	$1,983,896.01
Sep-05								
Oct-05								
Nov-05								
Dec-05								
Total of 2005	2262	557	913	$129,980.00	$3,360,815.00	$1,963,898.01	$1,363,427.09	
					% of Charges	59.03%	40.57%	

Exhibit 3 Southlake Hematology/Oncology Associates Estimated Receipts Less Expenses — Hammond		
Receipts	As of 8/31/05	Adjustments
David French	$1,983,896.00	1,010,972.00 (1)
Net Receipts:	1,983,896.00	
Expenses:		
Salaries — French	164,531.00	120,469.00 (2)
Salaries — staff	62,682.00	31,341.00 (3)
Payroll taxes — French	8,211.00	1,445.63 (4)
Payroll taxes — staff	5,230.00	2,397.59 (5)
Continuing Education	1,005.14	502.57 (3)
Dues & Subscriptions	600.00	300.00 (3)
Drug cost		1,765,273.00 (6)
Billing @ 5% of collections		149,743.40 (7)
Overhead @ 7% of collection		209,640.76 (8)
Rent Expense	32,297.80	16,148.90 (3)
Telephone	1,939.00	969.50 (3)
Utilities	2,485.27	1,242.64 (3)
Total Expenses:	278,981.21	
Excess Receipts Over Expenses		
Before Taxes:	$1,704,914.79	

(1) — Based on 3 month rolling average of 2005 collections from January through August 2005.

(2) — Was determined by subtracting Dr. French's salary through August from his yearly contractual amount of $285,000.

(3) — Determined by dividing amount through August by 8 and multiplying by 4.

(4) — Based on the Medicare portion of Social Security taxes (1.2%), multiplied by the adjustment amount.

(5) — Based on FICA and Medicare taxes (combined 7.65%) multiplied by the Salary — Staff adjustment of $31,341.

(6) — Estimated drug cost for the year was based on information supplied by Mr. James Lichardi CPA

(7) — Estimate to account for the cost of billing and collections.

(8) — Estimate to account for other expenses not included.

Exhibit 4
Southlake Hematology/Oncology Associates
Estimate of 2005 Hammond Collection
Based On Rolling Three Month Average Using January Through August 2005 Data

	Number of Patients			Total Patients	Charges	Average Charge per patient	Receipts	Average Receipt per patient	Adjusts	Average Adjusts per patient
	Office	Chemo	Hospital							
Jan-05	264	62	156	482	$360,604.00	$748.14	$200,564.15	$416.11	$126,988.58	$263.46
Feb-05	232	43	20	295	267,916.00	908.19	218,864.69	741.91	138,647.58	469.99
Mar-05	292	55	-16	331	351,307.00	1,061.35	244,886.36	739.84	158,288.10	478.21
Apr-05	267	69	109	445	337,353.00	758.10	249,228.19	560.06	189,736.25	426.37
May-05	313	91	272	676	537,801.00	795.56	266,886.53	394.80	161,369.25	238.71
Jun-05	327	86	239	652	518,671.00	795.51	283,843.83	435.34	199,219.56	305.55
Jul-05	274	78	18	370	471,099.00	1,273.24	256,928.47	694.40	172,084.42	465.09
Aug-05	293	73	115	481	516,064.00	1,072.90	262,693.79	546.14	217,092.99	451.34
Sep-05	287	71	120	478	421,671.89	911.97	252,743.28	568.06	171,743.67	385.08
Oct-05	287	71	120	478	421,671.89	911.97	252,743.28	568.06	171,743.67	385.08
Nov-05	287	71	120	478	421,671.89	911.97	252,743.28	568.06	171,743.67	385.08
Dec-05	287	71	120	478	421,671.89	911.97	252,743.28	568.06	171,743.67	385.08
Montly avg	3,410	841	1,393	5,644	$5,047,502.56	$921.74	$2,994,869.12	$566.74	$2,050,401.79	$386.59
Last 3 months avg	284	70	116	470	420,625	1,047	249,572	559	170,867	407
Rolling 3 month avg	298	79	124	501	501,945	1,047	267,822	559	196,132	407
Jan to Mar	263	53	53	369	$326,609	$906	$221,438	$633	$141,308	$404
Feb to April	264	56	38	357	318,859	909	237,660	681	162,224	458
Mar to May	291	72	122	484	408,820	872	253,667	565	169,798	381
April to June	302	82	207	591	464,608	783	266,653	463	183,442	324
May to July	305	85	176	566	509,190	955	269,220	508	177,558	336
June to Aug	298	79	124	501	501,945	1,047	267,822	559	196,132	407
Average	287	71	120	478	$421,672	$912	$252,743	$568	$171,744	$385

The following is the original petition filed in which Dr. French is made a defendant in the cause of action. The dates and name of the organization have been changed.

22nd JUDICIAL DISTRICT COURT PARISH OF ST. TAMMANY
STATE OF LOUISIANA

No. 2005-1566   DIVISION "B"

SOUTHLAKE HEMATOLOGY/ONCOLOGY ASSOCIATES
(A Professional Medical Corporation)

VERSUS   FILED

DAVID N. FRENCH, M.D.   SEP 1 2 2005

MALISE

Deputy

FILED: September 12, 2005   ~~PRIETO~~ - CLERK

DEPUTY CLERK

PETITION FOR TEMPORARY RESTRAINING ORDER,
PRELIMINARY INJUNCTION, PERMANENT INJUNCTION,
DAMAGES AND ATTORNEYS' FEES

NOW INTO COURT, through its undersigned counsel and pursuant to the Affidavits and Verifications attached hereto, comes Southlake Hematology/Oncology Associates (A Professional Medical Corporation), a Louisiana professional medical corporation, who, with respect, represents as follows:

1.

Made defendant herein is David N. French, M.D., a person of the full age of majority who has his. residence and domicile in the Parish of St. Tammany, State of Louisiana.

2.

Southlake Hematology/Oncology Associates (A Professional Medical Corporation) (hereinafter the "Employer") hired David N. French, M.D. (hereinafter the "Employee") to work with it in providing hematology and oncology medical services.

3.

The Employer and the Employee's relationship is documented by an Employment Agreement.

4.

The Employee began services under the Employment Agreement for the Employer on June 1, 2004.

5.

The Employment Agreement provides in pertinent part that the "Employee agrees to use his best efforts in practicing medicine for Employer providing professional hematology and medical oncology services and services incident thereto..."

6.

Pursuant to the Employment Contract, the Employee was to receive annual compensation in the amount of at least $225,000 a year, plus a bonus based upon performance.

7.

The Employment Agreement attached hereto was modified slightly at the request of Dr. French to enhance his bonus calculation on or around April 13, 2004. [not attached]

8.

The Employment Agreement provides at Article IX, Section A, paragraph 4, as follows:

> If Employee terminates this Agreement without cause, Employee agrees that he shall not, without Employer's prior written consent, engage in the practice of medicine, in any fashion whatsoever, directly or indirectly, for a period of one (1) year from the date of the termination of this Agreement in the parishes of St. Tammany and Tangipahoa, State of Louisiana and the County of Pearl River, State of Mississippi, as well as any and all other parish(es) or county(ies) in which Employer practices hematology and medical oncology services as of the date of the termination of this Agreement.

(Hereinafter the "Non- Competition Clause").

9.

The Employment Agreement further provides at Article IX, Section B, as follows:

> During the period of time beginning on the Commencement Date of this Agreement and extending during the term of Employee's employment and for a period of two (2) years after the termination of Employee's employment with Employer, regardless of the reason and whether voluntary or involuntary (hereinafter the "Restrictive Period"), Employee shall not (without obtaining the prior written consent of Employer) directly or indirectly,…either for himself, or for any person, firm or corporation, call upon, compete for, solicit,divert or take away, or attempt to divert or take away, any sources of patients developed by Employer within the parishes of Jefferson, St. Tammany, St. Charles, Tangipahoa or Orleans, State of Louisiana or the County of Pearl River, State of Mississippi.

(Hereinafter the "Non Solicitation Clause")

10.

The Employment Agreement provides that Article X, Section A that the Employee may not disclose any confidential information of the Employer (the "Non- Disclosure Clause").

11.

On July 25, 2005, the Employee sent a letter of resignation to the Employer resigning from his position with the Employer as of September 2, 2005.

12.

The Resignation Letter is consistent with the thirty (30) days' notice, provision required for the Employee to terminate without cause the Employment Agreement. See, Exhibit "1" Article VII (A)(1)(a). [not included]

13.

On August 17, 2005, the Employee sent correspondence to "all my patients" acknowledging that the patients' charts were the property of the Employer but requesting the patients to sign releases so that the Employee could take the files and the patients for his new competing practice.

14.

The Resignation Letter and the Solicitation Letter, as well as the Employee's intended initiation of a medical practice in competition with the Employer on Saturday, September 3, 2005, are violations of the Non-Competition Clause, the Non Solicitation Clause and, potentially, the Non -Disclosure Clause.

15.

The Employee advised principals of the Employer that he intends on September 3, 2005 to open up a competing hematology and oncology practice; all in violation of the Non-Competition Clause, the Restrictive Covenant Clause and, possibly, the Non- Disclosure Clause.

16.

The Employment Agreement provides a remedy for breach of the Non-Competition Clause or the Non Solicitation Clause of an injunction and damages. Specifically as to the remedy of an injunction, Article IXE states:

> The parties hereby agree that each of the foregoing covenants is important, material and confidential and gravely affect the effective and successful conduct of the business and affect Employer's reputation and goodwill. Employee understands that a breach of any one or more of the covenants contained herein will result in irreparable and continuing damage to Employer for which there will be no adequate remedy at law. In the event of any breach or threatened breach of Employee's obligations hereunder, Employer may, in addition to the other remedies which may be available to it, file suit to enjoin Employee from the breach or threatened breach of such covenants. In the event Employer files suit for injunctive relief, the parties expressly agree that, in the event a court grant[s] Employer's request for injunctive relief, said injunctive relief will be without posting of any bond by Employer (or alternatively, if a court requires posting of a bond, said bond will not exceed $1,000).

17.

In addition, Louisiana law provides at LSA-RS 23:921H the following:

Any agreement covered by Sections B, C, E, F or G of this Section shall be considered an obligation not to do, and failure to perform may entitle the obligee to recover damages for the loss sustained and the profit of which he has been deprived. In addition, upon proof of the obligor's failure to perform, and without the necessity of proving irreparable injury, a court of competent jurisdiction shall order injunctive relief enforcing the terms of the agreement

(emphasis added).

TEMPORARY RESTRAINING ORDER

18.

The Solicitation letter and the Employee's contemplated act on September 3, 2005 of setting up a competing medical practice, in violation of the Non-Competition Agreement, are presumed to be acts that cause irreparable injury to the Employer; not only by the Employment Agreement but as a matter of Louisiana law. Further, the Employment Agreement and Louisiana law provide that an injunction "shall" issue to enforce the terms of the Employment Agreement.

The Employer does not have time to file a preliminary injunction request and have same set and heard prior to September 3, 2005 and, as such, the Employer requires a temporary restraining order be issued pending hearing on the preliminary injunction to prevent the irreparable injury of the Employee competing.

19.

On August 31, 2005, after being forced to evacuate his home and offices due to Hurricane Katrina, undersigned counsel diligently attempted to locate and contact Employee in order to provide him with notice of Employer's intent to request a preliminary injunction on September 1, 2005, and to provide Employee with an invitation to appear and present himself in person or through counsel at a time that a Judge in the captioned court could be located. Said efforts to locate and contact Employee included (i) searching the internet via comprehensive search engines for contact information, especially email address(es) and the telephone number(s) for,

Employee; (ii) querying the American Medical Association's website for this information and not finding any; (iii) calling LU Hospital in Hammond, Louisiana where, upon information and belief, Employee is on staff for oncology patients treated there, but was advised that Employee, Dr. French had probably evacuated due to Hurricane Katrina and had not checked in with the hospital; and (iv) attempting to call "411" nationwide telephone number information without success due to the fact that all circuits were continually "busy" and/or overloaded from the aftermath of Hurricane Katrina. Undersigned counsel certifies that he has done everything he can think of to contact the defendant.

20.

No bond is necessary in association with this temporary restraining, order as same was waived by the Employee in the Employment Contract. Alternatively, the bond should be set at $1,000 considering that the obligation at issue is statutorily prohibited B with an injunction mandated by LSA-RS 23:921 and the Employment Agreement.

The Employer requests that this Court enter a temporary restraining order preventing, restraining and enjoining the Employee from engaging in the practice of hematology or medical oncology services, in any fashion whatsoever, directly or indirectly, in the Parishes of St. Tammany and Tangipahoa, State of Louisiana and the County of Pearl River, State of Mississippi.

PRELIMINARY INJUNCTION REQUEST

21.

For the foregoing reasons, the Employer requests that this Court, after notice and a hearing in accordance with law, issue a preliminary injunction, preventing, restraining and enjoining the Employee from engaging in the practice of hematology or medical oncology services, directly or indirectly, in any fashion whatsoever, for a period of one year from September 2, 2005, in the Parish of St. Tammany and Tangipahoa, State of Louisiana and the County of Pearl River, State of Mississippi.

22.

Further, the Employer requests that this Court prevent, restrain and enjoin the Employee for a period of two (2) years following September 2, 2005, from directly or indirectly, either himself, or for any other person, firm or corporation, calling upon, competing for, soliciting, diverting or taking away or attempting to divert or take away, any sources of patients or patients developed by Employer within the parishes of Jefferson, St. Tammany, St. Charles, Tangipahoa or Orleans, State of Louisiana and the County of Pearl River, State of Mississippi.

23.

Irreparable injury is presumed pursuant to Louisiana law (LSA-RS 23:921H) and in the Employment Agreement. Further, the Employee has waived the requirement for a bond.

PERMANENT INJUNCTION

24.

The Employer requests a permanent injunction, in the same form and substance of the preliminary injunction, after a full trial on the merits.

REQUEST FOR DAMAGES AND ATTORNEYS FEES

27.

Louisiana law provides the remedy of damages for violation of the Non-Competition Clause or the Non Solicitation Clause. LSA-RS 23:921H. These damages are in addition to an injunction. *id.*

28.

Similarly, the Employment Agreement at Article IX, Section E, provides as follows:

> Any breach of Employee's obligations under Article IX of this Agreement is a material breach of this Agreement, for which Employee shall also pay to Employer all damages (including but not limited to compensatory, incidental, consequential and lost profits damages), which arise from the breach, together with interest, costs and Employer's reasonable attorneys' fees (through appeal) to enforce this Agreement, in addition to stipulated and/or liquidated damages in the amount of one (1) year's salary of Employee determined at the time of the material breach. Any lawsuit for breach may be brought in St. Tammany Parish, Louisiana, which the parties agree shall be the proper venue.

29.

The actions of the Employee have and will result in damages to the Employer including, but not limited to, loss of profits, reputation and goodwill. In addition to those damages, the Employee is obligated to the Employer for his breach of the Employment Agreement and the amount equal to one (1) year's salary at the time of the breach — $250,000.

30.

In further addition, the Employee is obligated to pay the Employer's attorneys' fees for processing this action.

WHEREFORE, after proceedings in accordance with law, the Employer prays that this Court enter Judgment as follows:

1. Issue a temporary restraining order preventing, restraining and enjoining the Employee from engaging in the practice of hematology or medical oncology services, in any fashion whatsoever, directly or indirectly, in the Parishes of St. Tammany and Tangipahoa, State of Louisiana and the County of Pearl River, State of Mississippi;

2. Issue a preliminary injunction and, after a full trial a permanent injunction;

    (a) preventing, restraining and enjoining the Employee from engaging in the practice of hematology or medical oncology services, directly or indirectly, in any fashion whatsoever, for a period of one year from September 2, 2005, in the Parish of St. Tammany and Tangipahoa, State of Louisiana and the County of Pearl River, State of Mississippi; and

    (b) preventing, restraining and enjoining the Employee for a period of two (2) years following September 2, 2005, from directly or indirectly, either himself, or for any other person, firm or corporation, calling upon, competing for, soliciting, diverting or taking away or attempting to divert or take away, any sources of patients or patients developed by Employer within the parishes of Jefferson, St. Tammany, St. Charles, Tangipahoa or Orleans, State of Louisiana and the County of Pearl River, State of Mississippi.

3. Awarding money damages to the Employer for the Employee's breach of the Employment Agreement for amounts including, but not limited to, loss of profits, reputation and goodwill, as well as the additional stipulated damage fee of $250,000 and all attorneys' fees for this action; and,

4. For any other relief deemed appropriate by this Court.

The defendant, Dr. French's, expert submitted the following report in an attempt to refute the plaintiff's expert report and arrive at his own estimate of damages which was $0.

DEFENDANT'S EXPERT REPORT

August 4, 2005

Dear Mr. Tusa:

At your request I have read and analyzed the draft "Employment Agreement" between Southlake Hematology/Oncology Associates ("SHOA") and Dr. David N. French, MD ("French") as transmitted in a letter from Mr. Vince J. Brown to Dr. R. Dale Hebert dated April 13, 2005; the business valuation report of Kushner LaGraize, LLC ("KL") dated July 19, 2005; the United States Government Accountability Office ("GAO") report to the Judge in this case dated December 1, 2004 related to the impact of the Medicare Prescription Drug, Improvement, and Modernization Act on Medicare Chemotherapy Payments to Physicians; Louisiana. Revised Statues related to damages associated with restraint of business, competing business, etc.; pleadings in the above referenced case and other pertinent correspondence and financial documents. The purpose of this analysis was to:

1. Estimate damages, if any, that French might be obligated to compensate SHOA under the terms of the Employment Agreement if such agreement if found to be in effect and binding on both parties and
2. Estimate the value of the Hammond office as of August 31, 2006.

Following are my observations and findings related to these matters.

The final draft of the proposed Employment Agreement between SHOA and French contains an Article 131 entitled Restrictive Covenant which provides under section A. a definition oldie "Restrictive Period" as the one year period following the termination of French's employment. French notified SHOA on July 25, 2005 that he intended to resign his position with SHOA on September 2, 2005, which essentially established the year ending August 31, 2006 as the "restrictive period". The proposed agreement includes a "no compete" clause which would restrict French's medical practice in Tangipahoa and St Tammany Parishes daring this one year period.

The Hammond practice of SHOA was created and developed by French in connection with his initial employment by SHOA. As such, the SHOA Hammond practice began with French establishing his physician's practice at LU Hospital on June 1, 2004 and continues today, essentially unchanged, except for the name change on September 3, 2005.

Should a Court rule that the proposed Employment Agreement is in fact a binding document, I believe that SHOA would be entitled to profits earned, if any, from French's medical practice during the one year restrictive period ending August 31, 2006, and other damages provided for in the proposed Employment Agreement. The attached Exhibit entitled "Pontchartrain Hematology Oncology, Inc. Summary Financial Statement Information" presents the actual operating results of French's medical practice for the nine months ending May 31, 2006 as well as an annualized estimate of the operating results for the year ending August 31, 2006.

As shown on the attached Exhibit, French's medical practice at LU Hospital is expected to generate a modest operating profit of less than $10,000 during the one year restricted period. Even excluding certain depreciation costs which represent one time equipment charges, the practice would only have marginal profitability during the restricted period primarily due to the negative impact of recent changes in Medicare and third party payor reimbursements for hematology and oncology drugs and administration services. An exact determination of French's medical practice operating profit or loss for the restrictive period ending August 31, 2006 can be made after all accounting entries are completed at month end.

			Total	Annualized
Exhibit **Pontchartrain Hematology Oncology, Inc.** **Summary Financial Statement information**	Four Months Ending Dec. 31, 2005	Five Months Ending May 31, 2006	Nine Months Ending May 31, 2006	Year Ending August 31, 2006
Patient Revenue	$360,158	$ 2,003,645	$ 2,363,802	3,151,7313
Operating Expenses:	214,289	1,555,473	1,769,763	2,359,683
Drugs and Medical Supplies				
Percent of Patient Revenue	55.5%	77.8%	74.9%	74.e%
Salaries:				
Physicians	33,654	105,000	138,654	184,872
Medical	23,022	32,854	55,876	74,501
Clerical	9,721	43,094	52,815	70,420
Other	16,770	2,834	19,604	26,139
Total Salaries	83,167	183,782	266,949	356,932
Payroll Taxes	7,506	14,792	22,299	29,733
Rent	19,278	21,978	41,254	55,006
Insurance	14,729	23,108	37,336	50,448
Legal and Professional	17,835	23,913	41,751	55,867
Office Expense	11,037	8,543	19,580	28,108
Depreciation	100,453	4,817	105,270	110,003
Other Operating	30,270	44,425	74,695	99,593
Total Operating Expenses	498,567	1,880,829	2,379,396	3,142,168
Operating Income (Loss)	$(138,411)	$122,816	$15,594	$9,567

REQUIREMENTS

1. Determine whether Dr. French entered into a contract with SHOA and or Dr. Hebert. If so, define the terms and elements of the contract.

2. In your opinion if a breach of contract took place what is the measure of the damages that may have been suffered by SHOA? Could damages be limited to the non-compete period, and if so why or why not?

3. In this case, assuming damages resulted from breach of contract, how you would calculate damages?

4. Considering the practice started on June 1, 2004 and Dr. French's resignation on Sept. 1, 2005, what significance would you place on the revenue and expenses of that period?

5. Would you use any of that revenue and expense history and how would you apply it?

6. Utilizing the information furnished, calculate a value of the SHOA Hammond office as of August 31, 2005.

7. In order to calculate damages under the discounted cash flow method, how would you determine what capitalization rate to use?

8. Prepare an expert witness report for the court that could be used by Wilson A. LaGraize, the expert witness.